HIJACKING HISTORY

Hijacking History

American Culture and the War on Terror

LIANE TANGUAY

McGill-Queen's University Press
Montreal & Kingston · London · Ithaca

© McGill-Queen's University Press 2013

ISBN 978-0-7735-4073-6 (cloth)
ISBN 978-0-7735-4074-3 (paper)

Legal deposit first quarter 2013
Bibliothèque nationale du Québec

Printed in Canada on acid-free paper that is 100% ancient forest free
(100% post-consumer recycled), processed chlorine free

This book has been published with the help of a grant from the
Canadian Federation for the Humanities and Social Sciences, through
the Aid to Scholarly Publications Program, using funds provided by
the Social Sciences and Humanities Research Council of Canada.

McGill-Queen's University Press acknowledges the support of the
Canada Council for the Arts for our publishing program. We also
acknowledge the financial support of the Government of Canada
through the Canada Book Fund for our publishing activities.

Library and Archives Canada Cataloguing in Publication

Tanguay, Liane, 1976–

   Hijacking history : American culture and the war on terror / Liane
Tanguay.

Includes bibliographical references and index.
ISBN 978-0-7735-4073-6 (bound). – ISBN 978-0-7735-4074-3 (pbk.)

   1. War on Terrorism, 2001–2009, in mass media. 2. War on
Terrorism, 2001–2009 – Social aspects. 3. War on Terrorism,
2001–2009 – Influence. 4. Popular culture – Political aspects –
United States – History – 21st century. 5. Bush, George W. (George
Walker), 1946–. 6. United States – Politics and government –
2001–2009. 7. United States – Military policy – 21st century.
I. Title.

HV6432.T35 2013   363.325'1   C2012-903750-8

Typeset by Jay Tee Graphics Ltd. in 10.5/13 Sabon

For my parents, Jean and Judy

Contents

Acknowledgments

Sincere thanks to the staff at McGill-Queen's University Press, as well as to copyeditor Dorothy Turnbull and the manuscript reviewers. Many thanks to Professor Terry Eagleton for judicious oversight of my initial research and to Professor Tony Crowley for steadfast support and discerning advice. I could never have got (and kept) this book off the ground without continual encouragement from dear friends Andrea Byrne, Emily Cuming, Nina Sharma, Ulli Walker, and Nicole Weickgenannt. As for the many other friends and mentors in the UK, Ottawa, Toronto, Thunder Bay, Wolfville, and elsewhere whose support was invaluable but of whom I cannot provide a comprehensive list, I trust you know who you are.

Preface

What follows is first and foremost a retrospective on the first eight or so years of the twenty-first century, which witnessed (in my opinion) some of the most unapologetically aggressive acts of American military intervention to date. It reassesses the historical events that have defined them in light of the neo-conservative claim to an "end of history," which, for all its presumption and Eurocentrism, nonetheless resonates with a cultural illusion that we *have* reached the end of history, that despite whatever "events" may continue to take place, the status quo – the prevalence of liberal-democratic capitalism and its inevitable domination of the globe – is the only form that the future can take, an illusion that manifests itself at a number of levels, not least that of popular cultural production. Indeed, it is through an examination of the latter that I interrogate this "endist" paradigm as it applies not only to the "War on Terror" but to the decade that preceded it as well.

A few caveats: they say that hindsight is 20/20, but I certainly do not lay claim to this clarity of vision; I mean only to explore the possible connections between the present state of capitalism, the "structure of feeling" it generates, certain events (or phenomena) in America's world, and the ways in which America represents these aspects of contemporary history to itself. It is far less a history of American foreign policy, legal or illegal, than it is a history of the culture that crystallized around it, took the response to the terror attacks of 9/11 for granted, and cheered from the sidelines as America led its "coalition of the willing" into an unsanctioned, illegal invasion of Iraq on patently dubious premises, all the while curtailing civil liberties on the home front and violating long-standing conventions on torture and the treatment of prisoners of war – becoming, in short, a grisly mirror image of the enemy its leaders described. Although popular support slipped away over time, to the extent that Barack Obama's 2008 election victory was hailed as a triumph for a much-needed "change" and the focus shifted that year from international issues to a financial crisis that shook the nation to its core – the repercussions of which are still being felt at the time of writing – there was definitely, for a time, a solid core of Americans for whom Bush's master-narrative of victory over a barbarous enemy held tremendous resonance well into the twenty-first century. It is this, and the reasons for it, that I want to explore.

By the same token, this book does not lay claim to the future, to determining the outcome of the financial crisis, its implications for America's position in the world, the rise of powerful economies such as China, or the staying power of the Democrats in the face of the devastation the Bush administration left behind upon vacating the White House. It is still too early to gauge the meaning of these historical phenomena, of Obama's reforms, of the rise of Glenn Beck, of the coalescence of the "Tea Party" around a set of values not clearly defined but fearfully oppositional, of the inexplicably enduring popularity of former Alaska governor Sarah Palin. That is for another exploration – another book – to assess in comparable detail. Mine takes Gulf War I as a starting point and leaves off as the narratives sustaining the invasion in Iraq begin to lose their grip on the cultural imaginary. What the future holds and how it will resonate in the living rooms of Middle America appear, at the time of writing, to be anybody's guess.

However the future unfolds, there seem to be some fairly definitive indicators as to the correspondence between lived reality, the "structure of feeling" that mediates it, and mediation itself – the shifting lenses through which we apprehend the transformations taking place in society, at home, and in the world. What the following pages attempt to do is to illuminate this correspondence at a particular time in history – at the cusp of a new century in a world faced with a host of new geopolitical realities, in a nation accustomed to the idea of being at the "leading edge" of historical development, at a time of heightened material and social anxiety defused, in part, by the comforting illusion that "history" itself, as a sequence of world-altering events, has reached its endpoint – and at a time when the shattering of this illusion has given rise to a "new normal" in relation to which the most egregious of American endeavours have been allowed to take place. Such passivity, and I hope a good part of what sustained it, is ultimately the subject of this book.

HIJACKING HISTORY

Combative and woefully ignorant policy experts, whose world experience is limited to the Beltway, grind out books on "terrorism" and liberalism, or about Islamic fundamentalism and American foreign policy, or about the end of history, all of it vying for attention and influence quite without regard for truthfulness or reflection or real knowledge. What matters is how efficient and resourceful it sounds, and who might go for it, as it were. The worst aspect of this essentializing stuff is that human suffering in all its density and pain is spirited away. Memory and with it the historical past are effaced as in the common, dismissively contemptuous American phrase, "you're history."

Edward Said, *Orientalism* (preface to the 25th anniversary edition)

Introduction

The idea for this book emerged from a rather basic question, albeit one that desperately called for an answer: how were the "American people" (by which I mean, generally speaking, the cultural "mainstream") seduced into allowing what transpired in the early years of the War on Terror – the hijacking of power by a unitary executive, the subversion of constitutional and international law in a war that rapidly and increasingly lost any pretence to legitimacy, the demolition of core American values in the pursuit of a new, amorphous enemy, and a rising American death toll in this same pursuit? In other words, by what means were "mainstream" Americans persuaded to abandon their regard for freedom of the press, for information not micromanaged by the administration and the Pentagon, for the principles that this illegitimate war was ostensibly waged to defend? Why with such ease did they allow their personal freedoms to be so compromised, their international reputation to be all but destroyed, their patriotism redefined as a hostile, xenophobic nationalism manifesting itself above and beyond the rule of law? Why was so much of the available information – on the Internet or in much of the literature produced at the time – wilfully ignored or not sought out at all? How was what might be defined as an ideological "hegemony" – however imperfect, however short-lived – achieved during the early years of the war? And how, after the wreckage wrought by the Bush administration in the early years, could they have been persuaded to re-elect the same cabal to the White House in 2004?

I put "mainstream America" in quotation marks – as well as "hegemony" – to indicate that the definition of each term is heavily conditioned as well as problematic. I, for one, was not personally

acquainted with any American who supported Bush's response
to the attacks of 11 September 2001 or the wars in Central Asia
and the Middle East. From 9/11 onwards – not to mention before-
hand, as Chalmers Johnson's *Blowback* (2000)[1] illustrates – there
was a vocal cross-section of Americans who foresaw the imperialistic endeavours to come and quite rightly and lucidly denounced
them. But they do not represent what I refer to as the "mainstream
America" of the time. To see that there was indeed a substantial
core of Americans who "bought in" to the War on Terror and its
rhetoric as well as, crucially, its aesthetics, one has merely to note
that despite an increase in online news consumption, 78 per cent of
Americans still obtain at least some of their information from television (73 per cent from national networks)[2] and of that proportion, the majority turned to Fox News Channel during the period;[3]
that at least initially, the major corporate networks presented a unified front; and that numerous Hollywood films and television series served as allegories for what Michael Ignatieff famously called
"empire lite."[4] Further evidence comes from the blind eye turned
to abuses of power and violations of international law, the willingness to accept direct censorship by the Pentagon in terms of what
could be communicated over the airwaves, and absence of alarm
over the assumption of executive power and the erosion of the system of checks and balances so fundamental to the very concept of
an American republic. Despite the effort of a host of critics such
as Johnson and Noam Chomsky – not just the usual voices of the
left but even some who had recently occupied high offices, such as
Richard Clarke – the Bush administration pressed forward with its
agenda, and the majority remained silent.

  Hegemony is difficult if not impossible to maintain in a media-
saturated society, and the Internet, among other sources, was instru-
mental in undermining the dominant ideology under the Bush
administration, at least for those prepared to do the research. David
Holloway's *Cultures of the War on Terror*[5] summarizes and analyzes
the level of popular debate alongside the more blatant attempts by
the administration, the networks, and Hollywood to micromanage
the imagery from the wars in Afghanistan and Iraq for the viewing
public back home. Drawing on sources such as written critiques,
novels, and the visual arts as well as Hollywood films and network
television, Holloway amply demonstrates that a genuine "hegemony" was unachievable within the contemporary cultural context.

However, as he also points out, much of the debate was contained within a wider vision that saw the Bush administration and its imperial endeavours as an aberration, a "hijacking" of democracy, a deviation from an otherwise tolerable norm, rather than as a logical consequence of contradictions inherent in capitalist globalization (see David Harvey's *The New Imperialism*). I would add that even in critiques that were solid and situated in a historical context that took into account such contradictions – such as the *Blowback* trilogy, Harvey's book, and Chomsky's equally sustained critique – they were not the ideological sustenance of ordinary citizens. The very fact that the news networks and Hollywood, concerned chiefly with turning a profit, persisted in producing commodities corresponding to an "aesthetics of hegemony" would suggest that there was indeed a "mainstream" view of terrorism and the war waged upon it and that it prevailed sufficiently to be exploited for financial gain.

Despite the undercurrent of debate and dissent – in the academy, among popular historians and political scientists, even on public media such as the Public Broadcasting System and National Public Radio – the "aesthetics of hegemony" was and remains by definition quite powerful – and, I will argue, more in form than in content. To the relatively passive consumer, it was sufficient to perpetuate the illusion that those in power wished to project. In other words, the steady flow of information from Fox and the other networks as well as Hollywood captured the attention of what we might see as the "mainstream" American consumer and held it through the aftermath of 9/11 and the early years of the War on Terror. It is how this dominant aesthetics manifested itself throughout the 1990s and into the War on Terror that this book addresses, rather than what transpired within the corridors of power or what dominated the *New York Times* non-fiction bestseller lists. Popular culture in the form of network television and blockbuster films is where this aesthetics is chiefly manifested, and that will be the focus of the book's analysis. This is not to say that a fissure in the aesthetics was not always present, though it was more apparent toward the end of the second Bush administration. The fissure will be carefully considered later in the text for something it reveals about the maintenance of such an aesthetics – namely, that it is ultimately impossible to manage its unruly contradictions.

This book is not a historical chronicle, nor is it a treatise on political science. It will not argue that the "aesthetics of hegemony" was truly hegemonic to the extent of silencing all dissent. But it will argue that there was, and remains, such an aesthetics, and it will seek to explain how, within the bastion of popular cultural production, it maintained its dominance, obscuring the factual, obscuring the crisis within the republic, obscuring the contradictions inherent in capitalist globalization. If this book at times reads like a detective story – a question is asked (or a crime committed), and steps are taken to retrace the crime to its origin – it is no more of one than Joseph Conrad's *Heart of Darkness*, written at the cusp of literary modernism and the classic example of the detective story gone wrong, as we will see in chapter 5. It traces a narrative that compelled individual and collective identification, starting with the fall of communism and enabling the development of Walter Benjamin's "aestheticization of politics"[6] in the truest sense of the phrase.

A committed if unorthodox Marxist, Benjamin argued that what was most severely compromised in the aestheticization of politics was the irreducible fact of history itself – history being, in the Marxist sense of the word, the history of class struggle that would one day culminate in the liberation of the oppressed. History in the materialist sense can be reduced to just that: the relations among socioeconomic classes at any given time, all the more sharply thrown into relief first by the Industrial Revolution and then by the emergence of monopoly capitalism in the twentieth century, as well as by the imperialism that necessarily (as David Harvey has eloquently explained) must accompany it as a release valve for its excesses. The submersion of genuine "history" beneath the realm of the aesthetic is for Marxism just another means of perpetuating ignorance and oppression. In its stasis, its power to obscure and fascinate, the aesthetic can only ever be a weapon of the dominant classes. What is particularly pernicious about this aesthetic is its self-evident or apodictic quality, its pretence to mirror reality – a reality that it distorts and obfuscates. When it borders on the sublime – as we will see – it is at its most powerful, its most stifling, its most "real." Hence, what better occasion for the "aestheticization of politics" than the advent of terror on American shores?

By association, what better time for the obfuscation of history by such an aesthetic when history has officially been declared at an "end"? In the wake of Francis Fukuyama's treatise on the triumph of liberal-democratic capitalism at the "end of history," following the collapse of the Communist Bloc and interwoven through popular cultural production in the ensuing decade, the compelling notion of an "end" to history – history, with its connotations of war, discord, and sinister enemy powers, not to mention the shadows they cast over much of the twentieth century – came to influence not only politics in the form of neo-conservatism but popular culture as well. A kick-start was needed, and 9/11 in this context became the "crime" that once again set the narrative of history in motion, initially as a hunt for the perpetrator (Osama bin Laden) and ultimately as an intractable mess from which the US appears unable to extricate itself at all, never mind with any dignity. If a warlike administration and a popular press eager to toe the line can learn anything from how the War on Terror has unfolded to date, it is that their "victory narrative"[7] can never truly be righted again. The rush to the scene of the crime leads only to inexplicable dead ends. Not only did it take ten years to locate and eliminate Osama bin Laden, but in a deeper sense, imperialism has come face to face with itself – as Marlow did with Conrad's Kurtz and Willard with his reincarnation in Francis Ford Coppola's *Apocalypse Now*. The more recent body of Iraq War films bears witness to this ultimate futility, and although the box-office revenues of most of them revealed an American public reluctant to face the convoluted logic of its wars, the triumph of *The Hurt Locker* (2009) at the Academy Awards may suggest a gradual turning of the tide. It is also too early to assess the ultimate effects of the financial meltdown of 2008 or the Obama administration's approach to Bush's war, but an examination of popular culture over the past twenty years in relation to the turbulent events of the past decade can surely not be amiss, even if it promises no ultimate resolution. It is with these paradigms in mind that I approach such an analysis in the pages that follow.

Given the focus of this book, the methodology I employ will be chiefly defined by the discipline of cultural studies – one that seeks to explain, through analysis of the products themselves rather than through sociological methods such as surveys and focus groups, the way in which the "aesthetics of hegemony" has sought to dominate (as well as the way in which it ultimately failed). While I address the co-optation of power by the executive branch, the violation of constitutional and international law, the legitimization of acts formerly deemed unthinkable (namely, torture), and other quite material horrors associated with the Bush administration's rule, I turn to the realm of popular cultural production in search of clues that will lead to a possible answer to the book's central question. Box-office returns and television ratings are the main evidence for the popularity (or lack thereof) of given cultural products, possible reasons for which can then be proposed (although in many cases the system of distribution led to poor ratings for oppositional products). I do not point to a conspiracy (which is not to say that conspiracies were not afoot) but rather to the correspondence between what was happening, what was seen to be happening (allegorically or as "news"), and the degree of support for what was happening, support that declined but was nonetheless present, if substantially stronger at first.

Chapter 1 elaborates on the post–Cold War phenomenon of "post-history," both as defined by its main neo-conservative proponent, Francis Fukuyama, and as a "structure of feeling" appropriate to a media-saturated age. It sets out the theoretical parameters for the analysis of popular cultural texts that follows, from the news coverage of Gulf War I to the Vietnam-tinged, historical mire evoked by Kathryn Bigelow's Oscar-winning film *The Hurt Locker*. Chapter 2 links "the end of history" with Gulf War I and the coverage thereof, an unprecedented three-week media spectacle culminating in a triumph that according to George Bush Sr "kicked Vietnam Syndrome once and for all." Chapter 3 explores the uneasy balance over the ensuing decade between victory culture and the politics of fear during which America was simultaneously reassured of its global supremacy and terrorized by multiple, often invisible threats, blown out of proportion by the corporate media and by a sort of secular apocalypticism to which 9/11 – as I discuss in Chapter 4 – was perfectly suited. The rest of Chapter 4 consists of an analysis of popular culture and news coverage during the early years of the War on Terror. Chapter 5 then reveals the logical endpoint of a global venture based on misinformation and internal contradictions: namely, an arena of cultural production becomes the terrain of contention for dissenting views, for texts that break through the dominant aesthetics and reveal the intractable reality behind the image. While the book draws a chronological line at *The Hurt Locker*, it does not pretend to offer a definitive answer to the question that inspired it but rather suggests a means of understanding and interpreting the ongoing battle for the "hearts and minds" of mainstream America itself, a battle that may well outlast that country's endeavours in Afghanistan and Iraq.

1

The "Posthistorical" Structure of Feeling

THE END OF HISTORY?

Until 8:46:26 a.m. on 11 September 2001, America had been enjoying a protracted "holiday from history." At least such was the case if popular wisdom, as articulated in print and broadcast journalism in the immediate aftermath of the attacks that took place that morning, has any merit. Basking in the incandescence of a "posthistorical" future, the nation was unprepared for what many commentators described at the time as "the end of 'the end of history,'" as if a metaphysical concept had felled the Twin Towers rather than a pair of commercial airliners piloted by terrorists. Much like the "holiday from history," the latter phrase, though slightly more specific in terms of its referent, implies a perceived hiatus between the end of the Cold War and the morning of 11 September, and this apparent reprieve from the burden of "history" is a central concern of what follows.

The referent in question is a declaration made by a bold young academic in July 1989, published in *The National Interest* under the title "The End of History?"[1] The relative caution implied by the question mark had all but vanished by 1992, when Francis Fukuyama expanded and republished his argument in book form.[2] A member of the policy planning staff of the US Department of State and of the Political Science Department of the RAND Corporation, Fukuyama deftly interprets the impending collapse of communism as evidence of the triumph of "the liberal *idea*"[3] over all of its alternatives, real, imagined, or imaginable. In both the article and the subsequent book, Fukuyama heralds the inevitable triumph of freedom, democracy, and free markets worldwide, arguing that liberal-democratic capitalism represents the zenith of humanity's ideological evolution and the pinnacle of "progress" in the Enlightenment sense of the word. What Fukuyama refers to in his thesis as the "universal history of mankind"[4] tends always and invariably towards the realization of liberal-democratic capitalism on a global scale as the only political and economic order that satisfies the most fundamental human needs and desires. Of all possible systems, for Fukuyama, liberal-democratic capitalism is indeed the most compatible with human nature.

The idea of the "end of history," to be sure, has a fairly illustrious history of its own. Fukuyama lays claim to – and skilfully manipulates – a Hegelian legacy, as interpreted through Alexandre Kojève, who showed that, for Hegel, Napoleon's victory over Prussia in 1807 had formed "the basis for the universal spread of the principles of the French Revolution" and for the "regulative principle of a new political order."[5] As for Fukuyama some 200 years later, nothing as mundane as actual historical events counts – such as the rise and fall of European imperialism, the First and Second World Wars, or the Cold War – but rather the prevalence of the *idea*.

The "end of history" can be found elsewhere in contemporary thought as well. Lutz Niethammer's *Posthistoire*, published only months before Fukuyama's initial article, engages with a number of mid-century theorists and philosophers, including Kojève, who predicted, in one way or another, an imminent end to history, Carl Schmitt, Ernst Jünger, Henri de Man, and Henri Lefebvre, among others. Niethammer links these various thinkers with the central crisis of their own historical era – namely, the failure of radical hopes following two devastating wars fought in rapid succession and the consequent vision of a world beyond redemption.[6] Fukuyama's *posthistoire* is, by contrast, considerably more optimistic, and two further salient factors distinguish him from his predecessors. For one, this brazen newcomer was not an ivory tower intellect surveying an exhausted wasteland with disdain but rather a functionary in the US public service. And, more important, his work took off with electrifying speed. "Within a year," as Perry Anderson notes, "an arcane philosophical wisdom had become an exoteric image of the age, as Fukuyama's arguments sped round the media of the globe."[7] Translated into at least twenty languages, the book was an event unto itself.

This instant response, critical or otherwise, arose no doubt partly because the events of the post–Cold War period appeared to bear out Fukuyama's predictions, given the putative "triumph" of liberal-democratic capitalism over its long-standing enemy and its corresponding expansion into areas of the globe previously dominated by the communist system. The end of the Cold War increased the momentum of capitalist globalization, enabling the imperatives of the free market to take hold in areas formerly contested or out of bounds altogether. Alternatives, at this point, certainly *did* seem unthinkable, in no small part because – perhaps less popularly – the United States was at the leading edge of this expansion, now established in its role as the world's sole remaining superpower. Its unparalleled economic and military might allowed it to redefine itself (as will be discussed) as a sort of global "policeman,"[8] charged with the task of maintaining order and stability and enforcing it where necessary – of sustaining a global climate, in short, in which the free market would best be able to flourish. The Persian Gulf War was the first real demonstration of America's new status, confirming its global dominance while serving as a warning to those who might wish to challenge it in future and purportedly setting the foundations of what George H.W. Bush, on 11 September 1990, first designated the "new world order."[9]

Thus, the ensuing decade witnessed the further entrenchment of the American global agenda, according to which democracy and free-market values could, and would, be implemented worldwide, especially where they were actively challenged. Informing this view at base was, and remains, the principle that there could be no better system than liberal-democratic capitalism, even if it had to go through a series of redefinitions in order to find for itself a plausible ideological manifestation.[10]

"Events," of course, continued to take place over the course of the first "posthistorical" decade. Indeed, the argument that they persisted was often levelled against Fukuyama's thesis, usually by those who had failed to take into account the essential idealism of his argument – that is, the concept that the victory of liberal-democratic capitalism was a victory in principle if not yet in practice. For Fukuyama, such "events," however troubling – the war in Somalia, the genocide in Rwanda, the crisis in the Balkans, to name but a few – were not part of the deeper global configuration but were rather epiphenomenal and ultimately transient in nature. They took place in parts of the world "still stuck in history"[11] without ultimately affecting the broader trend toward the establishment

of liberal-democratic capitalism worldwide. Even the more apparently intransigent opponents of liberal-democratic capitalism, such
as ethnic nationalism and religious fundamentalism, did not constitute a serious or abiding threat to its ongoing conquest of the globe.
Events and trends appearing to counter the triumph of "the liberal
idea" were seen as passing aberrations or anomalies, not as viable
or insurmountable challenges to the principle of capitalist globalization itself.

It is certainly not the case that Fukuyama's thesis met with no
compelling opposition at all. Samuel Huntington's "clash of civilizations" thesis, appearing initially in article form in 1993 (also
accompanied by a question mark that was to vanish by the time
the full-length book came out),[12] pits a future of strife and conflict against Fukuyama's harmonious, "unipolar" world view. Interpreting the end of ideological conflict as the beginning of conflict
based on cultural identity and positing an intercivilizational conflagration that could ultimately engulf the globe, with allegiances
defined on cultural rather than political or even strictly economic
grounds, Huntington's thesis received quite as much critical and
popular attention as Fukuyama's. And even Fukuyama, as Anderson
notes, "appears to hesitate" on the question of cultural identity,
aware perhaps that "cultures form wider meaning-complexes whose
appeal cannot be reduced to the interests of liberty and plenty"; consequently, his case "fails to address just those human needs to which
a culture in the deeper sense answers."[13] In this respect, Fukuyama
is forced to acknowledge what he calls in a later article the "primacy of culture" as ranking among the "chief difficulties that liberal
democracy will face in the future," even to the point that "the real
difficulties affecting the quality of life in modern democracies have
to do with social and cultural *pathologies* that seem safely beyond
the reach of institutional solutions" and therefore, "the chief issue is
quickly becoming one of culture."[14] Ultimately, however, Fukuyama
manages to dismiss any substantive threat that these "pathologies"
might pose to liberal-democratic capitalism. Since the triumph of the
latter, as he argues in his principal oeuvre, there can be "no ideology *with pretensions to universality* that is in a position to challenge liberal democracy."[15] Although he acknowledges an increase
in "intolerant, aggressive nationalism" and admits that universal
democracy may be preceded in some cases by a "painful process of
national separation,"[16] he ultimately sees such difficulties as likely to

remain confined to those parts of the world "still stuck in history" and not destined to become a permanent part of the geopolitical landscape. Liberal-democratic capitalism might not answer directly to particular cultural needs, treating citizens instead as equal individuals and "[ignoring] the group-oriented character of real-world populations ... that finds great satisfaction in ascriptive collective identities"; nonetheless, he points out, nationalist states "[violating] liberal principles have not fared well," ethnic conflict is likely to be a "transitional phenomenon," and Islamic fundamentalism has no appeal for "anyone not culturally Islamic to begin with."[17] Religion and nationality remain historically significant only within the "historical" parts of the world and will eventually be eroded as the "desire for comfortable self-preservation" overrides the "desire to risk one's life in a battle for pure prestige."[18]

For Fukuyama, the reason for the triumph of the Western "idea," after all – as it had been for Hegel and later for the champions of European imperialism – is its universal applicability, above and beyond all particularist claims. Liberal-democratic capitalism presents itself, in Terry Eagleton's interpretation, as "cultureless"[19] – that is, as undetermined and ultimately unaffected by the contingent particularities of culture in the anthropological sense of the word; it is instead universal and universally applicable, appealing to human nature "as such" and transcending all contingent determinants of identity as well as any obstacles that they may impose. Ultimately, so convinced was Fukuyama of the viability of his thesis that even the terrorist attacks of 11 September 2001 failed to prompt him to reconsider (although he did later lash out at the Bush administration's response for violating the essential neo-conservative ethos and distance himself from the Republican neo-cons).[20] Islamic fundamentalism and the threats posed by "rogue" states are undoubtedly serious, he concedes in a response to the attacks, but cannot ultimately halt liberal-democratic capitalism in its tracks.[21]

Of the two propositions, Fukuyama's lends itself far more readily to the pursuit of America's global agenda in the years following the end of the Cold War and beyond (even though Huntington's helps to justify the superiority of liberal-democratic capitalism over the "bloody borders of Islam"[22]). The essence of his thesis is reflected in Bush Sr's "new world order," and even for Bush's successor, Bill Clinton, the end of the Cold War had ushered in a new era of peace, prosperity, and international cooperation. Intervention, military

or otherwise, would still be required from time to time to contain
any threats to the stability of that order or to bring other nations
into alignment with it, but broadly speaking, the realization of a
global free-market utopia was held to be imminent.[23] By this logic,
the "posthistorical" West held up a mirror to the still "historical"
rest, and the global pattern was one of a "worldwide liberal revolution"[24] that would see liberal-democratic capitalism assume its "special place" in the "universal history of mankind."[25]

Huntington's thesis, which maintains that the boundaries imposed
by cultural difference cannot be transcended by any single "idea"
and that liberal-democratic capitalism is not universal but rather
"unique" to Western civilization,[26] will be discussed at greater length
in chapter 3. But for present purposes, it is sufficient to note the
fact that two so thoroughly opposed interpretations of the post–
Cold War world order – one promising a future of peaceful, harmonious exchange, the other warning of a civilizational showdown
– could emerge at approximately the same time and both to similar degrees of popular critical reception. This suggests that neither
should be ignored or dismissed within the parameters of the current study as obsolete, whatever empirical evidence may be mobilized against them. That both propositions could enjoy such a broad
reception can be explained only by reference to the cultural context
in which the two visions took shape. In other words, both demand
to be accounted for in relation to their common socio-historical contexts, as symptomatic of an age, and one central aspect of this context is the notion of the end of ideology.

THE END OF IDEOLOGY

As noted in the introduction, what dominates the *New York Times*
non-fiction bestseller list is by no means an indication of what the
"mainstream," or the public at large, is consuming, and intellectual tracts such as Fukuyama's and Huntington's are certainly no
exception. However, if both are to be read as symptomatic, then
the broader cultural climate must be taken into consideration as
one in which each argument – however paradoxically – can be seen
as equally plausible. This climate, I would argue, is one in which
"ideology" as traditionally conceived has come to an end. I am not
suggesting that our mediated culture is not saturated with ideology
twenty-four hours a day but rather that it has erased itself from view,

a sleight of hand tantamount to, as the character Kaiser Söze puts it in the film *The Usual Suspects*, the devil "convincing the world he [doesn't] exist."

The essence of Fukuyama's argument, and of the neo-conservative agenda more broadly, is that there can be no system better than the current one, that liberal-democratic capitalism represents the "end point of mankind's *ideological* evolution."[27] By this logic, there can be no further ideological conflict, and there is thus no further need for ideology itself. In other words, there is no longer any need to justify or legitimate one system or another on ideological grounds, because there is only one system that works and liberal-democratic capitalism happens to be it. The emergence of a system that is both different *and better* than the current one is for Fukuyama and the adherents of the American global project a thoroughgoing impossibility.

The most immediately apparent objection to this argument is that it relies upon a very limited definition of ideology. Indeed, both Fukuyama and Huntington presume that ideology constitutes little more than the legitimating tenets of a given political or socio-economic system. For Fukuyama, the post–Cold War absence of any viable alternatives vitiates the need for ideology, whereas for Huntington the primary terrain of contention between peoples and nations shifts from an ideological one to the "fault lines" of cultural identity. Both ignore the mutual inextricability of identity and ideology and treat the latter as reducible to the paradigmatic co-ordinates of either capitalism (more favourably known as its ostensible political corollary, "liberal democracy") or communism (always referred to as a doomed economic system or, in an important variation, as coterminous with totalitarianism).

This limited understanding of "ideology" is given space and consideration in this book only because it goes largely uncontested and seems indeed to conform to the "popular" or "mainstream" understanding of ideology as a legitimating belief system and, in the form of "false consciousness," as an affliction particular to "other people" (i.e., not Americans). One's own belief system, by this logic, is not held to be ideological. Within the popular cultural texts I will address, this interpretation of "ideology" is implicitly or explicitly reaffirmed time and again, depending on the product; the term "ideology" is seldom if ever applied to one's own world view in cultural production. Yet if we embrace a more nuanced understanding of the term, declaring the "end of ideology" is certainly profoundly ideological in itself; indeed, if the "end of history" can be said to have a history of its own, the "end of ideology" has its own ideological tenets as well. And indeed it does, as well as a history: Daniel Bell proclaimed the end of ideology in 1960, arguing as Fukuyama would thirty years later that the inevitable triumph of liberal democracy, supported by and bound up with the capitalist mode of production, had made ideology redundant.[28] Bell's thesis, of course, was published before the upheavals of the 1960s and 1970s, both at home and abroad, dispelled any illusion that American society at the end of the 1950s represented the pinnacle of historical and political development. Further, unlike Fukuyama's, Bell's work was specifically concerned with the politics of Western intellectuals confronting the communist world and reflected the early years of the Cold War and the loyalty-oath politics it precipitated within the United States. This is an "end of ideology" different from the situation we are facing today in which ideology has simply slipped beneath the radar instead of presenting itself as one of two choices, albeit the only "legitimate" choice. Indeed, as Nick Dyer-Witheford points out, Fukuyama's "end of history" represents a "massively enlarged version of the 'end of ideology' thesis, now global in scope and engineered not by industrialism but by post-industrialism."[29] It therefore brings us full circle from Bell's declaration yet also opens up the question of whether this time around, in the context of the end of the Cold War and the triumph of capitalism, we might be dealing with a qualitatively different state of affairs altogether. The "end of history" may indeed have a history of its own, with the "end of ideology" its tacit corollary, but it is the way in which the latter is received and played out within post–Cold War, mainstream American popular culture that is of concern in this book. In other words, whatever the limitations of the mainstream understanding of the term "ideology," the notion of its "end" nonetheless warrants extensive consideration, both as an ideological proposition in itself and against a cultural backdrop to which it all too readily conforms. Broadly speaking, I propose that because the economic and, correspondingly, cultural configurations of late capitalism possess some distinctive characteristics that set them apart from the form they took during the Cold War and preceding eras, they come to inflect the present disavowal of ideology – certainly as evinced in mainstream cultural production – in particular ways. Consequently, an analysis of such products should reveal at least a dominant – albeit not hegemonic – "cultural imaginary" in which an ostensible absence of ideology can be said to prevail.

These configurations, taken together, constitute what is most usefully referred to as a "structure of feeling" and (given the present context, though without yielding to the logic of Fukuyama's own propositions) can be termed "posthistorical" (and post-ideological). Thus, I will put forth not so much an in-depth analysis of Fukuyama's argument but a consideration of his thesis as a "symptom" or a product of its time, minor as its broad cultural impact may be compared to that of Hollywood, video gaming, and network television. Rather than taking his central proclamation at face value, I will argue that it was made within a particular enabling socio-historical context – namely, that of "late" capitalism. And it is precisely in relation to this backdrop that his argument must be interpreted alongside other cultural products – popular, "official," and even at times "intellectual" – that manifest this "structure of feeling" in various forms.

THE "POSTHISTORICAL STRUCTURE OF FEELING"

The term "structure of feeling" originates with the Marxist critic Raymond Williams in his 1977 book *Marxism and Literature*. For Williams, it is more fundamental, more ingrained, and more meaningful than a fixed system of belief, education, explanation, or argument, even though the latter maintains an "effective presence" in social life. Along with institutions, formations, and traditions, they are often quite "fixed" and systematic, but they

> are not a whole inventory even of social consciousness in its simplest sense. For they become social consciousness only when they are *lived, actively, in real relationships*, and moreover in relationships which are more than systematic exchanges between fixed units ... Practical consciousness is almost always different from official consciousness, and this is not only a matter of relative freedom or control. For practical consciousness is *what is actually being lived, and not only what it is thought is being lived.*[30]

The idea, then, is to take "posthistory" not as a fixed or systematic set of beliefs and perceptions but rather in terms of the subject's negotiation with the social order and by no means "fixed" in itself. A "structure of feeling," for Williams as well as for the present analysis, involves "a particular quality of social experience and relationship, historically distinct from other particular qualities, which gives the sense of a generation or a period."[31] It is connected to a particular time and its determining factors but is not in any sense "fixed" by them, constituted as it is by subjective actions, which always unfold in space, through time.

"Structure of feeling" designates, in other words, the form of everyday "lived experience." For the purposes of this analysis, it is lived experience at the broadest cultural level: the experience not simply of "history" itself, or even necessarily of its mainstream cultural representations, but rather of the self in space and time, the self in society and the perceptible world: individual and social "reality" as mediated by a consciousness that both shapes and is (unconsciously or consciously) shaped, negotiation and navigation of space and time, as well as the parameters within which this negotiation and navigation takes place – that is, the limits of perception and the limits of intelligibility.[32] Further, for Williams,

> "feeling" is chosen to emphasize a distinction from more formal concepts of "world-view" or "ideology." It is not only that we must go beyond formally held and systematic beliefs, though of course we have always to include them. It is that we are concerned with *meanings and values as they are actively lived and felt, and the relations between these and formal or systematic belief* ... An alternative definition would be structures of *experience* ... We are talking about ... specifically affective elements of consciousness and relationships: not feeling against thought, but thought as felt and feeling as thought: practical consciousness of a present kind, in a living and interrelated continuity. We are then defining these elements as a "structure": as a set, with specific internal relations, at once interlocking and in tension.[33]

For the purposes of the present study, these elements, taken together, constitute the "sites" at which the dominant (not the hegemonic but the most widespread) set of "fixed," systematic beliefs, as propagated by news outlets, the administration, and the entertainment industry, as well as the socio-economic conditions they reproduce and legitimate, is translated into everyday social experience. It .

is at these sites that such beliefs are less consciously reflected upon than actively "lived," or "felt," at an aesthetic and sensory level, among others. And it is from the parameters of "lived experience" and "practical consciousness" that ideology *as* a set of beliefs (and this includes ideology's inbuilt disavowal of itself *as* ideology) draws its cultural force. In other words, any belief system must take root in this prevalent "structure of feeling" and be comprehensible within it and upon its terms; it is therefore ultimately inseparable from it. Although Williams was keen to identify "emergent" and "residual" structures of feeling alongside what might be called the "dominant" one,[34] for the purposes of my analysis of the "posthistorical structure of feeling" I will focus on the ideological disavowal of ideology (as discussed above) and how it appears to merge with lived experience in the arena of popular cultural production. First, however, it is necessary to identify some of the salient aspects of this dominant "structure" in relation to which such a disavowal can be effected in the first place.

I will principally consider the specific mechanisms of "late" capitalism; the sensory and perceptual parameters of its enabling technologies, particularly its communications technologies; and the effects of these forces on the lived experience and construction of time, place, identity, and, above all, linear, logical narrative as an epistemic framework and as a dominant aesthetic. All of these factors, I will suggest, generate equally plausible arguments as apparently antithetical as Fukuyama's and Huntington's, and they do so in their constitution of a structure of feeling for which ideology in its popular sense would appear to be redundant and genuine political alternatives inconceivable.

A key fundamental premise of the present structure of feeling, I would argue, involves a sense of narrative breakdown – a breakdown Tom Engelhardt associates with what he calls "the end of victory culture"[35] – and it is this that will both inform my discussion of the economic "base" of late capitalism and serve as a unifying principle for its superstructural manifestations, in particular those in the realm of popular culture. Postmodernism, it would seem – in the Lyotardian sense of the "end of grand narratives" – began to come into its own at this level with the end of the Cold War, the "end of history."

Such a claim may seem absurd when the US administration has invoked the grandest of grand narratives – indeed, revived

Engelhardt's central "victory" narrative of ambush and righteous slaughter in the tale of a war between Good and Evil – to justify its military endeavours abroad. However, I would argue, this, like Fukuyama's proclamation of the triumph of liberal-democratic capitalism, is to be viewed as symptomatic rather than deep-structural in nature. That is, there is no better time to invoke such a narrative than in an age for which the epistemic claims of narrative seem increasingly dubious.[36] If the metaphysical precepts of Bush's War on Terror belie the breakdown of narrative, then this is in large part what accounts for their broad appeal, at least at the level of network television, official statements to a captive audience, and the entertainment world. But it is in fact little more than yet another ideological sleight of hand, for Bush's narrative promises neither genuine progress nor a viable political alternative, both of which depend upon a sense of narrative that is absent from contemporary social experience. A profound loss of political direction lies concealed beneath a stultifying narrative that under scrutiny offers only more of the same – a neo-conservative paradigm of continuing global expansion. This commandeering of the truth of the global situation is what is meant by *Hijacking History* and is a central concern of this book. Before pursuing this line of inquiry, however, I will turn to establishing the connections between the logic of late capitalism, the epistemic parameters of its enabling technologies, and a structure of feeling in which "history," and linear narrative more broadly, has lost its bearings.

THE LOGIC OF "LATE" CAPITALISM

An updated, and arguably more lucid, use of the term "structure of feeling" can be found in Fredric Jameson's *Postmodernism, or, The Cultural Logic of Late Capitalism*, which emphasizes the need to "coordinate new forms of practice and social and mental habits ... with the new forms of economic production and organization thrown up by the modification of capitalism ... in recent years."[37] Let us, then, examine some of the nuances of this "modification," and there is perhaps no better place to begin than with David Harvey's notion of "time-space compression" – in other words, with the spatial and temporal reorganizations caused by the acceleration and expansion of capitalism and its enabling technologies.

According to Harvey, even leaving aside the analysis of contemporary conditions, "it is important to challenge the idea of a single and objective sense of time or space" and to recognize instead the "multiplicity of the objective qualities which space and time can express, and the role of human practices in their constitution."[38] That is, human practices shape space and time in certain ways that then come to act, reciprocally, upon consciousness and perception, giving rise to the structure of feeling appropriate to the era and the practices in question. As the irreducible media of Williams's "practical consciousness," neither space nor time, for Harvey, can "be understood ... independently of the qualities of material processes which serve to reproduce social life." Accordingly,

> [e]ach distinctive mode of production or social formation will ... embody a distinctive bundle of time and space practices and concepts. Since capitalism has been (and continues to be) a revolutionary mode of production in which the material practices and processes of social reproduction are always changing, it follows that the objective qualities as well as the meanings of space and time also change.[39]

The argument at its simplest is that what society does affects the way in which society experiences and apprehends time and space. Marshall McLuhan can be of assistance here, with his association of cartography with the world of print, which, in intensifying the visually oriented and linear conception of speech embodied in written language, allowed a similar – almost narrative – "segmentation" to evolve in representations of the world, which in turn corresponded to European exploration and conquest.[40] Now, at a very different stage of Western global domination, in an age in which the Earth has been seen and represented in its totality and in which audio-visual media have transformed the linear, temporal world of print into a simultaneity of what Raymond Williams calls "flow," time and space as depicted and understood – as experienced – take on another quality, which I will explore in greater detail later in this chapter.

For Harvey as well as Jameson and other contemporary Marxist critics such as Eagleton and Guy Debord, the latest great shift in the capitalist mode of production was the move from Fordism – a system based on the rationalization of labour control and management, the reproduction of labour power, and the standardization of production – to "flexible accumulation" as both a resolution to the economic crises of 1973 and a transcendence of the "rigidities" of its predecessor.[41] For these cultural critics, such a transition would engender a corresponding cultural shift at the intersection of material reality and the cultural imaginary. Again, if we take Harvey's (or McLuhan's) contention that the experience of time and space is shaped by human activity, in this case the mode of production, then it seems reasonable to suggest that cultural production would come to be inflected by material production in certain specific ways.

Flexible accumulation, as Harvey describes it,

> rests on flexibility with respect to labour processes, labour markets, products, and patterns of consumption. It is characterized by the emergence of entirely new sectors of production, new ways of providing financial services, new markets, and ... greatly intensified rates of commercial, technological, and organizational innovation ... It has also entailed a new round of what I shall call "time-space compression" ... in the capitalist world – the time horizons of both private and public decision-making have shrunk, while satellite communication and declining transport costs have made it increasingly possible to spread those decisions immediately over an ever wider and variegated space.[42]

These "early stirrings" in the 1970s and 1980s of "the passage to an entirely new regime of accumulation" brought with them, for Harvey as for many a Marxist thinker, a "quite different system of political and social regulation,"[43] as well as a shift in "norms, habits, and political and cultural attitudes."[44] The concepts of time and space associated with this new form of production and the different social and political systems it entailed – including, among other things, a loss of cohesion among the working class as industrial jobs were exported to the Third World and the service industry took on increasing prominence in the West – alter "lived experience" in significant ways. Leisure time, instant communication, and global travel, as well as global trade, inflect the dominant "structure of feeling," as we will see, in ways that return to us in the cultural products we consume and in how we consume them.

Jameson, for his part, characterizes the new regime of accumulation as constituting the economic base of "late capitalism." For Jameson, "late" is intended to convey "the sense that something has changed, that things are different, that we have gone through a transformation of the life world which is somehow decisive but incomparable with the older convulsions of modernization and industrialization, less perceptible and dramatic, somehow, but more permanent precisely because more thoroughgoing and all-pervasive."[45]

The transition from Fordism to flexible accumulation, in other words, lacked the dramatic upheavals of that associated with the Industrial Revolution – the mass migration of rural dwellers to urban centres, the reorganization of manual labour along the segmented assembly line, the rise of working-class consciousness – but for that very reason is to be seen as all the more invasive. Although a response to a crisis, it was a shift that could be apprehended more clearly in retrospect, after the proverbial dust had settled on a new, "flexible" mode of production. In other words, for critics like Harvey and Jameson, the impact on lived experience of "late" or "post-industrial" (at least for the developed world) capitalism is seen as more extensive than that of its predecessor, to have silently permeated more aspects of social life. And for both critics, this has largely to do with the "spatial and temporal displacement" effected by the new, post-Fordist regime of "flexible accumulation," which has reorganized every aspect of spatial and temporal experience and in turn has affected the dominant cultural imaginary in significant ways.

In *Millennial Dreams*, Paul Smith reminds us that at the "historical epicenter of the dream of capitalist development" is a conquest of space and time. Indeed, classical economics as articulated by Adam Smith in *The Wealth of Nations* is "predicated upon the possibility of expanding markets by way of improved communications, carriage, and navigation." Capitalism in its latest or "millennial" form, Paul Smith claims,

> now openly worships the graven image of a world where time and space are no barrier to the flow of capital, where political and social divisions are epiphenomenal and not structural or systemic; where, in short, the universal ideal of "a system from which all and everything follows" has been mythically (and willfully) installed. Time and space as obstacles to total domination were all that was left to be conquered; their fate is that they are now to be transcended in the *imaginary* of the perfectly global.[46]

I emphasize "imaginary" because it is, after all, quite strictly in the realm of the imaginary that capitalism has "conquered" its

last natural barriers. This assessment is indeed a prime example
of "endist" triumphalism of the sort that so captured Fukuyama's
imagination in 1989. The underlying economic system still depends,
in the last analysis, on material processes that require a massive
investment not only of capital but of time, resources, and energy,
such as, to name the most obvious and crucial one, the extraction
and transportation of fossil fuels. Multi-billion-dollar construction, extraction, and transportation projects must be designed and
approved at multiple bureaucratic levels for our basic energy commodities to be produced, shipped, and sold, and such projects – as
the recent BP Gulf of Mexico disaster indicates – are not without
significant environmental and economic risk. Further, it is increasingly in the realm of the "imaginary" that America, now effectively
an "economic back-seat driver,"[47] maintains the illusion of its own
economic dominance. In the "imaginary" that Paul Smith describes,
such matters are of little consequence, but the imaginary retains
its cultural power. That is why this book is principally concerned
with the dominant cultural imaginary, and these material realities
in and of themselves are not *yet* sufficient, I would argue, to undermine the patterns of lived experience that have emerged in the age
of instantaneity and extreme "time-space compression," however its
attendant crises may present themselves. The sense of "time-space
compression" and the structure of feeling it engenders do not fluctu-
ate with the actual fortunes of the self-proclaimed superpower any
more than does that power's willingness to assert what considerable
economic might that it possesses.

As Harvey notes, the "incentive to create the world market, to
reduce spatial barriers, and to annihilate space through time is omnipresent" in the history of capitalism, "as is the incentive to rational-
ize spatial organization into efficient configurations of production ...
circulation networks ... and consumption."[48] He further notes, justifying his choice of the word "compression," that

> the history of capitalism has been characterized by a speed-up
> in the pace of life, while so overcoming spatial barriers that the
> world sometimes seems to collapse inwards upon us. The time
> taken to traverse space ... and *the way we commonly represent
> that fact to ourselves* ... are useful indicators of the kind of phe-
> nomena I have in mind. As space appears to shrink to a "global
> village" of telecommunications and a "spaceship earth" of

economic and ecological interdependence ... and as time horizons shorten to the point where the present is all there is ... so we have to learn to cope with an overwhelming sense of *compression* of our spatial and temporal worlds."[49]

It is not an actual compression that concerns me here as much as the way in which it is experienced – the way in which we represent the "conquest" of time and space to ourselves and to the world, mainly in popular cultural production. The shortened time-space horizons of which Harvey speaks have brought, for instance, "the whole world's cuisine" (as commodities) into a single place "in almost exactly the same way that the world's geographical complexity is nightly reduced to a series of images on a static television screen." Further, for Harvey,

> [t]he general implication is that ... it is now possible to experience the world's geography vicariously, as a simulacrum [that is, as a simulation of the world that is not strictly "real" but that is nonetheless experienced as "real"]. The interweaving of simulacra in daily life brings together different worlds (of commodities) in the same space and time. [And] it does so in such a way as to conceal almost perfectly any trace of origin, of the labour processes that produced them, or of the social relations implicated in their production.[50]

We experience the world, in other words, as a screen – a flat screen projecting images behind which is only empty space. The concealment of any "trace of origin" is indeed part of the aesthetic of the screen, and a seductive aesthetic it is. The latest generations of Apple iMacs, for instance, exemplify this aesthetic with compelling perfection: the entire computer, all of its workings and machinations, is concealed just behind the screen itself rather than within the cumbersome towers of the PC world. Flat-screen televisions have replaced the bulky CRTs that once dominated family rooms, sometimes even mounted above the hearth instead of artwork. Labour processes have no part in such an aesthetic. Indeed, if one of capitalism's objectives has been to distance itself in the public imaginary from any trace of the social relations underpinning it, then it is precisely this aesthetic that enables the illusion of posthistory, at the level of lived experience or the "structure of feeling," to prevail despite the very real material barriers still faced by capital in its most fundamental endeavours. And this illusion is perhaps best manifested in the notion of a "global village" or a "communicational network" embracing the "globe" (the latter a representational construct in its own right). Sadly, even much of the "high theory" surrounding this illusion creates an impermeable bubble of its own into which reality is not allowed to penetrate. At any rate, this notion is certainly the most accessible means of conceiving the "world system" of multinational capitalism with which the technologies of time-space compression are inextricably linked and which, as Fredric Jameson asserts, is inconceivable through conventional means of perception.

Such a paradigm, as Jameson notes, becomes all the more necessary as conventional, "modern" notions of space and time break down, resulting in what he calls a "postmodern hyperspace" that has "finally succeeded in transcending the capacities of the individual human body to locate itself, to organize its immediate surroundings perceptually, and cognitively to map its position in a mappable external world."[51] The "mutation" entailed in the transition to flexible accumulation is one with which "we ... have not kept pace," which is "unaccompanied as yet by any equivalent mutation in the subject"; it is a totality for which we lack the "perceptual equipment."[52] This point is further elucidated by Harvey, who explains how the "rules of perspective" that shaped the modern era, beginning with the Renaissance, allowed for a conception of the world "from the [fixed or static] standpoint of the 'seeing eye' of the individual," emphasizing "the science of optics and the ability of the individual to represent what he or she sees as in some sense 'truthful.'" Indeed, he points to the emergence of accurate cartography during this period as implying "the ability to see the globe as a knowable totality,"[53] an ability corresponding with the imperative of power and its emphasis on the "conquest and rational ordering of space" as well as the "material and rational principles that might order the distribution of populations, ways of life, and political systems on the surface of the globe."[54] Indeed, McLuhan would associate this mode of perception with the spread of written language through the printed word, segmenting and ordering our perception of space along a visually and symbolically representational axis and the drive toward realism this entailed. But given what Harvey calls, following Marx, the "annihilation of space through time,"[55] this detached or "mediating" perspective, the illusion of distance, objectivity, and a fixed subject position from which the globe appears as a knowable and mappable totality, is lost. The detached perspective of the modern era is replaced by a tactile and total involvement to which the mind's representational capacities have not, as Jameson would have it, yet adapted. The result is an inability to "cognitively map" the new reality or "hyperspace" along with one's position within it.[56] In the world of postmodernist theory, this also fits well with Jean Baudrillard's concept of the "simulacrum," as mentioned above, in which there is no original, "real" referent but only a procession of indistinguishable simulations – mediated representations without an original.[57]

Such is the case for spatial organization, and, as noted, the structure of feeling so understood initiates a shift in the experience of temporality as well. For Harvey among others, some of the changes effected by the transition to flexible accumulation in the 1970s included an emphasis on "the new, the fleeting, the ephemeral, the fugitive, and the contingent in modern life, rather than the more solid values implanted under Fordism."[58] Older generations simply cannot comprehend the drive among youth to expose all facets of their personalities on social media such as Facebook – a seemingly transient medium but in which data is permanently stored. The emphasis on "speed-up," on the acceleration of "turnover time" in production, entails "parallel accelerations in exchange and consumption," making acceleration itself a central and determining factor. For Harvey,

[i]mproved systems of communication and information flow, coupled with rationalizations in techniques of distribution ... made it possible to circulate commodities through the market system with greater speed. Electronic banking and plastic money were some of the innovations that improved the speed of the inverse flow of money. Financial services and markets ... likewise speeded up ... The mobilization of fashion in mass ... markets provided a means to accelerate the pace of consumption not only in clothing, ornaments and decoration but also across a wide swathe of life-styles and recreational activities ... A second trend was a shift away from the consumption of goods and into the consumption of services – not only personal, business, educational and health services, but also into entertainments, spectacles, happenings, and distractions. The "lifetime" of such services ... is far harder to estimate than that of an automobile

or washing machine. If there are limits to the accumulation
and turnover of physical goods ... then it makes sense for cap-
italists to turn to the provision of very ephemeral services in
consumption.[59]

With the rise of the Internet, and Web 2.0 in particular, we are
always consuming – if not spending money, then at least generating it in the form of advertising revenues, more than we do when
we watch network television. In Harvey's words, the primary consequence of such shifts was, and remains, to "accentuate volatility and
ephemerality of fashions, products, production techniques, labour
processes, ideas and ideologies, values and established practices."
Instantaneity and disposability have come to apply not only to produced goods but also to "values, lifestyles, stable relationships, and
attachments to things, buildings, places, people, and received ways
of doing and being" (in short, to the "structure of feeling"). Consequently, "disposability, novelty, and the prospects for instant obsolescence" became central, along with the "bombardment of stimuli"
unleashed by the increasing prominence of the image in social life as
a commodity that could be "mass-marketed instantly over space."[60]
This sheer ephemerality, this fleetingness of the present moment in
both public and private life, is central to the "structure of feeling"
in question. Indeed, it pertains to a dominant cultural experience
of space and temporality without which the "end of history" and
the "end of ideology" would appear to have no basis in lived reality. This is why I focus in this book on the "cultural imaginary" so
generated rather than on material realities or any of the many sub-
cultures or dissenting voices that attempt (with often questionable
success) to counter this dominant aesthetic.

LATE CAPITALISM AND THE COMMUNICATIONS MEDIA

The phenomena described above are only reinforced at the level of
direct sensory experience as constructed by contemporary communications technologies, which correspond to the underlying logic of
flexible accumulation in their inherent ephemerality. While Marshall
McLuhan's alleged "technological determinism" (a misleading label,
since he openly acknowledges the commingling of capitalism and
consumerism in much of his work) might be seen by more traditional Marxist critics as undermining the usefulness of any critique,

his insights concerning the impact of the media on sensory experience are not only valid but necessary for a proper consideration of how the ideological tenets of capitalism's "millennial dream" are translated into lived experience (what I have been calling the interstices of material reality with the dominant cultural imaginary). McLuhan's insights into the media as "extensions of the human sensorium"[61] are most illuminating in this respect, revealing the "logic" of modern communications technologies in a way that corresponds to the spatio-temporal co-ordinates of late capitalism and, in turn, to the posthistorical "structure of feeling."

In his landmark work, *The Gutenberg Galaxy*, and in keeping with his central insight that technologies (from language onwards) are "extensions of man" and therefore profoundly affect the structures of cognition in a given society, McLuhan examines the impact of the printing press on Western culture. He writes that the visual codification of speech that began with the introduction of the phonetic alphabet foregrounded the visual at the expense of the "balanced interplay" of the other senses and the invention of the printing press in the fifteenth century made it a large-scale, standardized phenomenon: in terms of sense perception, it entailed an increased tendency to "separate level from level, and function from function, in a process of specialist exclusion."[62] For McLuhan, alphabetically literate societies are characterized by "[s]eparateness of the individual, continuity of space and time, and uniformity of codes," and the invention of the printing press, with its own contribution to space-time compression, made of these characteristics a more generalized cultural phenomenon. The perspectivism that enabled the aforementioned "mapping" of the Renaissance world, in other words, was consistent with the cognitive structures of phonetic literacy, which for McLuhan enabled the "breaking up of every kind of experience into uniform units in order to produce faster action and change of form,"[63] as well as the separation and apprehension of space and time as measurable, as "uniform and continuous."[64] For McLuhan, the "visual mode is successive"[65] – hence the evolution of "lineal, sequential habits" in Western culture that reached their peak in the Fordist assembly line, alongside the "visual homogenizing of experience" and the development of the "fixed position or 'point of view' so natural to the reader of typography" (and, by implication, cartography). Print, for McLuhan, "exists by virtue of the static separation of functions and fosters a mentality that gradually resists any but a

separative and compartmentalizing or specialist outlook"[66] germane
to the older means of capitalist accumulation and the consumption
of cultural products.

In other words, the now outdated "perceptual equipment" by
which we remain inclined to "make sense" of the world is premised upon a primarily visual sensibility, one that rationalizes or
organizes time and space in uniform and continuous ways, enabling
the subject to assume a fixed standpoint from which to effect such
organization. However, as McLuhan notes, "[b]oth time (as measured visually and segmentally) and space (as uniform, pictorial, and
enclosed) disappear in the electronic age of instant information,"[67]
or, to put it another way, in Jameson's ubiquitous "hyperspace" (as
well as the rough equivalents proposed by Harvey and Baudrillard,
among others). In an "instantaneous world," for McLuhan as well as
postmodern critics who succeeded him, albeit on different political
grounds, "space and time interpenetrate each other totally."[68] Whatever the flaws in his emphasis on the *primacy* of the "extensions of
man" as the driving force of socio-historical change, his observations on the modes of cognition to which they correspond conform
entirely to the modified experience of space and time that these later
critics, such as Jameson and Harvey, describe and in ways that can
be readily applied to the *dominant* "culture of feeling" or "cultural
imaginary."

McLuhan's characterization of the new media as primarily auditory and tactile in nature – rather than visual – corresponds, indeed,
to the ephemerality that both Jameson and Harvey emphasize, for
the fact that sound, as Walter Ong observes, "exists only as it is going
out of existence"[69] is equally applicable to the experience of contemporary communications media. That these media are often centred
on images does not prevent their being considered as extensions of
the auditory sense, because the structures of cognition they precipitate are at least to this extent primarily aural in nature. Their central characteristic, then, is one of ephemerality as distinct from the
properties of the communication system (print) that preceded them.
Before the advent of radio and television broadcasting, the rationalization and organization of content followed the logic of cognition
that McLuhan associated with print. As Raymond Williams notes,
"the essential items were discrete [in space and time]. A book or a
pamphlet was taken and read as a specific item. A meeting occurred
at a particular date and place. A play was performed in a particular

theatre at a set hour."[70] Now, however, the media generate Jameson's "series of unrelated presents in time,"[71] with commodified time-units organized into what Williams, discussing television, calls "flow." This "flow" constitutes the "defining characteristic of broadcasting, simultaneously as a technology and as a cultural form"; for him, "the real programme that is offered is a *sequence* or set of alternative sequences of these and other similar events, which are then available in a single dimension and in a single operation."[72] This is what unfolds onscreen, and it is at once a simulacrum – a flow of images behind which is no graspable sense of the operations of capital – and inherently transient. The ephemerality that Harvey sees as already established by the accelerating imperatives of capital is thus concentrated to an unprecedented degree in the "flow" of the electronic media. As media, therefore, they set forth an eternal present to which earlier models of rationalization and organization are antithetical; indeed, as Ong notes, "[t]here is no way to stop sound and possess sound."[73] The moment of its experience, in other words, is already the moment of its passing.

Media such as television further generate a sense of *im/mediacy* corresponding to the experience of space and time alike. While they may obsess about presentation, framing, graphics, and narrative text, they also seek to present themselves as *im/mediate* – that is, as *unmediated* and, in a sense that cannot be conveyed by the printed word, *real*. No longer is the subject disposed to conceive of space or time from a "fixed" standpoint outside of it; rather, the space becomes one of total involvement, one in which the subject is always directly caught up. For McLuhan the "auditory network" is one of "total interdependence and interrelation," a "resonating world of simultaneous relations"[74] that affords no opportunity for rational detachment or its corresponding, perspectivist approach to representation. The uniform space conceived by modern cartography has given way to Google Earth and even Google Street View, the user of which can "zero in," via satellite, to a city, street, or particular building with much the same precision as the Pentagon's "smart" weapons zero in on their targets. Granted, the images on Google are not presented in "real time," but it is not difficult to imagine that they will be in the not too distant future.

The space of multinational capitalism, as Eagleton notes, is indeed a "qualitatively different sort of space altogether," a "virtual or hyper-space ... whose borders and coordinates are constantly shifting, a well-nigh infinitely malleable dimension" in which "we live and breathe and have our being but too close to the eyeball to be represented or objectified."[75] It is Jameson's "hyperspace," Baudrillard's "simulacrum," Williams's "flow," Harvey's "time-space compression," McLuhan's "auditory network," and millennial capitalism's dream of a world in which time and space have been truly and decisively conquered. Nowhere is this more evident than in the realm of electronic communication, which in overcoming Euclidean space pretends to abolish it altogether. As noted, and in Harvey's words, "the world's geographical complexity is nightly reduced to a series of images on a static television screen"[76] in much the same way that the world's commodities come to rest side by side with local products in any shopping mall or supermarket, leaving no trace of the processes of production and transportation behind them. Further still, if, as Ong puts it, "[w]riting separates the knower from the known and thus sets up the conditions for objectivity,"[77] then objectivity vanishes in this new, inclusive "aural" world, which has no equivalent "mediating" function and involves its users instead in a spatio-temporal dynamic from which rational detachment is achievable only by conscious effort – an effort not everyone is willing to make. "Immediacy" in this respect, and as I will use it predominantly throughout this book, assumes its etymological sense of *non-mediation*: the "mediating" dimensions of "objective" space and time, as apprehended from a fixed perspective, as well as of any overarching or contextualizing "fixed" narrative premise, are absent from the experience of "flow," televisual or otherwise.

THE MEDIA AND "AURATIC DECAY"

Another way to approach the phenomenon of "im/mediacy" is through the work of Walter Benjamin, who in 1936 expressed it in terms of what he saw as the "aura" of traditional artworks, this "aura" being the literal and symbolic spatial *distance* from which such art derived its autonomy, authenticity, and authority; it constituted, in effect, the "unique existence" of the artwork "at the place where it happens to be."[78] The aura thus presupposes a certain fixity in time and space, a spatial distance or separation in relation to the observing subject, which I have argued is absent in the world of electronic communication. In other words, for a work of art to maintain its aura, it must have what Samuel Weber describes as "[its] unique and uniquely inimitable site in respect to which [its] uniqueness is constituted."[79] It must, in other words, be strictly unrepeatable. Yet photography and film, as Benjamin observed, replace uniqueness with plurality, allowing works of art to "meet the beholder ... in his own particular situation." In fulfilling the "desire of contemporary masses to bring things 'closer' spatially and humanly,"[80] they dispel the mediating, "auratic" illusion of autonomy, transcendence, and unspannable distance in which the work of art is traditionally enveloped. Although the emancipatory potential that Benjamin consequently discerned within the new technologies does not seem to have been realized, giving way instead to the apparently seamless totality that constitutes for Theodor Adorno and Max Horkheimer a monolithic "culture industry,"[81] this does not mean that the concept of the "aura" and some of Benjamin's other observations on aesthetics are not useful for an analysis of the situation I have been describing. Indeed, if the "aura" as conceived by Benjamin has been replaced by something still more mystifying, then this is in no small part precisely because of the apparent elimination of a "mediating" spatial and temporal distance. And the illusion of auratic decay applies to McLuhan's "orality" just as much as to the unrepresentable "hyperspace" that Jameson, Harvey, and Eagleton describe.

The resulting mystification, contrary to Benjamin's hopes of emancipation, arises precisely from the apodictic quality of sound, the fact that it coincides with its own referent rather than constituting a separable representation of it. Indeed, as the nineteenth-century essayist Walter Pater famously noted, "[a]ll art constantly aspires towards the condition of music,"[82] toward precisely this degree of self-identity between representation and referent, or, as Harvey interprets Pater's statement, "music ... contains its aesthetic effect precisely through its temporal movement."[83] This applies to the "movement" or "flow" of the audio-visual media as well, which enforces a spatial and temporal im/mediacy that is anti-auratic in its transcendence of distance but, rather than being in any sense revolutionary as a result of this new proximity, presents itself instead as fully authentic, at one with its referent. And if this "authenticity" is now a characteristic of the viewer's or user's individual experience of the work or text rather than the unique imprint of an author or producer, it is no less mystifying in the end than the "aura" deemed undemocratic by Walter Benjamin. The televised or cinematic image, in other words, functions similarly to sound in that it presents a fleeting coincidence of what *is* with what *appears*. The "im/mediacy" so effected – as "non-mediation" – thus corresponds to the elimination of detachment or objectivity from the experience of space and time as uniform, rationally organized containers and (most importantly) to the disavowal of ideology as effected by ideology itself in its apodictic pretence. That is, much as ideology denies its existence in the very act of its own articulation, the media, now more than ever – and despite their self-consciousness as branded commodities – increasingly deny their own mediating (that is, distorting) role.

COMMODIFICATION AND THE ILLUSION OF SOCIAL COHESION

With the media as an interface between material reality and the cultural imaginary, or between economics and culture, and with television as the main "vehicle" of capitalism's self-legitimation, despite the proliferation of computer technologies,[84] their "power of instantaneous communication," as Guy Debord noted, represents "an accumulation, in the hands of the existing system's administration, of the means which allow it to carry on this particular administration."[85] Although it may not be as dispiritingly totalizing a power as theorists of Debord's ilk tend to think, it is nonetheless a compelling one, demanding of the critical viewer a conscious effort and providing for the cultural mainstream an ongoing spectacle that shapes the dominant structure of feeling. And if the "spectacle" for Debord represents a particular stage in the accumulation of capital – indeed, "capital to such a degree of accumulation that it becomes an *image*"[86] – then the machinery of images that constitutes network television (and newer media) seems an appropriate focus for the present analysis. For Iain Boal and the authors of *Afflicted Powers*, a group known as "Retort," if "spectacle society" signifies first and foremost "the submission of more and more facets of human sociability ... to the deadly solicitations ... of the market," then television and subsequent image technologies, as the chief social means to "systematize and disseminate appearance, and to subject the texture of day-to-day living to a constant barrage of images, instructions, slogans, logos, promises, virtual realities, [and] miniature happiness-motifs,"[87] can be treated as the interface between the imperatives of consumer capitalism and the logic of daily lived experience. In other words, if "the world of images [has] long been a structural necessity of a capitalism oriented toward the overproduction of commodities,"[88] then the new technologies as a perpetual machinery of images best approaches, as Harvey notes, "that ideal of the 'twinkling of an eye' that Marx saw as optimal from the standpoint of capital circulation."[89] It corresponds almost perfectly, therefore, with the compressed temporality already described, a temporality structured, as Debord puts it, on "an infinite accumulation of equivalent intervals," its "exchangeable, homogeneous units" also commodities in themselves: "[i]n its most advanced sector, concentrated capitalism orients itself towards the sale of 'completely equipped' blocks of time, each one constituting a single unified commodity which integrates a number of diverse commodities." This is most patently the case in broadcasting, where "the reality of time has been replaced by the *advertisement* of time";[90] time is truly money in that it is exchanged in homogeneous units for the advertising revenues that keep the corporate networks up and running. The temporality of the broadcast media, therefore, perfectly complements that of capitalism more broadly with its "time-space compression," with its "flow," taking place as it does in "real time," constituting a central aspect of the structure of feeling of posthistory.

Taken together, then, these aspects constitute the dominant structure of feeling in relation to which a declaration such as Fukuyama's – that history has come to an end, along with ideology, or at least any need for it – can come to appear plausible. The time-space compression of multinational capitalism and its "spectacular" corollary at the level of the media indeed create the impression of, in Jameson's words, an "age that has forgotten to think historically in the first place,"[91] an age characterized in particular by a "new depthlessness," by a "weakening of history, both in our relationship to public History and in the new forms of our private temporality,"[92] and by a "mutation in space" for which we lack the "perceptual equipment" required to "map [our] position in a mappable external world."[93] Further, it is precisely these qualities of the contemporary experience of space and time that precipitate, crucially, a sense of narrative breakdown and that consequently facilitate the belief that "belief" itself, as a set of internally coherent discursive and narrative co-ordinates, is no longer viable or at least no longer central. This is not to say that mainstream America abandoned its beliefs in the wake of the Cold War but that in a sense it required none; there was no alternative set of beliefs against which a given one could be, or needed to be, asserted.

For Jameson, indeed, the sense of a "series of pure and unrelated presents in time," so pressed to an extreme, offers an experience that can be described as "schizophrenic" – a word that he uses not in the clinical sense but as a "suggestive aesthetic model" for describing lived reality under contemporary material conditions. Jameson describes this phenomenon at the level of the individual, defining personal identity as "the effect of a certain temporal unification of past and future with one's present"[94] that is now increasingly unachievable, and my contention here is that the same applies in a broader, social sense – that is, that society itself becomes "schizophrenic" under the imperatives of late capitalism, losing any sense of historical continuity and with it any sense of a future in any way distinct from the present. Instantaneity, volatility, and ephemerality as emphasized by the imperatives of capital are brought "home" to lived reality in the perpetual acceleration of production, consumption, and imagery. They contribute, then, to this breakdown in narrative, temporal, or historical understanding, the fallout of which is an apparent or "felt" end to history itself.

Complementing this development are the destabilizing effects of flexible accumulation in a very material sense – that is, with regard to class and social relations. While a new "transnational" class celebrates its conquest of the globe as a traversable totality, there are many others, indeed a majority, for whom flexible accumulation has meant only increasing insecurity, alienation, and disempowerment. The impact of flexible accumulation on the domestic labour market, as Harvey notes, has been defined since the outset by structural unemployment, de-skilling and re-skilling, minimal improvements in the real wage, and the fatal weakening of trade unions. Further, it depends to a substantial extent upon "flexible work regimes and labor contracts," relying increasingly on part-time, temporary, and contract work.[95] In other words, the permanent underclass created with the Industrial Revolution is now broader and differently defined, often in a way that obfuscates notions of "class" altogether, especially in America.

This too contributes to the overall sense of narrative breakdown and to the sense of transience and ephemerality already described. As Jean and John L. Comaroff observe,

[t]he workplace and labour, especially work-and-place securely rooted in a stable local context, are no longer prime sites for

the creation of value and identity ... The factory and the shop, far from secure centres of fabrication and family income, are increasingly experienced by virtue of their erasure: either by their removal to elsewhere – where labour is cheaper, less assertive, less taxed, more feminized, less protected by states and unions – or by their replacement at the hands of nonhuman or "nonstandard" means of manufacture. Which, in turn, has left behind, for ever more people, a legacy of irregular piecework, of menial "workfare," of relatively insecure, transient, gainless occupation.[96]

Corresponding to this is an undermining of any "useful" sense of collective identity – that is, one that can be mobilized in the interests of the redistribution of wealth – except insofar as it can be asserted by the fragmentary dynamics of identity politics, which is by no means always progressive. Undermined as well is any "useful" sense of "history" or indeed of capitalism itself. As capitalism progressively "[emancipates] itself from the working class,"[97] it erodes the very constituents of class identity, weakening those "[w]orking-class forms of organization" that for Harvey "depended heavily upon the massing of workers within the factory for their viability."[98] Further, as Harvey notes, it engenders a shift "from the collective norms and values, that were hegemonic at least in working-class organizations and other social movements of the 1950s and 1960s, towards a much more competitive individualism as the central value in an entrepreneurial culture that has penetrated many walks of life."[99]

As Benjamin well knew, a sense of collective social existence – a "useful sense of collective identity" – is integral to a sense of both public history and the possibility of historical progress. As he notes in "Theses on the Philosophy of History," this is why the ruling classes seek to abolish history altogether.[100] And a voracious capitalism that denies the very source of its survival – namely, human labour and oppression – achieves precisely this effect. The inherently alienating and atomizing tendencies of capitalism are pressed to an extreme under the imperatives of flexible accumulation, adding a profound sense of social fragmentation to an already disoriented and destabilized "mass" public. In this way, it differs from the "permanent underclass" identified in earlier Marxist thought.

Acceleration, ephemerality, compression of time and space, narrative breakdown, erosion of individual and collective identity: all of

these interrelated phenomena arising from the "logic" of late capitalism constitute the structure of feeling I have just described. The
absence of any "mediating" element in the subject–object relationship
and the end, as defined by Lyotard, of any contextualizing "grand
narratives" or "metanarratives"[101] allow for the disavowal of ideology so central to "posthistory" as the latest global configuration.

THE POLITICS OF FEAR

Lyotard, in his treatise on postmodernism, poses an intriguing question: "Where, after the metanarratives, can legitimacy reside?"[102]
This, indeed, is the central crisis faced by posthistorical culture
precisely as it seeks to universalize itself through the extension of
free markets around the globe. "Western civilization," notes Terry
Eagleton, "which has now embarked on a more ambitiously aggressive foreign policy, needs some spiritual legitimation for this project
at just the time when it is threatening to come apart at the cultural
seams"; it is "disabled at the very moment when it needs to affirm
its universal authority."[103] For a while, the united front presented
just after 9/11 served as precisely that, transcending the fragmentary
or centrifugal tendencies of identity politics, which had at least to
some extent stepped in to fill the void created when class identity left
the scene. But the declared end of history and ostensible end of any
need for ideology has made things difficult for the most full-throated
defenders of posthistory just as they seek the means to implement
their agenda on a global scale.

The West, in other words, is now faced with a critical problem
at the level of representation or ideological self-legitimation. What
Tom Engelhardt called "victory culture," largely based on a narrative
motif of Western-style "ambush" by easily distinguishable Others
followed by the justifiable eradication of those Others,[104] had faded
away or had come to be manifested in contradictory and confusing
cultural products positing a variety of potential enemies following
the collapse of communism as a threat to the American "way of life."
And it was precisely at this critical juncture that what is increasingly
known as the "politics of fear" came into play. Of course, the politics
of fear is nothing new in American history. From the Salem witch
hunts through Western expansion to the "Red Scare" of the 1950s
and the Soviet threat that hung over America throughout the second
half of the twentieth century,[105] it has surfaced time and again as an

instrument of social control. But it is the way in which such fear-mongering squares with the posthistorical structure of feeling in contemporary mass cultural production that is of interest here, substituting for the lack of a credible, teleological "grand narrative" that would project a genuinely desirable goal and emphasizing the preservation of the status quo by all necessary means against the possibility of its own destruction. To put it more bluntly, whereas "progress" in the Enlightenment sense of the word has allegedly "ended," we are facing not a utopian future but the perpetual threat of annihilation. Engelhardt claims that this politics of fear originated with the first deployment of atomic bombs over Japan in 1945,[106] and to a limited extent he is right in that it became inconceivable that any large-scale war could be fought without mass extinction as an overshadowing possibility. Yet at that time there was still an identifiable ideological enemy to be confronted, and "conventional" proxy wars were fought throughout the Cold War period, justified by the US on the grounds that any successful Soviet takeover in a region could trigger a "domino effect" (it didn't).[107] But now nuclear weapons (or other weapons of mass destruction [WMDs]) in the hands of terrorists,[108] ballistic missiles fired by "rogue" states, epidemics originating in the East, escalating crime and social breakdown, and similar dangers come to figure ever more prominently in the cultural imaginary as the sustaining narratives of "progress" fade into an idealized past. This imaginary becomes a matter of politics – that is, it comes to serve as an instrument of social control – in the legitimating narratives of the War on Terror in which the ruling system has found a means of justifying itself and its actions at home and abroad, supported by eager corporate news networks and the fabricators of Hollywood plots. (Obama's rhetoric has marked a "toning down" of this paradigm, if not yet accompanied by any substantive change in policy.) Following a supposedly posthistorical decade during which the gap between the real and the ideal became increasingly difficult to mask, the terrorist attacks of 11 September 2001 provided the Bush administration with sufficient ideological ammunition to defend its outward aggression over the course of the years up to the end of his administration in early 2009. And yet it is the very same structure of feeling that prompted the celebration of the "end of history" and the "new world order" that lends itself here equally seamlessly to the proliferation of a host of cultural fears and insecurities, which are in many instances a displacement of legitimate social anxieties onto more cathartic ones. As Jameson aptly puts it, the spectacle of late capitalist culture, "by transforming the past into visual mirages, stereotypes, or texts, effectively abolishes any practical sense of the future and of the collective project, thereby abandoning the thinking of future change to fantasies of sheer catastrophe and inexplicable cataclysm, from visions of 'terrorism' on the social level to those of cancer on the personal."[109]

In other words, even as the celebrants of the "end of history" envision the globe united as a harmonious electronic totality, so too do others envision a world that is hopelessly divided, imposing upon this fragmented totality a narrative of overall decay and decline that culminates in an apocalyptic finale. The simultaneous success in "intellectual" circles of such polarized theories as Fukuyama's and Huntington's can be at least partly explained by this dichotomy.

As noted, for ideology to be at all effective, it must be comprehensible in relation to socio-economic realities as well as the spatio-temporal co-ordinates of the contemporary structure of feeling. This is why the term "ideology" cannot be restricted to a notion of "false consciousness"; on the contrary, there is nothing "false" about it. Ideology itself is a real, material force, and it draws upon and reinforces a real consciousness corresponding to the broader structure of feeling linked to post-industrial capitalism in which it must take root to have any force. Further, and perhaps more importantly, it must meet certain real and legitimate needs arising from the socio-economic context and the structure of feeling in question – despite its inadequacies, its internal contradictions or antinomies, and the confusion or sense of dislocation and displacement that it generates. "Ideology" as I use it is therefore always inseparable from the structure of feeling – that is, the "dominant" structure of feeling; it constitutes a real, material force that provides a nonetheless illusory resolution to real, legitimate social needs and desires.

The fragmenting and alienating processes described in this chapter, combined with the inherently disorienting experience of space and time in their latest phase of "compression," generate specific needs and anxieties to which this dominant structure of feeling, and an ideology now premised on fear, presents itself as a response. Its self-disavowal removes any mediating framework within which the root causes of such anxieties can be properly apprehended and substitutes for it a host of increasingly interchangeable "bogeymen" that allegedly constitute an external threat to the self and society, ignoring any threat generated by the mechanisms of capitalism itself. I am by no means arguing that such insecurities and anxieties are in themselves illegitimate, nor do I wish to suggest that certain fears, such as of terrorism or environmental degradation, are unfounded. Rather, it is the way in which such fears are manipulated and made to serve the ruling interests that concerns me, particularly at the level of mass cultural production – in other words, the way in which a perceived threat becomes the site of a mass projection of anxieties at the expense of any "useful" understanding of their material, socio-economic origins.

As legitimation premised on fear exerts itself across the spectrum of popular culture, "official" rhetoric, and both print and broadcast journalism, we must therefore be careful not to dismiss "ideology," in Jameson's words, as "sheer manipulation, sheer commercial brainwashing," as "empty distraction or 'mere' false consciousness" (after all, as noted, it never was and can never be truly monolithic) but instead approach it as a "transformational work on social and political anxieties and fantasies which must then have some effective presence in [a given] mass cultural text in order subsequently to be 'managed' or 'repressed.'" This, he suggests, is the function of the "consumption-satisfaction" offered by commodities such as Hollywood film, which "[give] and [take] alike in a kind of psychic compromise or horse-trading, which strategically [arouse] fantasy content within careful symbolic containment structures which defuse it, gratifying intolerable, unrealizable, properly imperishable desires only to the degree to which they can again be laid to rest."[110]

What "mass culture" offers, in the main, is the invocation and effective acknowledgment (often by displacement) of structural anxieties, followed by their defusion by means of an illusion of collectivity in the face of increasing social atomization, and this, I would argue, is also a key function of the politics of fear. The evocation and maintenance of a "simulacrum of community" is a primary ideological function of the commodity world itself, and the need for this illusion of harmony grows all the more pressing as the "real" social order careens toward ever greater extremes of instability, insecurity, and fragmentation. Indeed, as Harvey notes, late capitalism generates nothing so much as a "search for personal or collective identity ... for secure moorings in a shifting world."[111] One might say, as Samuel Weber observes in a somewhat narrower context, that the commodity comes to "[present] itself as the antidote to the disorder to which it contributes."[112] That is, the more that late multinational or consumer capitalism atomizes and pulverizes, the more the commodity comes to serve the anodyne function of creating and preserving an illusion of social harmony at the level of the image and the simulacrum, and this merges seamlessly with the politics of fear, which reaffirms the illusion of collectivity in the face of an external factor that threatens to destroy it. This function is no longer the preserve of the "popular arts" alone but also of virtually any text designed for mass consumption, including news coverage and official rhetoric, which in many ways are commodities in themselves. My argument, then, is that the "consumption-satisfaction" discussed by Jameson in relation to Hollywood films applies across the board: that every aspect of dominant political and ideological legitimation has come to function as a commodity in its own right and in its constitution of a "deadly simulacrum" of cohesion defined, primarily, against an external threat.

SYNOPSIS

This chapter is intended as an outline of the broadest theoretical assumptions informing the present analysis – assumptions relating to the place of ideology within a structure of feeling premised on the logic of late capitalism, one that disrupts the uniformity and continuity of time and space in varying ways and in combination, moreover, with a disruptive and disempowering trend effected by flexible accumulation. Subsequent chapters will consider the socio-economic conditions of late capitalism, the structure of feeling that has arisen as a result, and the sensory impact of the communications media in relation to popular representations and perceptions of the post–Cold War period, from the first Gulf War through to the terrorist attacks of 11 September 2001 and well into Gulf War II. Such representations – that is, the most popular – will be considered throughout, both as commodities and in terms of their mainstream reception at the level of sensory experience – that is, as constituted by the structure of the media as technologies.

A primary assumption, then, is that there is an element of reciprocity or mutual support between the economics, the politics, and the culture of posthistory in America. The posthistorical structure of feeling just outlined lends substantial ideological and material force to the legitimating discourses of the American global enterprise as disseminated in the official rhetoric, the network news, and the popular arts. Yet the discursive co-ordinates of this structure of feeling and its grasp on the cultural imaginary are by no means free of internal contradictions or immune to opposition; neither the structure of feeling nor its accompanying ideology can lay claim to hegemonic status in a totalizing manner. I will reveal a great deal more about the fissures in the dominant aesthetic and ideology toward the end of this book with a closer examination of the dissent that began to arise as Gulf War II dragged interminably on. Nonetheless, this book will trace the particular ways in which the posthistorical structure of feeling feeds into mainstream American culture, thereby reproducing itself, as well as the ways in which various aspects are pressed into the service of the administration's interests, whether or not it was unanimously accepted (and it wasn't, although dissent was effectively silenced early on and thus not nearly as vocal as it later became).

The next chapter discusses the early years of the posthistorical period and in particular how the ostensible superiority of liberal-democratic capitalism over its alternatives was translated from the realm of systematic ideology into the cultural structure of feeling in the specific context of the collapse of communism and the first Gulf War as a media event. The "new world order" as declared and defined by the first Bush administration on 11 September 1990 will be examined in some detail, along with Gulf War I as the first decisive instantiation of that order, both in relation to posthistory more broadly and at the level of the dominant structure of feeling. I will also discuss the media coverage of the war in terms of the consumption-satisfaction it generated as a commodity – that is, in its creation of an illusion of a collectivity both positively and negatively defined. Overall, I will define this period as a short-lived but definitive moment of harmony between global events, the assimilation of these events into the ideological framework of late capitalism, and the immediate experience of them as a commodity and a media event.[113]

2

Brave New World Order

It is decidedly eerie to review a six-volume CNN video retrospective of the first Gulf War[1] some twenty years later – to review the network's original footage and commentary, the showcasing of American weaponry, the interviews with General Schwarzkopf and the now deceased Saddam Hussein. It is strange to view the coverage as unconscious of what was to come, the words of George H.W. Bush as untainted by the words of his son, and most of all the claim to victory as we now watch a much smaller US-led "coalition" effectively giving up on the deteriorating nation, receding without any clear "victory." Baudrillard's assertion that the war "did not take place"[2] remains controversial but is far more illuminating in hindsight. It *was* a spectacular war – a fact never really in dispute – but Schwarzkopf's famous "left hook" on Iraqi forces, a move that effectively ended the war, seems now to have deceived America more than its adversary, as I will explain in more detail later.

It was 2 August 1990 when Iraqi President Saddam Hussein ordered three divisions of his Republican Guard across the border of Kuwait, a tiny nation of key strategic interest to Iraq, partly as one of its creditors during the conflict with Iran in the 1980s and partly because of its oil reserves. Iraqi forces swiftly seized control of Kuwait City, including its government, military, and communications infrastructure, prompting fears that Saudi Arabia, a key US ally in the region, might be next on Hussein's hit list.

Ostensibly at Saudi Arabia's request, President George H.W. Bush authorized and implemented Operation Desert Shield, dispatching thousands of troops to the region on 7 August. In a landmark speech to Congress on 11 September 1990, Bush urged bipartisan support for the internationally sanctioned actions in the Gulf, actions undertaken, so he claimed, to "defend civilized values around the world and maintain our economic strength at home."[3]

As already noted, America's establishment as the world's only remaining superpower had occasioned a corresponding transition in how it would "justify" its actions to itself and to the world. The shift in its foreign policy from the Cold War strategies of containment and deterrence (punctuated by occasional covert interventions) to relatively open and active intervention seemed an opportunity to realize its "manifest destiny," ostensibly in the interests of all humanity. A key imperative would be to maintain a stable global environment in which the "new world order" could fruitfully take root, and for Bush, the new spirit of cooperation had become truly international. Now, "a new partnership of nations [had] begun," offering "a rare opportunity to move toward an historic period of cooperation," and further,

> [o]ut of these troubled times, our fifth objective – a *new world order* – can emerge: a new era – freer from the threat of terror, stronger in the pursuit of justice, and more secure in the quest for peace. An era in which the nations of the world, East and West, North and South, can prosper and live in harmony. A hundred generations have searched for this elusive path to peace, while a thousand wars raged across the span of human endeavor. Today that new world is struggling to be born, a world quite different from the one we've known. A world where the rule of law supplants the rule of the jungle. A world in which nations recognize the shared responsibility for freedom and justice. A world where the strong respect the rights of the weak.[4]

The irony in his invocation of "the rule of law" and his emphasis on "[respecting] the rights of the weak" hardly needs mentioning here, particularly in light of what has transpired since. But in any case, events up to that point seemed to confirm the president's vision of a "new world order" in the ascendance. As Perry Anderson points out, at the time of the crisis in the Gulf, "it looked as if the consensual reach of American diplomacy was greater than ever before."[5] Iraq's threat to oil pricing worldwide, as well as to the stability of the Gulf

region, allowed the US to secure the support of the United Nations
Security Council and to assemble a coalition of twenty-eight nations
willing to contribute to the war effort. Crisis and opportunity for
Bush came hand in hand as Iraq's invasion of Kuwait triggered an
international response designed, so it seemed, to further the objectives of the "new world order." It was, in his words, "the first assault
on the new world that we seek, the first test of our mettle," any
weakness in the face of which would be an undesirable "signal to
actual and potential despots around the world." Even four months
before the war, when diplomacy was still an option in principle, the
rhetoric was militant in tone: "America and the world must stand up
to aggression," declared Bush in the same September speech, "America will not be intimidated."[6] At stake were the foundations of this
"new world order" – freedom, justice, security, peace, and the rule of
law – and these values were to be defended at all costs. Indeed, by 11
September 1990, the world response seemed promising. For Bush,

> [r]ecent events have surely proven that there is no substitute for
> American leadership. In the face of tyranny, let no one doubt
> American credibility and reliability. Let no one doubt our stay-
> ing power. We will stand by our friends. One way or another,
> the leader of Iraq must learn this fundamental truth. From the
> outset, acting hand in hand with others, we've sought to fashion
> the broadest possible international response to Iraq's aggres-
> sion. The level of world cooperation and condemnation of Iraq
> is unprecedented. Armed forces from countries spanning four
> continents are there at the request of King Fahd of Saudi Arabia
> to deter and, if need be, to defend against attack. Moslems and
> non-Moslems, Arabs and non-Arabs, soldiers from many nations
> stand shoulder to shoulder, resolute against Saddam Hussein's
> ambitions.[7]

For Bush, the promise of a "United Nations that performs as
envisioned by its founders" – an ironic statement in light of his son's
rejection of the UN's efficacy twelve years later – was finally on the
verge of realization. A United Nations that "[backs] up its words
with action," imposing economic sanctions and authorizing the "use
of all means necessary to ensure compliance" with them[8] was for
Bush a United Nations that was relevant, up-to-date, and instrumen-
tal in the establishment and preservation of a "new world order."[9]

It was indeed in this same September speech that Bush first publicly outlined the terms of such an order in a way that might have met with more resistance had the "crisis in the Gulf" not already been in full swing. In the president's words, Iraq was "literally trying to wipe a country off the face of the Earth" and gain control of some 20 per cent of the world's proven oil reserves. Control of Kuwait's oil on top of its own would have given Iraq "the economic and military power, as well as the arrogance, to intimidate and coerce its neighbors – neighbors [including Saudi Arabia] who control the lion's share of the world's oil reserves."[10] Yet despite the emphasis on oil, it was (supposedly) not economic self-interest that prompted the US to take charge but rather the interests of the "civilized" world on the whole: "[w]e cannot permit a resource so vital to be dominated by one so ruthless" as Saddam Hussein, according to Bush, lest the "rule of the jungle" be granted free rein worldwide.[11]

Already it was clear that the "new world order" was about more than international cooperation, even of the sort that assumed a harmony of interests between former Cold War enemies or between Western states and Arab ones. Bush's rhetoric may have implied that such an order was emerging, but to some extent the end of the Cold War had already ensured its establishment, at least for a time, because the collapse of the USSR meant, as Anderson notes, that "there was no longer any countervailing force on earth capable of withstanding U.S. military might."[12] This fact in and of itself enabled the representation of the global situation within the discursive coordinates of an "order" whose integrity would not be undermined by the "rogue" actions of any one state acting unilaterally. The "end of history" would not permit such a disturbance. What the Gulf crisis afforded was an opportunity to instantiate the West's "new world order" in such a way as to set a global precedent and to demonstrate America's efficiency as a force for "good" in the world – a world in which an aggressive dictator such as Saddam Hussein could be compared only (and repeatedly) to a Hitler.[13]

This chapter is primarily concerned with the translation of this systematic ideological paradigm into "lived reality" through, in particular, the Persian Gulf War *as a media event* – not, I would emphasize, as a historical event but as the first "live" war to appear on American screens. It seems that this period witnessed a harmonious synchrony between global events, the ideology of liberal-democratic capitalism, and the "lived experience" of both. In a sense, the "structure of feeling" already described predated these key events and to a considerable extent actually enabled their representation within the framework of the "new world order" that Bush proclaimed. Nonetheless, within the realm of popular cultural production, it was the Persian Gulf War as a media event that truly brought posthistory "home" in certain definitive ways. Ideologically speaking, it was already a "posthistorical" war, and its coverage seemed to coincide almost seamlessly with the set of beliefs employed in its legitimation. The purpose of this chapter is to explore the ways in which this apparent harmony – apparent because the coverage was so tightly controlled by the Pentagon, with or without the networks' consent – was achieved.

LAW AND (THE NEW WORLD) ORDER

On the surface, the fact of war, particularly one in which the US was compelled to assume a leading role, would seem to contradict the declaration of an "end" to history, first made in *The National Interest* in 1989. However, the Persian Gulf War exemplified what Guy Debord, referring to the "spectacle" more broadly, termed the "choice already made."[14] One way in which this already irrevocable "choice" was asserted was by recourse to the familiar framework of "law and order." In other words, although the Bush response characterized Iraq's actions as imperialist in nature, thereby to better set the scene for war against a budding Hitler, the Persian Gulf War was in a broader sense less an actual war than an assertion of America's right to enforce the law and of the implications for future transgressors. Iraq's invasion of Kuwait was portrayed less as the assertion of imperial ambitions than as a criminal act. This is clear from the chosen wording: Iraq's taking of hostages was a "ruthless policy" by which America and the world [would] not be blackmailed"; its invasion of Kuwait was an "illegal conquest," the spoils of which Iraq would be forced to relinquish; and consequently, the "prudent multiyear defense program" for which Bush sought congressional approval had to reflect "not only the improvement in East–West relations but our broader responsibilities to deal with the continuing risks of outlaw action and regional conflict."[15] The enemy, by this logic, was no longer a superpower seeking to impose a different system or order on a region or the world but a "criminal" or "outlaw" state seeking to destabilize an order already in place, and the

US, by extension, had to assume the role of a "policeman" seeking to restore law and order and preserve it for future generations, using Iraq as an example.

Accordingly, America's objectives – and those of the twenty-seven other countries supporting its actions in the Gulf – were quite "clear" from the outset: to expel Iraqi forces from Kuwait and to restore the latter's "legitimate government" and "freedom."[16] (Never mind that Kuwait was anything but a "free" state at the time of Iraq's invasion; footage of the "peaceful" nation taken prior to the war shows women clad in the very same sort of burqas that would later serve as a rallying cry for the "liberation" of Afghanistan from Taliban rule but that drew no attention at that time.) A further long-term goal was to have Iraq "comply with all relevant United Nations resolutions" and become a "peaceful and cooperative member of the family of nations"[17] – a tall order for a country armed through-out the previous decade by none other than the United States itself. However, in the context and by the logic of the "new world order," such goals were fully realistic. Saddam Hussein's Iraq represented not the emergence of a new and enduring antagonist to world peace but rather a criminal aberration, a temporary and resolvable viola-tion of law and order of the sort that Fukuyama would never con-sider capital-H "History." The cooperation of both the former Soviet Union and other Arab nations suggested that neither political nor cultural difference could stand in the way of global harmony, of the "universal" precepts of liberal-democratic capitalism – law, order, and freedom. Indeed, Bush made much of the fact that other Arab nations supported the United States, whose response was in no way directed against "the Iraqi people" but rather against "Iraq's dictator and ... his aggression."[18]

Despite this suggestion of transience, the comparison with a real "historical" enemy – Hitler – was also crucial in building up a *casus belli* within the cultural imaginary. As John MacArthur notes as well, a clear image of Kuwait as a "democracy" had to be projected, and it was.[19] I will examine these projections in greater detail in the following pages. For now, what counts is that the enemy-image of Saddam Hussein, murderous as indeed he was, came to be juxta-posed with the ideal of a reformed and redeemed Iraq, sharing in global peace and prosperity. Whereas Iraq – the "Iraqi people" – could in principle assume a useful role in the "new world order," the country's dictator most assuredly could not. And although there

is no doubt that his reign was one of terror, this is less relevant
to the present analysis – which focuses on the American cultural
imaginary – than the way in which the official rhetoric focused on
Hussein himself as a "rogue" individual at the expense of any useful
consideration of the actual historical context of his actions, including America's support for his regime during the Iran–Iraq war.
"Saddam," designated more often than not by his first name – as
an individual rather than as the head of a political party – stood
alone as the man who single-handedly "raped, pillaged, and plundered a tiny nation, no threat to his own," subjecting its citizens
to "unspeakable atrocities"[20] (such as the oft-disputed baby incu-
bator incident described by the daughter of the Kuwaiti ambas-
sador to the US, who was not identified by name at the time).[21]
His "ruthless, systematic rape of a peaceful neighbor" had "violated
everything the community of nations holds dear,"[22] including, presumably, women's rights (note the rape imagery), even though the
lack of recognition of such rights in Kuwait failed to register on the
administration's radar. The Iraqi invasion of Kuwait was thereby
portrayed as an isolated criminal's outright and defiant rejection
of the shared and undisputed "values" of the international community. To some extent, of course, this is precisely what it was,
at least insofar as the Iraqi leader had acted in violation of international law and the principle of national sovereignty, not to mention human rights, but the tireless emphasis on Saddam Hussein in
and of himself as a defiant and dangerous criminal had ideological
implications well beyond the localized terms of the crisis at hand.
The paradigm of law enforcement implied by his portrayal as an
outlaw facilitated the ongoing transition to a discursive framework
enabling America to present itself in the dominant cultural imaginary as a global "policeman" for years to come.

Within the more immediate context of the ongoing crisis, what
this paradigm permitted was a simplistic narrative in which America, backed by the United Nations, could impose an ultimatum
on the Iraqi leader, could respond to or ignore any efforts on his
part toward a diplomatic solution,[23] and, finally, could crack down
on the recalcitrant dictator should he not withdraw uncondition-
ally from Kuwait. The long-anticipated outbreak of hostilities on
16 January 1991 thus represented for Bush a "historic moment"
in the forging of a "new world order" in which "the rule of law,
not the law of the jungle, governs the conduct of nations."[24] The

implications in the cultural imaginary were to prevail over dissenting voices.[25] "Rogue" states would remain a threat to be defused by American firepower alone. Diplomacy, as Bush announced on the first night of the Persian Gulf War, had failed, leaving no option but attack. The air strikes on Iraq, he took care to emphasize, had the blessing of both the United Nations and Congress, following as they did "months of constant and virtually endless diplomatic activity on the part of the United Nations, the United States, and many, many other countries":

Arab leaders sought what became known as the Arab solution, only to conclude that Saddam Hussein was unwilling to leave Kuwait. Others traveled to Baghdad in a variety of efforts to restore peace and justice. Our Secretary of State, James Baker, held an historic meeting in Geneva, only to be totally rebuffed. This past weekend, in a last-ditch effort, the Secretary-General of the United Nations went to the Middle East with peace in his heart – his second such mission. And he came back from Baghdad with no progress at all in getting Saddam Hussein to withdraw from Kuwait ... While the world waited, while Saddam stalled, more damage was being done to the fragile economies of the Third World, emerging democracies of Eastern Europe, to the entire world, including our own economy.[26]

The war, then, was the Iraqi dictator's own choice: "[w]hile the world prayed for peace," Bush stated, "Saddam prepared for war" – as if the amassing of some 250,000 American troops in Saudi Arabia was not war preparation – and "arrogantly rejected all warnings" as well as "every overture of peace."[27] In the face of an enemy so determined to wreak havoc on the region and the world, America and its allies had no choice but to restore order by military force. And indeed, throughout the conflict, "Saddam" the individual remained the sole focus of the American-led war effort. According to Bush, "[w]e are determined to knock out Saddam Hussein's nuclear bomb potential. We will also destroy his chemical weapons facilities. Much of Saddam's artillery and tanks will be destroyed. Our operations are designed to best protect the lives of all the coalition forces by targeting Saddam's vast military arsenal."[28]

Once again, the image of the criminal Saddam was juxtaposed with the "people of Iraq," with whom, Bush reiterated, the American-led coalition "[had] no argument." The goal was "not the conquest of Iraq" but the "liberation of Kuwait," a defenseless nation "raped, pillaged, and plundered" by a ruthless criminal.[29]

Thus, on 16 January 1991 the escalating narrative of the Gulf crisis came to a head. And well before the end of the war – in his 29 January State of the Union Address – Bush was already heralding a new "American century," calling for "new initiatives" and for "every American to prepare" to lead the world into the future.[30] This future, to which America alone held the keys, would be one in which (as the Persian Gulf War would show) "brutality [would] go unrewarded and aggression [would] meet collective resistance."[31] Further, only the United States could lead in this effort, because it alone possessed "both the moral standing and the means to back it up" in its capacity as "the only nation on this Earth that [could] assemble the forces of peace."[32] Less than two weeks into the war, "the world now [stood] as one"; together, it was working "to achieve another victory, a victory over tyranny and savage aggression."[33]

From the outset, victory was already more or less guaranteed. It was only a matter of weeks before the "forces of peace" would achieve their stated aim in the Gulf. The aerial war in Iraq, which saw an average of one bombing sortie per minute from its inception on 16 January,[34] continued unabated until Iraqi "targets" were deemed sufficiently depleted for a successful ground invasion to take place. A last-minute effort at diplomatic resolution, aided by the Soviets, was rejected by Bush, who claimed on 22 February that Iraq had imposed a number of "unacceptable" conditions on its withdrawal from Kuwait and that, furthermore, Saddam Hussein was now implementing a "scorched-earth" policy on its annexed neighbour.[35] Bush then set a deadline of noon on Saturday, 23 February, for Saddam Hussein to publicly announce both his withdrawal from Kuwait and his unconditional capitulation to UN demands. When the deadline passed, the "liberation of Kuwait," according to Bush, "entered a final phase,"[36] with the commencement of a ground war designed, as was evident by noon the next day, not only to "liberate" the country but to decimate retreating Iraqi forces in the process.[37]

The overwhelming success promised by the Bush administration quickly materialized. By 25 February, the networks were reporting numerous triumphs on the part of the US-led coalition. Apart from a Scud attack on a residential complex outside Dhahran that killed twenty-eight American soldiers, the situation appeared to be improving by the hour. Saddam Hussein ordered his troops out of Kuwait that same afternoon. Yet the US maintained its offensive, continuing to kill Iraqi forces as they retreated to Basra. On 27 February, the US announced that its coalition had blocked off Iraqi escape routes and was now engaged in large-scale battle. That evening, Bush appeared on live television to declare success in the "liberation" of Kuwait as well as the wholesale defeat of Iraqi forces. General Norman Schwarzkopf then presented a live, blow-by-blow account of the coalition's overwhelming victory. The war was thus won less than a week after the ground offensive began, with George H.W. Bush emerging triumphant as the leader of his proclaimed "new world order." The United States' role as the world's leading superpower was effectively confirmed by its victory in the Gulf, while the cooperation of some twenty-seven other nations was cited as evidence of a new era of international consensus and harmony. For Bush, indeed, the American-led victory was also "a victory for every country in the coalition, for the United Nations" and for "unprecedented international cooperation" and, ironically, "diplomacy." Further, it marked "a victory for the rule of law and for what is right," following which "[o]ur uncommon coalition must now work in common purpose: to forge a future that should never again be held hostage to the darker side of human nature."[38]

Bush summarized the ultimate significance of the war in relation to the narrative of the "new world order" in the following terms:

[t]he consequences of the conflict in the Gulf reached far beyond the confines of the Middle East. Twice before in this century, an entire world was convulsed by war. Twice this century, out of the horrors of war hope emerged for enduring peace. Twice before, these hopes proved a distant dream, beyond the grasp of man. Until now, the world we've known has been a world divided – a world of barbed wire and concrete block, conflict, and cold war. Now, we can see a new world coming into view. A world in which there is the very real prospect of a new world order ... A world where the United Nations, freed from cold war stalemate, is poised to fulfill the historic vision of its founders. A world in which freedom and respect for human rights find a home among all nations. The Gulf War put this new world to its first test. And, my fellow Americans, we passed that test.[39]

For Bush, posthistory in the neo-conservative sense was now in full swing: America remained "what Lincoln said it was more than a century ago, 'the last best hope on Earth.'"[40] The "American leadership that undermined the confidence and capacity of the Communist regimes" was now a "beacon of hope for all the peoples of the world," and "[t]he end of the cold war ... has placed in our hands a unique opportunity to see the principles for which America has stood for two centuries, democracy, free enterprise, and the rule of law, spread more widely than ever before in human history."[41] American leadership, for Bush, was not only ideal but also necessary in order to guarantee the security of the American people: "[a] retreat from American leadership, from American involvement"[42] could destabilize the "democratic revolution" underway and "pose a direct threat to the safety of every single American."[43] Challenges remained, but they were challenges that America could overcome in its mission to lead the world in a "new order." They were certainly not "challenges" along the lines of 9/11.

Although the Persian Gulf War as a historical event seemed to contradict the declaration of posthistory, its legitimating narratives and its discursive co-ordinates nonetheless assured it a logical place in the establishment of a triumphant, unipolar "new world order." From Iraq's invasion of Kuwait in August 1990 until America's "victory" the following February, the Bush administration presented its public with what seemed a clear-cut and morally unambiguous narrative: a murderous criminal, not altogether unlike Hitler in his cruelty, his cold-bloodedness, and his naked ambition, had violated the principles of international law as founded on national sovereignty and in so doing had posed a threat to international security; his refusal to comply with Security Council resolutions had left America no choice but to wage war, with the backing of the international community; and his swift and decisive defeat by a broad, US-led coalition had heralded a golden age of consensus and cooperation among the nations of the world. This narrative involved, as MacArthur points out, a "tireless" effort to "awaken the docile journalists to a previously little known danger named Saddam Hussein" and to fix Kuwait's "image problem" for those in the US who knew of the country's existence:[44]

As recently as May 1990, [Hussein] had been portrayed by the Pentagon as a rather ordinary Middle Eastern dictator who happened to kill political opponents with poison gas. Just four months later he was cast by the Administration as the uniquely evil equivalent of Adolf Hitler; suddenly the Iraqi President relished the use of gas on ethnic minorities, particularly Kurds and – if he could get away with it – Israeli Jews.[45]

In citing the administration's unyielding efforts to demonize Saddam Hussein, I do not mean to downplay his egregious human rights violations but rather to show that this "historic opportunity," at the end of "history" proper, was already posthistorical in its logic. That is, the narrative of America's seizure of this "opportunity" was little more than a representation in readily comprehensible terms of a new situation, one in which, for better or for worse, America was now free to pursue its objectives and further its interests virtually without restraint. The parallels drawn to Hitler pointed to inevitability, to the choice "already made" – the choice, commendable in principle, never to permit such atrocities again. But this "choice" was restricted, by means of this comparison, to the realm of the cultural imaginary: it was not a "choice" that was exercised in parts of the world where America had no "interests" to protect. As Anderson points out, the Bush administration's emphasis on international consensus and collaboration masked a more profound transformation in international relations, one that shifted the balance of American hegemony toward coercion and away from consent.[46] Still further, it imbued the Gulf conflict with an overriding historical "necessity," presenting it as the culmination of a series of attempts to achieve global harmony. The Persian Gulf War was to the Bush administration what the end of the Cold War was to Fukuyama: namely, the logical conclusion to a universal narrative in which America, by dint of its "manifest destiny," would assume the leading role in global affairs. That this narrative had "ended" happily in this case was not cause for complacency; America would have to remain vigilant, neutralizing any threats to global stability and security as they arose. But it was certainly cause for celebration. There was clearly but one solution to the problems of the world, and it was the establishment and preservation of the "freedom" defined by the now inseparable principles of free markets, free elections, and human rights.[47]

More important still in terms of the cultural imaginary, the sheer swiftness and decisiveness of America's victory in the Gulf – a war that "kicked the Vietnam Syndrome once and for all"[48] – seemed to indicate that no dictator would go unpunished, that any man fool enough to challenge America's leadership would meet irresistible force. Indeed, "kicking Vietnam Syndrome" was a way of "kicking" history itself, a history that had held American morale hostage for far too long. History was over not only in the sense that there would be no further great struggles: by the logic of the Bush administration, its nightmarish grip on the present had also been undone by the triumph of the new world order.

Vietnam Syndrome, widely understood as a broad public reluctance to engage in combat missions following the quagmire of the Vietnam War and usually (incorrectly) attributed by Pentagon and administration strategists to the products of an uncensored American media,[49] was still high on the official agenda at the start of the Persian Gulf War. Bush more than once assured Americans that Iraq would not be "another Vietnam," and he was the first to pronounce the syndrome "dead" in the wake of victory. But it took a highly concerted effort, in official rhetoric as well as on the ground, to keep the syndrome in its grave. At the official level, the law enforcement paradigm – easily accessible to the dominant cultural imaginary – made of the Persian Gulf War a defining posthistorical event. Apart from rendering the conflict in culturally assimilable terms, which the paradigm undoubtedly did,[50] it also furthered the illusion of the "choice already made," the absence of alternatives. The disavowal of ideology as effected by Fukuyama's declaration of the triumph of "the liberal *idea*" was replicated in the legitimating narratives of the Persian Gulf War and to a considerable extent in the framing of the event as a crime drama. After all, in a conflict between an "outlaw" and the guardians of a "new world order," there can be no question of "ideology" in the sense of a set of beliefs; rather, the conflict is a global extrapolation of the logic of law enforcement on the home front. Even if laws themselves, and the policies used to implement them, can be ideologically inflected, law *enforcement* in and of itself is not: it is little more than a means of preventing, stopping, and punishing criminal activity so as to defuse its threat to the stability of a given order. The disavowal of ideology upon which posthistory is founded thus manifests itself in an ideological framework according to which the threat to stability is always and invariably criminal in nature. There can be no "choice" in such matters; they no longer represent a conflict between two systems but rather a conflict between the "rule of law" and the "law of the jungle."[51]

This paradigm, in Jean and John Comaroff's words, "[reduces] difference to sameness by recourse to the language of legality," presenting a "universal standard in terms of which incommensurable sorts of value ... may be mediated."[52] In the case of the Persian Gulf War, it universalized a position that might otherwise have been classified as mere belligerence, making it a matter of "law" rather than of simple disagreement. Iraq's invasion of Kuwait was indeed a violation of international law, but it is the ideological effect of framing it as such in the mainstream media, and of framing America's response in terms of law enforcement, that is of primary significance here, since it would continue to inform America's representation of itself to itself and to the world throughout the 1990s and indeed into the War on Terror.

The Bush administration's repeated references to the "law of the jungle" added a further, reinforcing dimension to the structure already in place. Not only, by this logic, were Saddam Hussein's actions illegal, they were also essentially primitive and barbaric. Again, ideology could have no place in such a conflict as it had in the long, "cold" struggle between capitalism and communism. The "law of the jungle" is as bereft of ideological considerations as the corresponding necessity of a struggle against it, and victory in this struggle would constitute a triumph for "civilization" in the most normative sense of the word. A return to the "jungle," after all, would also be a return to the past – a notion quite as unthinkable as, if not more so than, the outbreak of criminal anarchy. The choice, in such a paradigm, is already "made": in effect, there is no "choice" at all. The paradigm of civilization versus barbarism may be an ancient one indeed, echoing the overtones of what Edward Said called "Orientalism,"[53] but in light of the declaration of "posthistory" it takes on another inflection: not only would the triumph of the "law of the jungle" entail the undoing of Western modernity, but it is presented as the only *alternative* to the system currently in place and maintained by the "rule of law." The Persian Gulf War, in other words, would not be fought in the name of a qualitatively better future, one that, if it were within the scope of the imaginable, would constitute a genuine alternative to the status quo. It was rather a question of defending the status quo, the "present," against an incursion of the past – the past as seen from the "pinnacle" of historical "progress" as the only conceivable alternative that remained, one that, while surely "imaginable," could not be entertained as a viable possibility.

Indeed, another neo-conservative, still plugging the values espoused by Fukuyama but some fifteen years later, speaks of the "gaps," of "disconnectedness," of those trapped in the "past" as the ones against whom the Pentagon should be prepared to wage war.[54] At the end of history, to keep the "law of the jungle" at bay is to assert the present system as the only viable one.

Another way in which the official narrative of the Persian Gulf War reinforced the posthistorical illusion was by abstracting the situation from history entirely. For example, the focus on "Saddam" the megalomaniacal tyrant – rapist, pillager, plunderer, thief – lifted him directly out of an undeniably more complex and contradictory context, which included, among other things, America's previous support for the dictator against the threat ostensibly posed by Islamic fundamentalism in Iran. His apparently unprovoked and therefore purely acquisitive annexation of Kuwait marked him as a "rogue" element in an already unstable region, a man whose actions had to be countered with the full force of the "law." Historical continuity was set aside in favour of a narrative framework that did away with all ambiguity, moral or otherwise, and left only the option of military force – and by definition, as noted, to have only one option is to have no option at all. Further contributing to this sense of the "choice already made" were the parallels drawn between Hussein and Hitler,[55] both in the official rhetoric and in the popular media. "Appeasement does not work," Bush Sr stated in only one of many comparisons, "As was the case in the 1930s, we see in Saddam Hussein an aggressive dictator threatening his neighbors."[56] Bolstering the parallel, the *New Republic* – supposedly a "flagship magazine of the liberal establishment"[57] – famously airbrushed Hussein's moustache on its cover so that it would better resemble Hitler's. Such historical misappropriations fly in the face of the radical incomparability of the respective historical contexts. Once the seed of the comparison had been planted in the dominant popular imaginary, however, any question of "choice" was decisively removed from the equation. In the face of pure evil there could be no "choice," particularly if this modern-day Hitler was indeed seeking the means to add to his "chemical weapons arsenal" an "infinitely more dangerous weapon of mass destruction – a nuclear weapon."[58] Although the fear of nuclear proliferation in unstable regions is certainly not unreasonable,[59] the problem – as it was in the second round in the Gulf – was that the mere prospect of a nuclearized Hitler was sufficient to legitimate even the most drastic of measures taken against him. The fact that it would have been suicidal for Iraq to deploy nuclear weapons even if it possessed them was lost on the American public when the threat was conflated with the unmistakable image of the German dictator, architect of the greatest evil perpetrated in modern times. In this way, then, the focus on Saddam – both as a criminal and as a Hitler – dehistoricized him to the utmost degree, confirming in the process the undisputable superiority of the current system over its alternatives and the need to preserve it by all necessary means.

My analysis is certainly not intended to defend either Saddam Hussein or his actions – against Iranians, against Iraqi Kurds, or against Shi'ites. Rather, my concern is with the way in which the legitimating narratives of the Persian Gulf War cast a monumental shift in international relations – namely, the collapse of the Soviet Union – in distinctly posthistorical terms, equating the end of communism with the onset of a new era characterized by the following principles: first, the undisputable triumph of liberal-democratic capitalism and its establishment as the only viable means of socio-economic organization; second, the criminalization of any individual or state not wholeheartedly committed to the development and preservation of this system; third, American leadership in global law enforcement, along with the responsibility of the world community to assist it in its new capacity; and, finally, the equating of opposition to that order with unmitigated evil of the sort associated, in popular memory and imagination, with German fascism. All of this was manifested on the screens of the nation, and although there was criticism and opposition, by the time of the invasion fully 76 per cent of Americans supported US actions, according to an ABC News/ *Washington Post* poll.[60]

On the subject of abstraction from historical context, it is also significant to note what the narratives of the first Gulf War simultaneously concealed. Kellner sums up a more complex set of interests behind the endeavour, defining the "new world order" as

a hegemonic project organized around the use of military force to resolve political conflicts and to assert U.S. interests ... with the U.S. as the world's sole superpower [and to] highlight the importance of the military for U.S. foreign policy in which the U.S. would ... become the policeman of the world ... Bush's Gulf War policies were able to enlist the support of old Cold Warriors looking for new enemies, as well as military-industrial complex interests, big oil, banking and finance, and other interests directly served by a strong U.S. role in the Middle East and other hot spots of the world.[61]

What the narratives concealed, then, were some of the deeper implications of the end of the Cold War, chief among which was the removal of all serious impediments to American foreign policy objectives dating from the end of the Second World War: namely, making the world safe for capitalism and ensuring American primacy within the global capitalist system.[62] It masked a historical continuity that would otherwise have betrayed the place of the Persian Gulf War within a broader tradition of Western imperialism and compromised the ostensible moral clarity of the American response to Iraq's violation of international law.

The end of the Cold War, after all, was never a straightforward "victory" even though it was repeatedly and insistently presented as such following the "evil empire" rhetoric of the Reagan years. As Anderson points out, its ambiguity posed a significant challenge to the hitherto almost seamless compatibility of America's twin goals. In the absence of the communist threat, he argues, "American primacy ceased to be an automatic requirement of the security of the established order," allowing Europe and East Asia to "contemplate degrees of independence unthinkable during the time of totalitarian peril." And the corollary was the enhancement of America's "coercive superiority,"[63] establishing that country alone at the helm of international affairs, unchallenged by any comparable military force.

Economically, however, America's status was a bit less auspicious. By the end of the 1980s, America had become the largest debtor state in the world, with an accumulated debt of just under $2 trillion, a figure that would more than double by the middle of 1992. Its GDP at the end of Reagan's presidency represented less than 23 per cent of world output and its trade less than 12 per cent of the international total. Europe and Japan were emerging as notable competitors, and the Soviet policies of *perestroika* and *glasnost* had put the US in a difficult position with regard to its $300-billion military budget.[64] The Persian Gulf War itself was mostly financed not from America's own coffers but by Germany, Japan, and the Arab oil states.[65] America's economic primacy, in short, was already seriously compromised and seemed set to decline further still. Whatever the posthistorical illusions of the late-capitalist superstructure, the fact remains that as a material force, capitalism is also an irreducibly historical one, and it doesn't always behave in the way that its guardians would like it to. "History," either at home or elsewhere, will always subject it to variations and fluctuations that can threaten any one nation's position relative to the rest of the world at any time. This is even more the case in recent times as a globalized capitalism, its operations dispersed throughout even the more volatile regions of the world, is exposed to the slings and arrows of the very force – "history" – from which it relentlessly strives to abstract itself.

In a very real sense, then, America's assertion of military supremacy in the first Gulf War concealed from itself and from the world its economic vulnerability, while the narratives deployed in its legitimation served to displace some of the less palatable implications of the momentous historical shift that had just taken place. It was also a means of confirming the dominance of a "new world order" over any threat, which could therefore be perceived only as inherently criminal in nature. Faced with economic decline and a potential crisis in legitimation brought on by the lack of a serious and enduring enemy against which it could both define American virtues and values and justify continued military expenditures, America waged a war that would enable the maintenance of its military budget despite the demise of its Cold War enemy, the assertion of its superpower status in the face of overall decline, the "exorcism" of so-called Vietnam Syndrome through the deployment of a more compliant press to cover its inevitable (and sanitized) "victory," the establishment of control over oil flow in the Middle East, and the promotion of modern American weaponry. Meanwhile, as a narrative, the story of the Persian Gulf War from start to finish served as a pleasing and plausible instantiation of a seemingly utopian dream – namely, harmonious international cooperation transcending cultural boundaries – and of an end to war as such.

In all of these ways, the logic of posthistory was brought to bear on the official legitimation for the Persian Gulf War. The paradigm of law and order, the undoing of a past defeat, the assertion of a "choice already made," the disavowal of historical context, and the proclamation of a "new world order" all presented the "end of history" within the terms of a readily comprehensible interpretive framework.

Yet the story in itself would have amounted to very little without the wholehearted support of the mainstream American media throughout the crisis. From the very beginning, the national media in the US faithfully endorsed Bush's vision of a "new world order," applauding America's performance in the Persian Gulf War and presenting it uncritically as a necessary step toward the final abolition of instability and evil in the world. The following section addresses the relationship between the media, particularly television, and the legitimating narratives of the Bush administration, with particular emphasis on the role of the media in presenting the war in a way conducive to the Bush administration's ideological aims. In both content and form, television during the Persian Gulf War brought posthistory into "lived experience" and to a degree that was without precedent at the time.

GOOD RIDDANCE, VIETNAM! THE PERSIAN GULF WAR ON THE NETWORK NEWS

Capitalism's attempt to extricate itself from the mire of history and the impact of this abstraction on the structure of feeling particular to Western "postmodern" culture – the loss of a sense of temporality, the erosion of working-class identity in the developed world, the increasing ephemerality of "throwaway" society – are replicated in, and complemented by, the operations of the mainstream media. In the same way that capitalism disavows its material, historical constraints, so too do the media increasingly deny their mediating role in their pursuit of authenticity as well as the irreducible embeddedness of the production process in material reality. Further, just as the Persian Gulf War itself was part of a broader historical continuity involving America's pursuit of long-standing strategic goals, so too were the ways in which it was represented part of a continuity within the economic and technological development of the corporate media, not to mention the development of a new "relationship" between these media and the Pentagon in times of conflict. The media as corporations and as technologies, of course, fit within the broader structures of the capitalist economy and therefore cannot be considered independently of it. The combined impact of the news networks on the structure of feeling, however, should illuminate their function at the time of the war, throughout the remainder of the first posthistorical decade, and into the War on Terror as well.

The Persian Gulf War marked a decisive moment within this broader continuity, given its status as the first war televised in real time. Although Vietnam is known as the first "television" war, visual coverage was substantially delayed in its presentation, allowing for at least a remnant of critical distance that Benjamin's "aura" supposedly provides. The invasions of Grenada and Panama in 1983 and 1989, respectively, were also media "events," although the relationship between the media and the Pentagon was not yet what it would be in Gulf War I. They did, however, foretell what was to come. Grenada was a "resounding success" in terms of news management, according to John MacArthur:

> There simply *wasn't* any news; the invasion was kept secret even from the press offices at the White House and the Pentagon until an hour after it began ... Over the next four days the Reagan Administration did everything in its power to keep reporters off the island ... When reporters finally were allowed on the island, they were able to refute one of the rationales for the invasion – that Grenada had become a supply dump for Soviet and Cuban weapons, a veritable staging ground for subversion. But by then so many newspeople had repeated the Reagan Administration's lie about warehouses stacked to the ceiling with sophisticated Soviet weapons, and hordes of Cuban military advisors roaming the island, that the truth had little impact.[66]

The news blackout resulted in the resignation of White House communications director David Gergen and a subsequent inquiry on war reporting under the direction of Major General Winant Sidle. As MacArthur reports, the Sidle Commission

> recommended the creation of the National Media Pool, which was still functioning as of February 1992. In principle, this rotating group of trusted and knowledgeable military reporters – all regular Pentagon correspondents – was now on call to depart at a moment's notice for American surprise attacks in parts unknown. In theory, the Pentagon would be honor-bound to bring them along in a timely fashion.[67]

Censorship was not addressed, and the system was put to the test in Panama. The departure of the National Media Pool was delayed for two hours following the invasion, and the reporters were then kept on a US base for five more hours upon arrival. "Outside of

Pentagon pictures spoon-fed to journalists," notes MacArthur, "little real information reached the American public."[68] The number of Panamanian casualties, civilian and military, was underreported, and the coverage at home was untainted by any focus on American casualties. In other words, the system that would perfect itself in the coverage of Gulf War I was already well in place by January of 1991. At any rate, it is hardly disputed that the media were anything but complicit, overall, with the administration's goals throughout the Iraq crisis, cementing a relationship between the networks and existing power structures that became the object of much critical observation and commentary before, during, and after the conflict. If one takes MacArthur's account at face value, it becomes apparent that this was not always the media's choice;[69] however, the degree of effective censorship combined with the technology of real-time, televised coverage helped to make Gulf War I, to American audiences, the success that it was.

While television as a technology is by no means inherently disposed toward the reproduction of the dominant ideology, this was certainly the purpose it served throughout Gulf War I, not only because of the pool system but also because of the thoroughgoing commodity status of its products. Granted, by the same token the networks' political stance could shift away from that of the administration if public demand occasioned such a shift, and by and large it has in recent years. However, at the time one could almost say a deal had been struck between the Pentagon and the press. The development of real-time coverage as the unassailable standard for news presentation combined with the ever-accelerating imperatives of commodity production and consumption to reproduce a structure of feeling fully amenable to the posthistorical thrust of post–Cold War geopolitics. If the technologies themselves are not the motor of this development, their role in the reinforcement of the dominant, posthistorical ideology nonetheless warrants close scrutiny. From the most "visible" elements of their complicity – that is, at the level of content – through the deeper structural elements, such as their sensory impact and their place within the economy at large, the mainstream media reinforced the vision of a "new world order" as articulated by the Bush administration at the onset of the Gulf crisis. Indeed, the Persian Gulf War as a media event represented a nearly seamless integration of the dominant (administrative) ideology, the media, the posthistorical structure of feeling, and global events themselves. The "sprawling realism"[70] that the Pentagon and the administration believed had brought about Vietnam Syndrome would no longer be a problem. By the time of the Persian Gulf War, and after a couple of practice rounds in Grenada and Panama, the "realism" was much more tightly controlled and was purported as the "truth" of war while concealing its ambiguities, moral or otherwise. This legitimating function of the media in times of crisis would serve successive administrations throughout the 1990s and into the War on Terror as well.

THE PRESS AND THE PENTAGON: PARTNERS IN TIME

The most obvious factor influencing the cooperation between the media and the military throughout Gulf War I was surely the strategy of direct intervention and censorship on the part of the White House and the Pentagon as described above. Determined not to repeat the mistakes of Vietnam and allow the kind of unflinching coverage that subsequent administrations blamed for the erosion of popular support during that conflict,[71] the Pentagon ensured that its "pool" system would give only minimal access to potentially sensitive sites. As Kellner notes, "[r]eporters critical of the deployment were not given access to top military brass or allowed to join the pools, while compliant reporters were rewarded with pool assignments and interviews." Further, he notes, reporters who flouted the rules were detained or told to leave and in some instances had their credentials temporarily lifted.[72] Most correspondents, MacArthur notes, "acceded passively to the Pentagon management program" and moreover "were made to appear ... bumbling and information-less in the televised press briefings, contrasted as they were with the purposeful and self-assured military briefers" in Saudi Arabia.[73] In addition, the Pentagon ensured that no journalist could travel unaccompanied by a military chaperone or be granted unsupervised access to the troops or to civilians. Finally, a strict layer of censorship was imposed by a Joint Information Bureau (JIB) through which all correspondence had to be filtered before its release to the general public.[74] Ostensibly, many of these controls were instituted in the name of national security, but among their more immediate effects was the presentation of the war by the mainstream media in such a way as to sustain maximum popular support. The Bush administration knew from the outset that it would need the unwavering support of the media in order to legitimate its enterprise, and military censorship on the ground was one of the most straightforward ways by which it could be achieved. There was no question of repeating the disaster of Vietnam; this time, the military would control the presentation of the war from beginning to end, while creating the illusion – unlike during the invasion of Grenada – that the public was witnessing a real war in real time.

A further indication of military–media cooperation was the media's reliance on a variety of "experts" to explain and comment on the action as it unfolded. Patrick O'Heffernan, commenting on the role of television in the Gulf conflict, discusses the reliance on former diplomatic and military officials and its effect on the presentation of the war. First, O'Heffernan notes, it "gave copious air time to men ... who were seen as and were in many cases former administration spokesmen, reinforcing the administration's perceived credibility." Second, it "[failed] to provide any meaningful time to experts with opposing opinions," giving "the impression that all of the facts, knowledge, and expertise lay with the pro-war administration."[75]

Compounding these factors was a layer of "self-censorship" imposed by, in some cases, the relationship between the networks themselves and broader corporate, even military-industrial, interests. These relationships, as Kellner points out, included direct ownership, which led to a reluctance to broadcast information that might undermine the economic interests of parent companies. NBC is a prime example, owned as it is by General Electric (GE) and RCA, both military contractors that stand to benefit from military enterprises. As Kellner suggests, NBC not only supported the war effort but effectively provided "free advertisements" for major weapons systems produced by GE.[76] MacArthur, who interviewed news division president Michael Gartner, claims that the latter "dismissed out of hand the contention that General Electric interfered with coverage or policy, but deep down I couldn't abandon the image of a heavy-handed corporate owner issuing subtle hints, at the very least, through Gartner to his news executives."[77]

To compound the issue, as Kellner notes, "[m]any GE board members sit on the boards of other corporate media like the *Washington Post* and are connected with U.S. government agencies and oil corporations as well." Nor is this an isolated phenomenon: the board of directors at both ABC and CBS have their own connections to the oil and defense industries.[78] Consequently, the more direct controls imposed on the media by the Pentagon were complemented by a set of controls the media imposed on themselves.

One could be forgiven for surmising that the networks' uncritical coverage of the Persian Gulf War arose from quasi-conspiratorial behaviour on the part of the networks, the Pentagon, the administration, and the military-industrial complex as a whole. But the usual response to accusations of censorship and conspiracy is the assertion that what sets America apart from totalitarian states is its right to free speech and freedom of the press. And it is certainly true that apart from the major corporate networks and direct restrictions imposed in the Gulf region, opposition to the war effort could not have been (and was not) entirely suppressed. Nor, even among the corporate networks, was there no opportunity for dissent. MacArthur's interviews with news executives following the war bear this out.[79] Censorship was rife, but it was by no means the sole determining factor. At a less obvious level is a set of structural constraints imposed by the status of the media as a producer of commodities for mass consumption.

What this means is that regardless of the networks' ties to military and corporate interests, their driving imperative as businesses is not the promotion of any one political agenda over another but rather to sell their products. Like any other company, they are motivated first and foremost by profit, not to any particular administration or even to their parent corporation. Accordingly, in order to achieve the viewer ratings necessary to attract advertising dollars, their products must respond to what is popular at any given time, and at the time of the Persian Gulf War, it was the war effort itself. Of course, it stands to reason that had the war proved – against the explicit wishes of the administration and the Pentagon – to be another "quagmire" on the scale of Vietnam, the media would not have been able to maintain high viewer ratings by continuing to present it in a positive light (as is now evident with the double quagmire in Afghanistan and Iraq). Had the war effort in the Gulf for whatever reason become unpopular, the glorified and morally unambiguous narrative framework in which it was presented to the public would have ceased to sell. It is therefore always possible for the media to turn against the interests of the administration. Even Kellner, an unrelenting critic of the media's apparently unquestioning stance, notes that there can be "structural economic reasons for occasional critical discourse" as well as "rewards for breaking stories and for presenting

novel or challenging views."[80] Until such time as an oppositional
view becomes popular, however, the media seem likely to avoid taking unnecessary risks.

The unprecedented level of harmony between the Pentagon and
the media was undoubtedly a factor in the failure of such views to
emerge. But again, it is not a matter of simple causality. In a country
that values freedom of the press, such blatant censorship – exemplified more by footage of military officials briefing journalists on the
day's events than by "pool" footage itself – should have prompted
the emergence of dissenting viewpoints, leading to more balanced
coverage at the very least. Further, if the high viewer ratings of the
"real-time" conflict spoke to a widespread desire on the part of the
public to bear witness to the "reality" or "truth" of the event – or
to what Benjamin called the "desire of the masses to bring things
'closer' spatially and humanly" – then censorship of the sort that
was so visibly implemented during the Persian Gulf War should not
have been as widely tolerated as indeed it was. For the media to submit so readily to such constraints, and for the wider public to take
the administration's message at face value in light of such flagrant
censorship, other factors almost certainly had to be in play. Indeed,
as MacArthur points out, the networks eventually did resist the constraints imposed upon them by the Pentagon:

> It is true that a new committee was formed to protest the Penta-
> gon restrictions and that this time it did include two owners,
> Katharine Graham, chairman of the Washington Post Company,
> and Donald Newhouse of the powerful Newhouse publishing
> family ... On September 12, 1991, representatives of this latest
> ad hoc assembly met with Secretary of Defense Dick Cheney to
> make their case against the Pentagon's conduct toward repor-
> ters in the Persian gulf. The formal rhetoric of protest remained
> rather timid, however ... The committee ... accepted the con-
> tinued existence of the Department of Defense National Media
> Pool system and asked that the Sidle commission recommenda-
> tion of temporary pools ... be respected.[81]

The Sidle Commission had recommended that pools be dis-
banded after the first twenty-four to thirty-six hours of war, and the
committee, representing reporters who had spent six weeks under
Pentagon control, were objecting to the fact that this had been over-

looked. However, the committee's concession effectively gave the Pentagon the right to "invoke the exigencies of combat to justify extensions."[82] Overall, opposition was tepid, if more pronounced after the fact. CBS journalist Dan Rather, in MacArthur's account, offered the bluntest criticism of the pool system but conceded that "'unless the audience and the readership begin to say to the people who own the [news] entities [that] this isn't the best way,' things are not likely to change."[83] The protests came too late, and little had changed by the time of the War on Terror. What the audience did want, broadly speaking, was "patriotism" – defined as solidarity with and support for the troops, which the Pentagon could provide by filtering what the networks could present.

Censorship, in other words, cannot be held solely responsible for the media's largely uncritical stance or for its success in maintaining high ratings throughout the war.[84] The implications of censorship and control are therefore less straightforward than they may initially seem and go beyond the mere omission of "sensitive" information or the promotion of military successes. It is as a commodity that the coverage must therefore be examined if we are to further illuminate the relationship between the media as corporations, the "official" narrative of the war, and, ultimately, the posthistorical structure of feeling.

COVERAGE AS COMMODITY: THE AESTHETICIZATION OF POLITICS

There was a complicity between the Persian Gulf War as the first instantiation of Bush's "new world order" and its reception and consumption as a media event, a complicity that went beyond the mainstream networks' explicit support for the war effort through censorship and control and therefore beyond the immediate content of the coverage alone. This is not to say that the content was irrelevant but rather that at the time of the war, content was determined by its form and by its structural conditions in certain specific ways. It was the commodity form in particular that inflected the content of the coverage in favour of the war effort and in a variety of inter-related ways.

First of all, the complicity between the Pentagon and the media was often a two-way street; that is, the controls imposed by the Pentagon offered certain specific advantages to the media as corporate

entities out to sell their products, advantages that helped to ensure
the overwhelmingly positive nature of the coverage as commodity. The Pentagon gave the networks first and foremost a readily
"saleable" account of events, including dramatic and novel footage
(for instance, the now iconic image of the "bomb's-eye view" taken
from the nose-cameras of the Pentagon's "smart weapons"), real-
time updates, and a clear, unambiguous, narrative structure.[85] Tom
Engelhardt notes,

> [i]f the Persian Gulf war revealed the media's ability to mount
> technical operations on an unprecedented scale, it also exposed
> the need of these financially pressed media giants ... for spon-
> sorship on a scale hitherto unimaginable. This is what the Bush
> administration seemed to offer in the Gulf War – an outside
> production company able to organize a well-produced, subsid-
> ized total event that could be channeled to the U.S. (and increas-
> ingly, the global) public at, relatively speaking, bargain-basement
> prices.[86]

The Persian Gulf War, in other words, "offered the media giants
new possibilities in the production of entertainment,"[87] creating a
real-time, real-life action film that was also simultaneously an advertisement for both the networks and the military-industrial complex.
And the military, as well as the media, had to adjust to this new state
of affairs. The Pentagon as a "production company" had to offer
"round-the-clock, on-location support systems across a vast theatre
of operations; ... a preedited flow of visuals available to all chan-
nels ... control over access to the set of the production, thus lim-
iting intranetwork competition and consequently network costs ...
and, finally, the sort of precise scheduling and closure that television
craves."[88]

It was precisely, as Engelhardt suggests, the "lack of closure" that
had made the Vietnam War an "event unnervingly at odds with television,"[89] and such a mistake would not be repeated in the coverage
of the war in the Gulf. The Persian Gulf War as a "real" event thus
coincided almost seamlessly with its presentation as a media event
and as a commodity. Although this was by no means the first time that
the government had intervened in war reporting, it certainly marked
a new stage in the development of military–media cooperation. This
war, more than any preceding one, seemed designed as much for

television as for the expulsion of Saddam Hussein from Kuwait. "In the Gulf War," as Engelhardt observes, "it felt like the United States went into battle in tandem with an American media."[90]

It was in large part according to the logic of the commodity that the form of the war as a media event came to dictate the content of the coverage. The Persian Gulf War was by no means the first media event to be consumed as a commodity, but it was nonetheless unique in its scale, its duration, and the quality of the consumption-satisfaction it afforded. As the first war to begin, escalate, and conclude on live television, it provided on a large scale, and over a prolonged period of time, all the entertainment of a well-executed Hollywood film: "[m]ore than any other conflict in human history," Chesterman declares, if perhaps a bit hyperbolically, "this authorized bloodshed was scripted for consumption by a willing global audience."[91] The historical fact of an essentially "exterministic"[92] war between the First World and the Third was forced into the narrative structure of a Hollywood film, with a clear build-up (the "crisis" that led to the war), an explosive climax (the air war, followed by the ground war), and a dénouement (the aftermath), all shot through with narrative suspense (opportunities for a diplomatic solution) and drama (the "human interest" stories involving individual soldiers and their families). In sharp contrast to the Vietnam War narrative, which, as Michelle Kendrick puts it, has "come to represent chaos and lack of closure,"[93] the story of the Persian Gulf War as it unfolded on the network news represented a satisfactory completion and a restoration of order.

The relationship between the Pentagon, the administration, and the media was therefore on the whole mutually beneficial, whatever the restrictions placed on independent access to information and the objections raised by some commentators. The Pentagon's careful filtering of information for release to the general public – as well as its provision of novel and dramatic footage such as the crosshair shots – allowed for the presentation of a non-contradictory, morally unambiguous narrative that benefited its global purveyors, the networks, as much as it did the architects of the war itself. Censorship, in other words, contributed to the production of a saleable commodity of the sort that would guarantee a broad and receptive audience.

A further formal aspect of the coverage as commodity was the imperative of real-time transmission, for which CNN, over the course

of the 1980s, had become the "standard-setter"[94] and which led
the media to rely on the Pentagon for continuous updates (since
the Pentagon was the sole source of updates). The crisis climate of
warfare left the reporters largely hostage to whatever information
official sources felt they could provide. Those who ventured out on
their own or were reporting from outside the pool system drew fire,
even though, as MacArthur points out, both CNN and NBC kept a
correspondent in Baghdad for as long as possible after the bombing began.[95] Generally, however, reporters who "[turned] on their
sources" or who were "too critical of official policies" risked "[dis-
rupting] their connections and [losing] important conduits of information," thus compromising their employers' capacity to compete
with other networks. The temporality of late-breaking stories in
particular cemented the networks' dependence on "official sources
which are thus able to manipulate and control the agenda."[96] The
cooperation of official sources with television reporters thus enabled
the networks, in general, to maintain a competitive edge in their
presentation of "breaking news" to the public, while ensuring that
the coverage endorsed the administration's position. The real-time
imperative and the consequent reliance on official sources, combined with the "packageability" of the Persian Gulf War as a media
event, allowed for an overall coherence in the narrative as well as
a degree of ostensible moral clarity and simplicity that the events
in and of themselves, framed differently, would not have been able
to provide. Much like the Hollywood blockbuster, which is seldom
concerned with questions of moral relativity or existential doubt,
the media event of the Persian Gulf War offered a clear-cut and harmonious resolution untarnished either by its own historical circumstances or by any potentially delegitimizing aspects of its conduct.

Further still, the Pentagon's direct involvement in the coverage
facilitated a focus on technology that shifted the emphasis from a
moral question to the simpler question of efficiency. This question,
like the broader narrative of the war, dispensed with all moral ambiguity, shifting the central question, as George Cheney aptly notes,
from "Is it right?" to "Does it work?"[97] As Lyotard also notes, the
"operativity criterion" in postmodernity is "technological; it has
no relevance for judging what is true or just."[98] And the answer to
the question "Does it work?", at least at the level of popular representation, was resoundingly affirmative. Coverage emphasized the
plethora of means available to "pound" Iraqi forces from the outset,

with missiles, warships, submarines, bombers, tanks, and fighter jets repeatedly pictured in action. Stressed as well was the effectiveness of centralized command and control, achieved through long-distance co-ordination by means of real-time satellite and computer technology. What moral ambiguity might have remained was nullified with the image of the "bomb's-eye view": in contrast to the primitive, brute, and indiscriminate power of conventional ("dumb") weaponry, viewers were shown a weapon apparently capable of making the "right" choice. The "smart" weapon, in other words, was invested with a moral capacity seen to be lacking in conventional firepower; it reinforced the ostensible moral clarity of the enterprise itself, an enterprise supposedly undertaken not out of naked self-interest but to guarantee a future in which "the strong respect the rights of the weak."[99] Instead of the "sprawling realism" of mass slaughter in Vietnam, the psychic "trauma" of which overshadowed America's sense of moral rectitude for years afterwards, viewers were presented with the "smart" bomb that could seek out strategic (military) targets and annihilate them in what then appeared a bloodless strike. The victory was moral as well as military in that by "kicking" Vietnam Syndrome it had asserted the essential rightness of America's global project minus the "grey area" of "collateral damage." Note, of course, that

twenty-five hundred to thirty-five hundred Iraqi civilians were accidentally killed by allied bombs, according to William M. Arkin, military research director of the environmental organization Greenpeace. [*Life* reporter Ed] Barnes rightly, it appears, decried the "smart bomb" hype as "crazy." After the war the Air Force announced that laser- and radar-guided bombs and missiles made up just 7 percent of all U.S. explosives dropped on Iraq and Kuwait. The other 93 percent were conventional "dumb" bombs, dropped primarily by high-flying B-52s from the Vietnam era. Ten percent of the "smart" bombs missed their targets, the Air Force said, while 75 percent of the dumb bombs were off-target. In all, about sixty-two thousand tons of explosives – or 70 percent – missed their targets. The story of the smart/dumb ratio, one of the biggest untold stories of the Gulf War, would have been difficult to pin down precisely, but a few unsupervised interviews at air bases, or a little digging in Washington, might have yielded some of the information.[100]

This was certainly not what the broadcast Pentagon briefings displayed. The multiple "crosshair" shots displayed by senior officials showed bombs annihilating their targets with a video-game precision that utterly sanitized the fact that there were human beings occupying those targets (and that they were not necessarily all military facilities). Such an aesthetic also, arguably, invited a degree of participation – and hence identification – with the troops carrying out the attacks; this would become even more the case in the war in Afghanistan and in Operation Iraqi Freedom a little more than a decade later.

The preceding points certainly help to account in large part for the fact that the coverage was positive on the whole. Moreover, the sense of a global communication network that the coverage engendered did contribute to the persistence of the illusion that a "new world order" would soon be in place. But the positive coverage was not the sole factor in the persistence of the illusion, nor does it explain the "feeling" that "history," in the sense of great, transformative movements, would soon come to an end (with the end of the Cold War representing the last great, transformative movement). Censorship and government control, in other words – including the mutual benefits they bestowed on the media and the administration alike – cannot fully account for how the dominant posthistorical ideology came to be "felt" at the level of lived experience. There are other aspects of the commodity-form and its influence on content that are more closely connected to the popular reception and assimilation of the "new world order" at the level of the structure of feeling, one of which is the rather insidious phenomenon of the aestheticization of coverage for mass consumption. That is, like almost any commodity designed to satisfy needs extraneous to basic subsistence, it must appeal to a fundamentally aesthetic sensibility. As Jameson puts it, in relation to commodities more generally,

> commodity production is now a cultural phenomenon, in which you buy the product fully as much for its image as for its immediate use. An entire industry has come into being to design commodities' images and to strategize their sale: advertising has become a fundamental mediation between culture and economics, and it is surely to be numbered among the myriad forms of aesthetic production ... We talk a good deal – loosely – about the commodification of politics, or ideas, or even emotions and

private life; what we must now add is that commodification today is also an aestheticization – that the commodity, too, is now "aesthetically" consumed.[101]

By this logic, war too – as presented on the mainstream networks – is "aesthetically consumed"; like virtually everything else, as Jameson says elsewhere, it is "reduced to a means for its own consumption."[102] News coverage, particularly at times of high tension, is experienced as a commodity by the mass audiences it attracts, even if its "sale" is in some sense indirect (the revenues are determined by the monetary value of advertising time). And if this commodification is also an aestheticization, then the media become not only the "site of politics,"[103] as McKenzie Wark has said, but also the site of what Benjamin called an aestheticized politics.[104]

For Benjamin, writing at the time of German fascism, the aestheticization of politics was partly a function of what he called the "Führer cult,"[105] the "selection before the [photographic] equipment from which ... the dictator [emerges] victorious."[106] However, it involved more than simply the "spell of a personality"[107] as projected by the new technologies in lieu of the vanished aura. Rather, it constituted what he saw as a new and insidious means of social control. The process of auratic decay initiated by the new technologies of photography and film threatened, for Benjamin, to eradicate the cult value of art and, by extension, the traditional social hierarchy in which it was situated. This process on the one hand bore the promise of emancipation, jeopardizing as it did art's antidemocratic function as an object of ritual. The simultaneous emergence of masses and mass media offered the possibility of art's reception by a newly self-conscious and active mass public. This is the "useful" notion of class to which the first chapter alluded in its analysis of post-Fordist capitalism. However, for any totalitarian system to maintain an adequate degree of social consensus, it had to "organize the newly proletarian masses without affecting the property structure which the masses strive to eliminate," and new technologies could therefore be pressed into the service of the system's needs as well. The system could respond, that is, with the "introduction of aesthetics into political life" – by "[giving the masses] an [aesthetic] expression while preserving property [relations]."[108] In other words, it gave the public aesthetic rather than properly political rights. And like the aesthetics of the aura, fascist aesthetics, according to Benjamin, imposed form and structure at the expense of truth and justice; communication and praxis were effectively pre-empted in the submission to spectacle. The result was a necessary illusion of agency at the cost of agency itself – an illusion of collective identity that, *as* an illusion, effectively pre-empted any meaningful form of collective praxis (individual instances of dissent aside).

To transpose Benjamin's reading of this insidious phenomenon to the present day, the aestheticization of politics – now a function more of universal commodification than of direct totalitarian control – generates what the authors of *Afflicted Powers* refer to as "weak citizenship," an "impoverished and hygienized public realm" in which "only the ghosts of a more idiosyncratic society live on." That is, while on the one hand the state depends on social atomization to maintain its control, it must nonetheless "[sew] the citizen back (unobtrusively, 'individually') into a deadly simulacrum of community"[109] – create an illusion of harmony where only alienation exists – thus maintaining the degree of social stability required for the continued operation and reproduction of the system as it stands.

Benjamin's essay was concerned mainly with photography and film and at a time when the rise of fascism in his native Germany was proceeding at an alarming rate. Although it would be inappropriate, to say the least, to draw a direct comparison between 1930s European fascism and contemporary liberal-democratic capitalism, it is nonetheless not unreasonable to suggest that the idea of the "aestheticization of politics," just as much as that of the "aura," remains fully applicable in the present day. As Russell Berman notes, "[t]he aesthetic packaging of political discourse, the priority of image over substance, and the metamorphosis of the political speaker into an actor for the mass media all point to the continued relevance of Benjamin's insight for contemporary culture ... i.e., the demise of a public of rational debate, replaced by a consumerist culture of manipulation and acclamatory politics."[110]

Benjamin recognized back in 1936 that despite what he considered the revolutionary potential of the new technologies, a vestige of aura could still be preserved through commodification as well as through fascism. For him, the "capitalistic exploitation of the film" was already resulting in a situation in which "illusion-promoting spectacles and dubious speculations" were becoming the medium's primary attraction.[111] This meant that commodification could seriously mitigate any potential challenge to the social order; the liberating

"shock effect"[112] accompanying the penetration into reality, or, as
he called it, the "deepening of apperception,"[113] was already at risk
of being pre-empted by the spectacular and its associated perils.
And indeed, it would seem that his fears rather than his hopes have
since materialized. Although the aestheticization of politics today
is the almost ineluctable consequence of universal commodification rather than of totalitarian state control, the result is nonetheless structurally the same. Politics proper becomes inseparable from
its aestheticized representation, often to the point that aesthetic concerns precede and even to some extent determine the development
of a given event (as I will demonstrate in my reading of the 9/11
media spectacle in chapter 4). Further, the distinction between news
coverage and entertainment is progressively eroded by the aesthetic
imperative – such as the sanitized video-game aesthetic "covering"
the reality of war in the Gulf – leading to what some have termed
the "Hollywoodization" of network news, or a process involving
more than the mere "framing" of events with colourful graphics,
theme music, and so forth. Presented and consumed as a commodity,
news coverage takes on a thoroughly incapacitating or "immobiliz-
ing" function. Much like the Hollywood film or the video game, it
appeals to impulse over deliberation, emotion over intellect; because
its primary motivation is to "sell" itself, after all, it must appeal to a
sensibility beyond the strictly rational.

This is the function of the "psychic horse-trading" Jameson discusses in relation to Hollywood films, a mechanism I would argue is
equally present in commodified coverage. The true ideological function of such commodities, according to Jameson, is not a matter
of perpetuating "false consciousness" but rather the sublimation of
genuine social needs into a "deadly simulacrum" of their resolution.

Relying on Freud's model of the work of art as the "symbolic fulfillment of the repressed wish ... whereby desire could ... achieve
some measure of a purely symbolic satisfaction," Jameson goes on
to "conceive how (commercial) works of art can possibly be said to
manipulate their publics":

> the psychic function of the work of art must be described in
> such a way that ... two inconsistent ... features of aesthetic grati-
> fication – on the one hand, its wish-fulfilling function, but on
> the other the necessity that its symbolic structure protect the
> psyche against the frightening and potentially damaging eruption

of powerful archaic desires and wish-material – be somehow
harmonized and assigned their place as twin drives of a single
structure.[114]

What Benjamin saw as the substitution of genuine political rights
with the illusory "right" to self-expression is conceived by Jameson
as a trade-off: "[t]o rewrite the concept of a management of desire
in social terms" brings "repression and wish-fulfillment together
within the unity of a single mechanism," one that "[gratifies] the
intolerable, unrealizable, properly imperishable desires only to the
degree to which they can again be laid to rest."[115]

Much as Benjamin's masses see themselves "reflected" in the cinematic spectacles of fascist Germany, Jameson's mass audiences find
an "optical illusion of social harmony"[116] in the cultural products
they consume, a "ritual celebration of the renewal of the social
order"[117] that constitutes for him the "Utopian dimension" of such
products. As social atomization continues apace, undermining, consistently with the logic of capital itself, the grounds for any sense
of collective or class identity, this mechanism "effectively displaces
the class antagonisms between rich and poor which persist in consumer society ... by substituting for them a new and spurious kind
of fraternity in which the viewer rejoices without understanding that
he or she is excluded from it."[118] This is in effect what is meant by
"weak citizenship," the "sewing" of the citizen into a "deadly simulacrum of community."[119] For Benjamin, the technologies of "mass
reproduction," though potentially emancipatory, could also lend
themselves to such ends, in his time, through the "reproduction of
masses": in "big parades and monster rallies," he wrote, "in sports
events, and in war, all of which nowadays are captured by the camera and sound recording, the masses are brought face to face with
themselves."[120] Or, as Samuel Weber puts it in his gloss of Benjamin,
fascism "allows the mass to look itself in the face and thereby to find
a gaze that ostensibly looks back," as if in a mirror, "thus [reinstat-
ing] the aura of the world-picture by means of the very media that
undermine it." The result is that "what is in its innermost structure
dispersed and distracted [i.e., the atomized public] is given a form
and a shape, a voice and a face,"[121] that invites the illusion, not dis-
similar to Lacan's "mirror stage" of infant development, of organic
community and agency. The screen, in other words, constitutes a
"mirror" that reflects the "mass" as an aesthetic, organic totality.

And because this totality is strictly illusory, substituting that "deadly simulacrum" of community for a genuine sense of collective identity, it also conceals the essential ephemerality of the consumption-satisfaction so effected beneath an illusion of historical agency. The sense of collectivity reflected back onto society during the Persian Gulf War, in spectacles such as the "human flag" composed by several thousand people clad in red, white, and blue or in the mass proliferation of yellow ribbons across the country, helps to "overcome difference or alienation ... on an imaginary level," as Jochen and Linda Schulte-Sasse explain, "[affording] millions of viewers an imaginary participation in a mass ornament and an imaginary experience of community."[122]

Further, they observe, the constitution of the collective subject so constructed prompts a regressive impulse based on exclusion, entailing as it does "the fortification of the national body as 'Oneness' on the basis of excluding or marginalising alien elements as 'Otherness,'" and this is how violence – specifically, the violence of warfare – comes to serve as the "ultimate means of aestheticizing politics."[123] Indeed, for Benjamin, "[w]ar and only war can set a goal for mass movements on the largest scale while respecting the traditional property system," and "[o]nly war makes it possible to mobilize all of today's technical resources while maintaining" that system.[124] In creating a spurious "community" of believers, it becomes the ultimate aesthetic achievement of fascism (in Benjamin's time), securing and maintaining the balance between mobilization and suppression (or immobilization) and thereby ensuring the continued domination of power relations as they stand. War, rendered in unreal, abstract, and aestheticized terms and disseminated through the mass media in our own time, mobilizes on a mass scale a collectivity that is safely and necessarily false – that is, it will not subsequently threaten the dominant order on any meaningful level. And like the Lacanian "imaginary," it is in the realm of the *image* – in particular the mass-generated popular cultural image – that this illusion of coherence and continuity is fostered and perpetuated; in the "gaze that ostensibly looks back" is found a means of expression that is purely aesthetic, sublimating anarchic, revolutionary drives within an "optical illusion" of harmony. It masks a fundamental internal antagonism as the source of collective anxiety and is therefore purely "aesthetic" in the traditional sense of the word. Whether *every* single citizen submits to this unspoken doctrine (and indeed not everyone does) is immaterial. What concerns me is the way in which it is perpetuated and disseminated – the power of the "media-military-industrial complex" that lies behind it.

This fantasy of collectivity, in effect, is structurally akin to the ideology of the work of art, a primarily spatial or synchronic phenomenon in which all parts are supposedly organically integrated and which is immune to transformation along the diachronic axis, consisting in "that privileged condition in which the law of the whole is nothing but the interrelations of the parts."[125] As Slavoj Žižek puts it, what is at stake is a "vision of society which *does* exist," which "is not split by an antagonistic division," and "in which the relation between its parts is organic, complementary." The vision is one of society as "an organic Whole, a social Body in which the different classes are like extremities, members each contributing to the Whole according to its function."[126] This entails the displacement of social negativity onto an external enemy; in the case of anti-Semitism, for instance, the "trick" is to "displace social antagonism into antagonism between the sound social texture, the social body, and the Jew as the force corroding it, the force of corruption."[127] It defines that collective subject, then, in negative terms, even if it simultaneously conceals that fact beneath the illusion of agency. A sense of community experienced aesthetically, at the expense of an external "other" onto whom internal contradictions are projected, may in one sense appear to have an empowering function, but this comes only at the cost of subordinating that community's constituent members to a spatialized and totalizing principle or law.

This is certainly the logic behind the illusion of collectivity presented by Hollywood film, and it manifests itself in the Persian Gulf War coverage partly by means of the familiar narrative framework of policeman versus criminal. Presidential speeches presenting Saddam Hussein as a "rogue" element were complemented in the media by the presentation of a "simple, transparent interaction between two men, Saddam Hussein and George Bush," one "a criminal, perhaps a lunatic as well" who had "committed a robbery and a rape," the other "a policeman, a global policeman who thus [acted] not in his own interest but in the interest of 'the world.'"[128] And the imposition of such a framework constitutes more than a mere oversimplification of the facts. For Link, "[t]he application of such simple base schemes of our normalistic cultures to exterministic wars in effect amounts to the normalization of such wars. Even without military censorship, the war's exterministic dimension could be disguised as long as the simple interactional scheme of global sheriff and global criminal, for example, underlies nearly all commentaries, news, and 'expert' opinions."[129]

Further, such "normalization" is structurally identical to Benjamin's "aestheticization," imposing form and structure upon what is in fact a violation of form (even more in the second Gulf War). This involves more than the mere "addition" of an aesthetic dimension to the narrative "after the fact" so as to render it in more culturally intelligible and assimilable terms. Rather, the result is an intersection of fiction and reality in which the aesthetic to a certain extent precedes the facts or is at least inseparable from them.

This cultural assimilability and the moral unambiguity of the law enforcement paradigm were further complemented by the media's careful construction of a suitable enemy image around Saddam Hussein himself, much of which can be illuminated by Edward Said's framework of Orientalism – a Foucauldian interpretation of the system of representing the "Other", a "created body of theory and practice in which ... there has been a considerable material investment. Continued investment made Orientalism ... an accepted grid for filtering through the Orient into Western consciousness, just as that same investment multiplied ... the statements proliferating out from Orientalism into the general culture."[130]

The purpose of such a discourse, for Said, is to generate an idea (through the course of European imperialism) of "European identity as a superior one in comparison with all the non-European peoples and cultures," creating an "idea of Europe, a collective notion identifying 'us' Europeans as against all those non-Europeans."[131] He sees in Orientalist discourse the "division of races into advanced and backward," the latter linked to other "elements in Western society (delinquents, the insane, women, the poor) having in common an identity best described as lamentably alien."[132] So while Bush in his speeches focused on "Saddam's" arsenal, "Saddam's" atrocities, "Saddam's" deception and the broadcast media embraced and developed an image of the Iraqi dictator that reduced the terms of the conflict to those of a battle between a "good" West and an "evil" Iraq, using highly selective images of Hussein and foregrounding his crimes at the expense of any complicating contextual (historical) factors, this image also had to correspond to "character stereotypes and collective symbols," to "pictures that are culturally 'anchored'

... and that act as carriers of symbolic meaning."[133] As Link notes, "[i]f murder were the salient issue, our repertoire of 'enemies' would have to ... include many rulers ... whom our cultures tend to regard more as 'friends.'"[134] While comparing Hussein and Hitler – "*the* global referent of evil and the most convenient embodiment of an Other"[135] – was intended to function on an emotive rather than an intellectual level, abstracting both dictators from their respective historical contexts in a disabling strike against rational analysis and lending a distinctive Hollywood quality to the coverage at times, the Orientalist bias was necessary in order to round out the "enemy image" and, ironically, replicated some of the ideological strategies employed by the Nazis themselves in their displacement of internal antagonisms onto the figure of the Jew. The American collective identity was constructed not just against one dictator but against a more generalized portrayal of cultural difference informed by Orientalist tropes. Saddam Hussein was more than just an updated incarnation of the evil of communism or even of fascism. While the communist enemy could be seen as an essentially rational being, however sinister his motives, Saddam Hussein was invested with that "inscrutable" quality corresponding to the perception of the East as not only antithetical to but also as immune to rational (Western) inquiry as evil itself. The characterization of Hussein as a present-day Hitler was thus compounded by his portrayal as an enigmatic Eastern "other," invested with an intellectually impenetrable "foreignness" and the inscrutability evident in Western cultural representations of the "Arab" more generally. Although his regime was predominantly secular in nature, he took on in his portrayal certain representational aspects of the Islamic fundamentalist that helped to make him the antithesis of the "civilized," "rational" West. His "unreadability," indeed, was captured perhaps most strikingly in an image, shown on CNN, of his face carved up as a jigsaw puzzle.[136] The putative threat of the "Oriental" to white, Western women – also mobilized in the long, brutal history of slavery and segregation practised in the West – was displaced onto the dictator's "rape" of Kuwait (which, although not "white," was portrayed, contradictorily, as feminine for the purposes of the war). Such portrayals of "the Arab" as irrational, menacing, and deceitful as well as anti-Western and "backward" form the basis of such cultural representations as well as supposedly scholarly texts such as Fukuyama's and Huntington's. As Said further notes, the hold these instruments have on the mind is increased by the institutions built around them. For every Orientalist, quite literally, there is a support system of staggering power, considering the ephemerality of the myths that Orientalism propagates. The system now culminates into the very institutions of the state. To write about the Arab Oriental world, therefore, is to write with the authority of a nation, and not with the affirmation of a strident ideology but with the unquestioning certainty of absolute truth backed by absolute force ... One would find this kind of procedure less objectionable as political propaganda – which is what it is, of course – were it not accompanied by sermons on the objectivity, the fairness, the impartiality of a real historian, the implication always being that Muslims and Arabs cannot be objective but that Orientalists ... writing about Muslims are, by definition, by training, by the mere fact of their Westernness. This is the culmination of Orientalism as a dogma that not only degrades its subject matter but also blinds its practitioners.[137]

"Scholarly" texts, popular cultural representations, and the actual institutions of power thus unite around this long-standing, deep-rooted image of the "Arab" (or "non-Westerner") as, paradoxically, both helpless and dangerous, both subservient and hostile to Western demands.

The construction of an evil and inscrutable enemy, as effected by the representation of Saddam Hussein according to the conventions of popular culture, primarily evoked an emotive response impervious to potentially mitigating or relativizing questions such as the issue of American support for the dictator prior to the war or atrocities committed by Americans themselves. Implicit and explicit comparisons with Hitler in particular effected a moral absolutism that dictated precisely the swift and punitive response that the American-led coalition carried out. In this way, among others, was the narrative of the Persian Gulf War thoroughly dehistoricized, abstracted from its wider context and presented in terms according to which a military strike seemed the only justifiable response. The equation of Saddam Hussein with sheer, unadulterated evil made the American-led invasion an unquestionable necessity as well as an assertion of unassailable moral virtue. At the same time, the presentation of the dictator according to the logic of Orientalism – as an unreadable, enigmatic, dangerous, and clearly irrational force – added a cultural superiority to the moral one, contributing in the process to the construction of an American collectivity defined by a shared "way of life" and by shared values and beliefs. His enemy image, for the duration of the Persian Gulf War, "[merged] the chill of the terrorist without subject status and the evil adversarial with subject status for the benefit of psychological motivation"[138] and – as the overall popularity of the war effort seems to demonstrate – to considerable ideological effect.

The complicating factor of the Iraqi people, "innocent" according to the rhetoric of the Bush administration, was resolved in part by negating their existence entirely. According to another convention of mainstream popular culture, enemy forces were routinely dehumanized. Indeed, Orientalism can ascribe to the other what Link defines as a "chaotic" or "non-subjective" quality akin to that of "germs, viruses, poisons, floods, deserts, storms, fires, vermin," and other amorphous and threatening entities.[139] The Pentagon's refusal to provide a body count was complemented by a dispassionate presentation of Iraqi casualties – many of them conscripts – as unavoidable consequences of the war. Civilian casualties, supposedly kept at a minimum by the use of "smart" weaponry, were grouped under the rubric of "collateral damage," a phrase that, as Chesterman shows, is remarkably effective in disguising its referent:

> [a]pparently simple language games in the reportage of the war were seen to be disturbingly effective in blunting public sentiment for Iraqi civilian dead. An American poll found that only 21% of those polled were "very concerned" about the amount of "collateral damage" produced by the war. By contrast, 49% were "very concerned" about "the number of civilian casualties and other unintended damage" in Iraq.[140]

Indeed, in CNN's *War in the Gulf* and CBS's *Desert Triumph*, images of oil-soaked seabirds – victims, allegedly, of Saddam Hussein's ecological crimes – were invested with greater emotive value than those of dead Iraqi troops. The latter were shown as evidence of allied "victory" at the end of the ground war, while imagery of struggling wildlife was accompanied by a sentimental soundtrack designed to elicit pity and compassion. The dehumanization of the "inevitable" human victims of the allied war effort thus contributed to the sense of moral integrity on the American side while simultaneously containing the conflict within the symbolic framework of the simplest of Hollywood narratives. Indeed, this "moral integrity" was emphasized by Bush in reference to yet another of the iconic scenes of the Persian Gulf War:

> [t]he men and women in our Armed Forces have demonstrated their ability to master the challenges of modern warfare. And at the same time, and whether on the battlefield of Iraq or some tiny little village in Somalia, America's soldiers have always brought a quality of caring and kindness to their mission. Who will ever forget – I know I won't – those terrified soldiers surrendering to American troops? And who will forget the way the American soldier held out his arms and said "It's okay. You're all right now."[141]

Here Bush neglected to mention that the Iraqi troops were surrendering in terror amid the wholesale and criminal slaughter of "Saddam's" retreating forces. Further, the scene "humanized" the American soldier more than it did the troops themselves, who in classic Orientalist gestures of submission were searched and brought to their knees before the cameras – some in tears, all clearly terrified, and all surrendering their dignity to the global media at the same time that they surrendered their arms to the Americans.[142]

Further, the age-old strategy of dehumanization was complemented in many instances by the removal of humanity from the picture altogether. As Bernd Hüppauf notes,

> [d]emonstrated technological supremacy of the West was identified with a moral nobility of its position in opposition to that of a dark, inane, and morally inferior enemy ... The distribution of right and wrong was straightforward and provided an ideal basis for presenting the aesthetic nature of abstract images of a war in which modern technology demonstrated its purity splendidly through its confrontation with images of an enemy characterized by backwardness, cowardice, and inhumanity ... Technological progress and modernity were not associated with fascism and aggression but were strongly identified with the ideals of humanity and material superiority. There was no need to provide a space for the suffering individual in this war.[143]

In the famous cross-hair image, for instance, the point of impact dissolved into white noise and blank screen, obliterating the "cries and groans and the flesh of the dying"[144] along with the dying themselves. The spectacular dimension of high-tech warfare as represented on the network news thus replicated the effects of technological triumph in Hollywood film, inscribing technological advantage with moral virtue.

To summarize, the "consumption-satisfaction" precipitated by the coverage of the Persian Gulf War as commodity consisted in the illusory resolution of internal contradictions, the sublimation of legitimate social anxieties and needs. It was the "optical illusion of social harmony" that Jameson sees as a central ideological mechanism in Hollywood film, that the Retort group sees as "weak citizenship," that Benjamin saw as an "aestheticized politics," and that Žižek sees as the result of a projection of internal contradictions onto an external enemy. This aspect of the commodity-form more than any other, I would argue, is what determined the overall slant of the coverage, which just as much as any Hollywood blockbuster of its time involved the projection of internal contradictions outwards, as well as the constitution of an illusory collective subject. To some extent, of course, the construction of a "we-group" in wartime has long been a deliberate ideological strategy. However, such an intention has not always been present or at least fully central. Further, the commodity-form itself in this case – the aestheticization of the coverage under the imperatives of profit – is what led to the creation of this illusory collective subject, a primary factor in its consumption-satisfaction. The content, in other words, was determined largely by the commodity-form itself and based on the following mechanisms: a "scripted" Hollywood narrative framework corresponding to the "collectively anchored" symbolic co-ordinates of cop versus criminal; an opponent characterized by pure, unmitigated evil, whose immunity to rational inquiry also corresponded with the supposedly "enigmatic" quality of the East in general; a swift and decisive victory on the part of the rational West, achieved through cutting-edge technology; and the dehumanization of casualties both military and civilian as well as an outright denial of their suffering. The ideological effect of all this went far beyond the sheer entertainment value of the spectacle; more fundamentally, it came in the form of a pseudo-utopian consumption-satisfaction premised on an "optical illusion of social harmony," on the negation of internal contradictions through their outward projection, and on an imaginary resolution consisting in an ultimately aesthetic fantasy of social cohesion.

While this strategy undoubtedly allowed for the representation of the Persian Gulf War in an overwhelmingly favourable light, its implications for the "new world order" and the posthistorical structure of feeling were broader still. First of all, as a commodity in itself, the coverage corresponded to the structure of feeling as already described – that is, it played into the sense of ephemerality generated by the ever-accelerating turnover time of consumer goods and services. As a "packaged" and then "repackageable" narrative – re-released in video compilations such as CNN's *War in the Gulf* and CBS's *Desert Triumph* – it was abstracted from history proper, and once the war ended, Iraq was promptly forgotten by the mainstream audiences, along with the suffering of its civilian population (with whom "we" had no "quarrel"), who struggled under economic sanctions that remained in place until Gulf War II some twelve years later.

Despite the essentially transient nature of the commodity in general, the consumption-satisfaction that the coverage supplied in the form of an illusion of social harmony was somewhat more lasting. Or, to put it another way, the fact that it took the form of a "true story," and over an extended period at that, made the illusion of collectivity all the more credible. Mass displays of public support such as the "human flag" implied that "real" Americans – not Hollywood celebrities – were speaking as one, while other "real" Americans risked their lives in an actual war. Meanwhile, the existence of a "real" rogue element embodying all of the traits most antithetical to the American "way of life" served to reinforce the essential moral "rightness" of America as a nation. This consumption-satisfaction was reinforced repeatedly and on a daily basis, lending consistency to an illusion that in itself had some distinctly posthistorical attributes: on the one hand, it contributed to a sense that "progress" within the West would no longer be a requirement, that perfection was already at hand, and on the other, it presented the impossibility of an alternative to the status quo, save a return to the past, to the "law of the jungle," and to barbarism. Finally, as a fundamentally aesthetic illusion, it took on the attributes of time "out of time," of an atemporal, synchronic or static paradigm immune to the effects of chronology itself. The commodity-status of the coverage as implied by its consumption in "leisure time" – time outside the time of production – was complemented by an essentially aesthetic consumption-satisfaction that reinforced the illusion of atemporality at the level of the popular experience of history. The Persian Gulf War, in its construction of an aesthetic collectivity in place of a genuinely political one, reinforced the illusion of history at an end.

This sleight of hand conceals the atomizing function of the commodity-form beneath the illusion of social cohesion, or, to put it another way, if the atomizing and ephemeral nature of "late" capitalist consumption undoes the sense of collective identity essential to properly historical agency, then the "optical illusion" of collectivity effected by commodified coverage, an illusion as ephemeral as any other, presents us with a substitute that inhibits *actual* agency and that endures only as an incapacitating, collective "dreamwork." The very force that undermines social cohesion, by abstracting itself from "history" and its enabling material conditions in one stroke, must simultaneously compensate for this loss with an "illusion" that in turn lends credence to the legitimating narratives on which it relies.

BEING THE FIRST TO KNOW: THE FIRST "INSTANT" WAR

None of these developments would have been possible without the enabling vehicle of the narratives – television. I have already noted one way in which the real-time imperative of contemporary news coverage to some extent determined its content – that is, the reliance of the networks on "official" sources for up-to-date information, which led to a notable lack of critical voices. Indeed, the media's perpetual thirst for "late-breaking" information accounted in large part for the generally unquestioning endorsement of the official position on the war. But it is also important to note that the narrative framework just discussed, through which was effected the consumption-satisfaction of an illusory collectivity, was also in part attributable to the real-time imperative. As McKenzie Wark notes, the speed of network coverage depends on "simple but subtle, standardized but interchangeable stories to prevent the event from rupturing the seamlessness of televisual discourse," which leads to events being "quickly captured and interpreted in an acceptable narrative framework"[145] – a framework that includes, in this case, stock perceptions of the "other" that reinforce an Orientalist bias and that also assist in the production of a commodified, Hollywood narrative according to which "good" must defeat "evil" by means of unrivalled cunning and massive firepower. However, there is another way in which real-time coverage contributes more directly, if at the same time more insidiously, to the illusion of posthistory, and this is in the quality of the sensory experience it offers as a medium and independently of its content.

Increasingly, I would argue, the commodification of history itself is complemented by a consumption-satisfaction deriving from the speed at which a given network can process its raw materials and transmit them to the viewer. Speed and instantaneity become a virtue unto themselves, independent of the explicit content of the coverage or even the rhetorical terms in which it is framed. One of the main slogans of CNN, the first network to establish a real-time, global presence, is "Be the first to know," which implies something of the commodity structure. There is certainly an element of possession at work, a hidden affinity between being "the first to know" and being "the first to own" in terms of consumer goods and high-tech goods in particular. Even the term "breaking news" suggests a certain aesthetic gratification, perhaps a hidden element of shattering or transgression. And the beginning of the Persian Gulf War was "breaking news" par excellence, with more than a billion viewers in 108 countries worldwide according to one source.[146] As Kellner points out, it was indeed "appropriate" that, within North American time zones at least, the air assault on Baghdad was launched during prime time.[147]

The commodification of history as discussed above, when combined with its representation in "real time," makes for what George Gerbner calls "instant history" – in his words, "memorable moving imagery" into which "past, present and future can now be packaged, witnessed, and frozen."[148] One might say that the act of "reporting" or "writing" history has converged with the act of "making" it: it is simultaneously written, made, and given narrative form through the media, and this narrative form insidiously takes precedence over historical "reality." Unfolding and received history become one and the same, leaving no opportunity for revision or deliberation. For Gerbner, "[i]nstant history is image history. The crisis unfolds before our eyes, too fast for thoughtful consideration of antecedents, alternatives, or long-range consequences but just in time for conditioned reflex. The show is on, we are in it, and the deed must be done before second thoughts, counteracts, and regrets can derail the action."[149]

This transformation in the temporality of historical representation necessarily has an impact on its reception at the level of sensory
experience. If in what McLuhan called the "typographic" world, history was conceived as linear and sequential,[150] it is now, as conveyed through the "flow" of televisual coverage, transmitted in "real
time," simultaneously with its occurrence, with only "episodic" surface narratives invoked to frame events. Thus, its real-time presentation affects immediate sensory experience in a way that enhances
the posthistorical structure of feeling, since despite the apparent predominance of the visual image in televised coverage, what happens
in the age of real-time history, as noted, is structurally akin to the
auditory sense: the televised image, like sound, exists "only as it is
going out of existence" and thus cannot be stopped in its progression or retained. The time horizons, as Harvey takes care to emphasize, have indeed shrunk.

Combined with its commodity-status as an episodic narrative,
then, the real-time coverage of the Persian Gulf War contributed
both to its high viewer ratings and to the illusion of posthistory in
the broader sense as the first great "instant-historical" media event
from beginning to end. In a real-time narrative such as the conflict
provided, the emphasis is only ever on what happens "next"; the
coverage "sells" largely on the basis of perpetual imminence and
anticipation. "Instant history" is commodified history, appealing to
its consumers through the constant provision of "breaking news,"
which at a time of crisis such as that of the Persian Gulf War keeps
the viewer in thrall to the immediate future. Of course, the sheer
"spectacular" value of the war – massive explosions, "tracers," bil-
lowing smoke over Baghdad – was sufficient to guarantee a wide
audience, particularly during the early days of the war when it was
still a novelty. But beyond this was the status of the coverage as
instant, commodified history providing instant gratification. While
other "spectacular" events took place in real time in previous years
– such as the Challenger disaster of 1986 – this was the first erup-
tion of hostilities in real time, unfolding as part of a suspenseful narrative sequence built up by the networks over the preceding months
during the "crisis in the Gulf." For a large cross-section of the public,
the televised war held the same riveting appeal that a live sporting
event holds for sports fans. Again, the parallel with "cutting-edge"
commodities is apparent: "breaking news" is not unlike cutting-edge
technology, with its own obsolescence built into its very design; in

the moment of its presentation, it is already consigned to the past and can never be experienced in quite the same way again, no matter how many times it is replayed. In the age of "instant history," both the viewers and the networks – the latter in their drive to meet viewer demand – come to inhabit the immediate future, neglecting in the process what is occurring in the present or what has previously occurred. The presentation of historical events simultaneously with their occurrence means, in effect, that the present is already the past and that by association, the future must already be the present. The immediate future, in other words, is (to borrow again from Harvey) "discounted"[151] into the present and this at the same time that the present is discounted into the past.

Again, the speculations of Benjamin and McLuhan are relevant. Part of the emancipatory potential with which Benjamin invested the new technologies consisted, after all, in the decay of the "aura," and the "time-space compression" offered by real-time communication technology may indeed be seen as "anti-auratic" to the extent that the idea of any "original," fixed in time and space, can now be done away with. Television certainly "[brings] things 'closer' spatially and humanly,"[152] satisfying what Benjamin saw as a potentially revolutionary desire on the part of the "masses." However, this very rapprochement, far from evoking a "deepening of apperception,"[153] substitutes for the aura an equally deceptive illusion of reality, of harmony or self-identity between the object and its representation. I cannot emphasize too much how fundamental this is to the appeal of live, televisual coverage to a sensibility that is largely auditory in nature: one of the properties of sound, as noted, is that sign and referent are one and the same; there is no constitutive "gap," no space of non-identity, between the representation and what is represented. As the media event subsumes the "real" event – in other words, as "instant history" subsumes history itself – the concept of "coverage" becomes pure simulacrum, relating to Baudrillard's version of Borges's tale in which the map drawn up by the emperor's cartographers comes to cover the entire world[154] or, as Debord puts it, "the spectacle is the map of this new world, a map which exactly covers its territory."[155] Representation, according to the illusion so generated, achieves self-identity with its object, subsuming in the process the material reality of the object itself. The media thus take on a quasi-performative role, enacting history at the same time that it unfolds. So ultimately, the disappearance of Benjamin's "aura," a democratizing process in at least some ways, is also paradoxically a sleight of hand to the extent that the elimination of *any* "mediating" distance removes the means of objective apprehension.

The consumption-satisfaction of "breaking news," however, remains and is in part related to the consumption-satisfaction of the commodity-form in general – that is, as a transient phenomenon that satisfies its manufactured needs only ephemerally without ultimately hindering its own self-propulsion. As "cutting-edge" technologies often differ from their "obsolete" predecessors only in quantitative terms – they are usually only smaller or faster or both – they represent nothing qualitatively new but only a renewal of the same consumption-satisfaction produced by the previous purchase, a satisfaction that comes undone at almost the same time that it is achieved. That is, the next "cutting-edge" product is always just around the corner, and the consumer is always on some level aware of the inevitable fate of his or her latest purchase: relegation to the dustbin of technological progress. The satisfaction is only ever temporary, and the consumer is always aware of its transience. The perpetual newness of the commodity-world has as its corollary the perceptual sameness of the life-world – a "sameness" identical to that proposed by posthistory, as punctuated at intervals by "breaking news." As the media event "breaks" or "irrupts" into the endless sameness of consumer society, only to be rapidly consigned to oblivion in anticipation of the next big event, the consumer-spectator receives a certain ephemeral satisfaction the precise quality of which can be repeated only in the event of still more "breaking news" that exceeds its predecessor in scale and spectacular value. In the face of each technological innovation and each new "breaking" event, consumers essentially resign themselves, for better or for worse, to the determination of the future-present by forces well beyond their comprehension or control.

This element of resignation is compounded by the fact that in the age of real-time coverage, the "story" is always already in place, leaving no opportunity for change. In Gerbner's words, "[t]he boiling point is reached when the power to create a crisis merges with the power to direct the movie about it,"[156] and this is precisely what occurs when real-time technology meets the new world order. The imposition of narrative form in real time by the networks, the real-time "story system" according to which events can be decoded, effectively pre-empts the opportunity for change; it is always already too late for alternatives. The future, in real time, is already present, and it is beyond the power of collective agency to change it, however persistent the illusion of a collective historical subject commodified coverage might provide.

The Persian Gulf War as covered in real time, then, presented its viewers with a certain "im/mediacy," both spatial and temporal, that disavowed mediation itself while pre-empting any consideration of alternatives. And it is in this way more than any other that the medium of television corresponds to posthistory at the level of the structure of feeling. Combined with the undoubtedly sensational or spectacular appeal of warfare, the relentless forward momentum of "instant history" proves nearly impossible to withstand; real-time coverage sweeps up history proper with cyclonic force, entangling it inextricably within the "vectors" that for McKenzie Wark now constitute the "site of politics itself." And when the "site" of politics ceases to be anything remotely like a site at all, any useful concept of politics as progress seems to vanish along with it. If the immediate future is all that matters, within the abstract transnational space of information transmission, the notion of narrative continuity – of a logical sequence comprising past, present, and future – is degraded into irrelevance. Against the "real-time" narrative that keeps the viewer in thrall to the future, then, is in fact the loss of narrative in a broader sense – in the sense, that is, of history "proper," an essential element of a useful socio-economic consciousness and of a broader continuity between past and present within which a qualitatively different future might otherwise be discerned.

The Persian Gulf War, as represented both in the official rhetoric and on television, confirmed the "end of history" as a structure of feeling in a variety of ways. Ideologically, it presented a forced choice between the "rule of law" and the "rule of the jungle" according to a law enforcement framework independent of any genuine political considerations. As a commodity, it was consumed "out of time" and in a way that emphasized a sense of ephemerality at the expense of historical continuity. Also as a commodity, it effected an aesthetic illusion of collectivity that was itself "out of time" and according to which genuine change seemed neither necessary nor possible. And finally, as "instant history," it presented the consumer with a certain "im/mediacy" (non-mediation) while foregrounding the "immediate" future at the expense of present and past conceived historically. The "end of history" was thus implicitly confirmed by a medium that, paradoxically, claims to present history as it unfolds.

The "end of history" so effected, the posthistorical structure of feeling as reinforced in this moment of harmony between events, ideology, and representation, is also the "end of politics," the "end of ideology," the "end of mediation." If by the logic of the "millennial dream," events such as the Persian Gulf War are "epiphenomenal and not structural or systemic," it is in large part because the medium makes them so. In claiming, as Samuel Weber explains, to "make up for [the lack of a unifying totalizing world instance]" by presenting themselves as "[models] for such totalization,"[157] the networks cast what is, in effect, a "posthistorical" eye on the world. The temporal dynamic of history is spatialized in the networks' lateral appropriation of places and the events that unfold therein and in their processing and presentation of such events as commodities.

In its abstraction of the "Gulf crisis" from a broader historical continuity, in its construction of an aestheticized collective through the projection of internal contradictions outwards, in the capacity of this collective to mask its own loss of agency, in the presentation of a "choice already made" in all of these respects, and in the disavowal of ideology, politics, and even mediation, the Persian Gulf War brought the "end of history" home to "lived experience." Of course, it is for the Western (more specifically, American) world that this structure of feeling was, and continues to be, reinforced. Posthistory places America at the fixed, stable centre of a world in which "events" are peripheral, contingent, and aberrant, much like Saddam Hussein's illegal invasion of the little-known Emirate of Kuwait. Yet, as Žižek notes,

[a]ll phenomena which appear to everyday bourgeois consciousness as simple deviations, contingent deformations and degenerations of the "normal" functioning of society (economic crises, wars, and so on), and as such abolishable through amelioration of the system, are necessary products of the system itself – the points at which the "truth," the immanent antagonistic character of the system, erupts.[158]

Or, one might say, the points at which the "truth" *threatens* to erupt and is subsequently contained by the mechanisms of a thoroughly commodified and aestheticized politics. Hence, the Persian Gulf War repressed the essential connectedness between the "crisis in the Gulf" and the broader history of Western imperialism as it has shaped and defined the Middle East over many decades.

However, the "truth," or the "immanent antagonistic character of the system," cannot be repressed indefinitely, and it continues to manifest itself in a variety of unsettling, disturbing, often mystifying forms. In that regard, the next chapter deals with the increase in cultural paranoia during the 1990s and accounts for the prevalence of fear over security despite the ostensible end of the nuclear threat, America's unquestioned victory in the Gulf, and the more anodyne rhetoric of the Clinton administration, which promised a new era of peace and security. Popular intellectuals such as Samuel Huntington began at this time to posit a decidedly less utopian global future, while the media saturated popular consciousness with all manner of forebodings, from crime and disease to terrorism and ecological meltdown. These fears, too, lent themselves to commodification in such a way as to create a consumption-satisfaction that would release social anxieties only temporarily, paving the way for a wholesale appropriation of cultural fear as an instrument of social and political control. In other words, the "end of history" can be just as much a source of terror as a source of optimism, and its assertion of an end to systemic alternatives results in a logic according to which the only alternative to the present system is that system's outright negation. Hence the emergence of a climate of fear despite and within the apparent "end of history" and the ostensible establishment of a *Pax Americana*.

3

Climate of Fear

POSTHISTORY ACCORDING TO WILLIAM J. CLINTON

The first Gulf War as a media event (a non-event, in Baudrillard's terms[1]) seemed to confirm, both ideologically and at the level of the structure of feeling, the "end of history" in Fukuyama's sense of the term – that is, the realization of a "new world order" character-ized by peace, democracy, and free trade among nations and dom-inated by an America that would not shy away from using military force, where necessary, to contain and defuse any threats. Events, even crises, might continue to occur, but as essentially peripheral phenomena they would also be a thing of the past, confined to those "historical" or "disconnected"[2] parts of the world that would some-day catch up to the advanced capitalist democracies, given just the right sort of encouragement.

This impression would not change under the Clinton administra-tion after the transition from a Republican to a Democratic leader-ship. The ideological co-ordinates that sustained George H.W. Bush's proclamation of a "new world order" would remain more or less in place while America adjusted to its new role as a "global police-man" and mastered the finer points of the rhetoric required to legit-imate its cause. Indeed, for Clinton, the Second World War and the Cold War had led to a global situation in which America would have to continually "renew [its] leadership abroad." And the bene-fits of this "leadership" were already evident, if we are to believe the official rhetoric: by 1994, according to Clinton, "the American people [were] more secure than they were before," owing to Amer-ica's support for "democratic renewal and human rights and sustain-able development all around the world,"[3] whether by diplomacy or force. This was to remain a constant theme in Clinton's State of the Union addresses; indeed, in 1997 he saw fit to announce that "more people than ever embrace our ideals and share our interests" and further, that the spread of these ideals was, and remained, conditional upon that of free-market capitalism: "[b]y expanding trade, we can advance the cause of freedom and democracy around the world."[4]

The Clinton administration's foreign policy as it developed over the course of the 1990s was in many ways, as Perry Anderson notes, simply an extension of what had gone before, even though the rhetorical framework had changed somewhat and served essentially the same broader interests. The Gulf and Balkan wars had "helped to crystallize an ever more comprehensive doctrine, linking free markets (the ark of neoliberalism since the Reagan-Thatcher period) to free elections (the leitmotif of liberation in Central-Eastern Europe) to human rights (the battle-cry in Kurdistan and the Balkans)."[5]

If anything, it was the third element in the trio – human rights – that was the "principal innovation" of the 1990s (though of course not a new concept), enabling what Anderson describes as the "legitimate pursuit by the international community of universal justice and human rights, wherever they were in jeopardy, regardless of state borders, as a condition of a democratic peace." For Anderson, it was this, "the most emollient of ideologies, whose every second word was international understanding and democratic goodwill,"[6] that sustained the American enterprise over the course of the first posthistorical decade. American military endeavours in 1994 alone, Clinton insisted, "[showed] America at its best – helping to save hundreds of thousands of people in Rwanda, moving with lightning speed to head off another threat to Kuwait, giving freedom and democracy back to the people of Haiti."[7] America's future, as a result, had been made "more confident and more secure,"[8] and only continued American "leadership" could guarantee prosperity and peace in the years to come. "For the first time since the dawn of the nuclear age," Clinton noted in 1996 – however inaccurately – "there is not a single Russian missile pointed at America's children,"[9] and this was all a result of America's continued "leadership" in global affairs.

As far as the "end of history" is concerned, the addition of "human rights" to the equation of free markets and free elections quite simply served to reinforce the idea of liberal-democratic capitalism as the only viable system, contributing further to the sense of a "choice already made." Within a framework so defined, any alternatives were, for all intents and purposes, at least *presented* as unthinkable. The concept of universal human rights, of course, was not new, nor had the question of transgressing national sovereignty in its name not been extensively debated. But its history as a popular concept bears scrutiny. As John MacArthur notes:

> Universal human rights ... came into fashion in America during the Carter Administration. After the creation of the United Nations in 1945, and the adoption of the Universal Declaration of Human Rights in 1948 [clearly influenced by the atrocities of Nazi Germany], American Presidents had piously invoked the Declaration to condemn Communist depredations while overlooking the crimes of right-wing allies. But Carter was the first to apply human rights doctrine more or less without prejudice ... Under Reagan and Bush the pendulum swung back toward highly selective application ... President Bush was ... deaf to the entreaties of human rights representatives when they interfered with Administration objectives ... he was practiced in the art of realpolitik, which cannot exist in harmony with the notion of a universal standard of human rights ... [they] were not much more than a political angle to the Bush Administration.[10]

They would remain a "political angle" during the Clinton years too but more in the public eye than before. The Rwandan genocide notwithstanding, it was the "cultural mnemonic"[11] of the Holocaust that was implicitly and – given the comparisons of Saddam Hussein with Hitler – quite plausibly invoked in the justification of military endeavours in various parts of the world throughout the 1990s, with parallels between that inescapable trauma and contemporary abuses repeatedly invoked throughout Clinton's term in office. By some sleight of hand, and despite the as yet unresolved moral ambiguity of intervening militarily in the name of human rights – a debate that is outside the scope of this work[12] – such action was *portrayed* as morally unassailable: to turn a blind eye to human rights abuses would be unforgivable, signalling a willingness to tolerate or even condone crimes of the sort committed under German fascism. As Clinton noted in 1996, stressing the undeniable benefits of American leadership, "we stood up for peace in Bosnia. Remember the skeletal prisoners, the mass graves, the campaign to rape and torture, the endless lines of refugees, the threat of a spreading war. All these threats, all these horrors have now begun to give way to the promise of peace."[13]

The imagery invoked by Clinton – none of which was invented, of course, but did correspond quite accurately to the news networks' coverage of the conflict – was sufficient, at the popular level, to discredit any alternative. It was, in effect, inseparable from the imagery of the Holocaust, the defining trauma of the twentieth century, in popular memory and at a time when Holocaust memorialization was shaping into an industry. The same parallels would be drawn in relation to the Kosovo crisis a few years later when, as Andreas Huyssen notes, "[s]treams of refugees across borders, women and children packed into trains for deportation, and stories of atrocities, systematic rape, and wanton destruction all mobilized a politics of guilt in Europe and the United States associated with non-intervention in the 1930s and 1940s."[14]

I do not mean to trivialize such abuses or to suggest that abstaining from intervention is always preferable in such cases. Rather, I want to illustrate the force of the "human rights" argument within a context that is posthistorical anyway to the extent that liberal-democratic capitalism admits of no alternatives. Given as well the rise of the "Holocaust industry" (what Jewish scholar Norman Finkelstein describes as the exploitation of the memory of the Holocaust for political and financial gain[15] – in other words, an ideological construct that is manifested, for example, in multiple-award-winning films such as *Schindler's List*), the popular association of contemporary human rights abuses with those committed under fascism in the 1930s and 1940s lends to posthistory an element of desirability that the ideological co-ordinates of the free market alone, even when linked to free elections, cannot provide. The desire for a world free of such abuses should certainly not be dismissed as delusional or "utopian," but mobilizing that desire in support of liberal-democratic capitalism as the only viable system nonetheless warrants careful scrutiny. It is, in effect, another assertion of a "choice already made" and as such is detrimental to any serious consideration of the proliferation of human rights abuses worldwide within the context of their specific contemporary conditions of possibility. Not only is the alternative – that is, tolerance of another Holocaust – to be avoided at all costs, but it also evokes a "past" that, in the advanced Western democracies, has ostensibly been overcome and must now be transcended by those nations still "stuck in history" before the "new world order" can be implemented to its full potential. Much as the comparisons between Saddam Hussein and Hitler helped to legitimate the war in the Gulf in spite of the major disservice to historical analysis they entailed, so too does the association of modern-day victims with those of the Nazis give America a "free hand" (as well as the "upper hand," in relation to Engelhardt's "victory narratives") in its global endeavours. A singular and traumatic episode in modern Western history is thus projected onto a wholly different, if similarly intolerable, situation and thereby associated with the ideological imperatives of the American superpower. And the detrimental abstraction of both situations from their respective historical contexts has implications beyond the merely "academic": it negates the underlying "necessity" that constitutes history proper – that is, the real, historical forces of capitalist globalization – and presents "events" instead as peripheral aberrations simply in need of surgical "correction."

As already noted, those who dismissed Fukuyama's thesis on the basis of the persistence of "events" were therefore seen as misguided: events, as Fukuyama himself acknowledged, could always continue to take place.[16] But they would always be "epiphenomenal," unrelated to the deep-structural configuration of the times, which was the new world order. Even when they demanded a military response from the West, on whatever grounds, they were not to be seen as in any way intrinsic to that order. It was always by choice, the choice already made, that America and its "posthistorical" allies would intervene in the "historical" parts of the world and always with a view to bringing them "up to speed" in the interests of all concerned. Only the West's response to a given event could be seen as consistent with the new world order, never the event itself.

The logic by which Saddam Hussein was portrayed as a criminal in the first Gulf War thus continued to apply under the Clinton administration in relation to a variety of events that prompted a military response: what these events had in common was that they constituted significant anomalies and aberrations that had to be stamped out lest they spiral out of control, threatening "America's interests" abroad. This is the thrust of Barnett's *The Pentagon's New Map*, which brings together Fukuyama and Huntington to the extent that it identifies "disconnected" parts of the world as the source of danger (what Fukuyama would call those parts still "stuck in history") but differs from Huntington only in that it advocates military intervention.[17] At any rate, the logic by which Saddam Hussein was portrayed as a modern-day Hitler was re-invoked as appropriate, with imagery indissociable from that of the Holocaust lending increasing authority to the appeal for "human rights."[18]

The preservation of human rights must not be taken lightly under any circumstances, but the manipulation of imagery and memory such as took place under both Bush Sr and Bill Clinton is also a serious matter. If anything, it is the cavalier assimilation of one historical situation into another that does a disservice not only to historical analysis but, more urgently, to the very principle of human rights, emptying it of analytical force and any potential for serious engagement with a world in which such atrocities are anything but anomalous.

For Clinton, to be sure, there was no denying that such events, if "epiphenomenal," were nonetheless significant. Apart from the gut-level intolerability of human rights abuses such as those beamed around the world throughout the 1990s, the need for military intervention was also characterized, where necessary, as a matter of national security. For those for whom human rights abuse in small, distant countries was insufficient cause for military intervention, Clinton stressed the possibility that inaction could bring the threat home to American soil. "The threats we face today," he intoned in 1996, "respect no nation's borders. Think of them: terrorism, the spread of weapons of mass destruction, organized crime, drug trafficking, ethnic and religious hatred, aggression by rogue states, environmental degradation. If we fail to address these threats today, we will suffer the consequences in all our tomorrows."[19]

"All over the world," he noted a year later, "people are being torn asunder by racial, ethnic, and religious conflicts that fuel fanaticism and terror." This constituted a sharp contrast to his earlier assertion that no nuclear weapons were "pointed at America's children" or that America had never been more "secure," but for Clinton, posthistorical America still held the answer, with the rest of the world "[looking] to us to show that it is possible to live and advance together across those kinds of differences."[20] America must therefore "continue to be an unrelenting force for peace," lest it be "drawn into far more costly conflicts" down the road.[21] Despite the ostensible (not, obviously, real) end of the nuclear threat, America "must maintain a strong and ready military," finding the will and the means to make the world "a better place."[22] America's "success" in this mission over the preceding half-century did not mean that it could afford to become complacent or short-sighted. Invoking "history" as the narrative of America's rise to world leadership, in effect as America's "manifest destiny," Clinton set forth his commitment to a better and more secure future for all:

> [a]lmost exactly 50 years ago in the first winter of the Cold War President Truman stood before a Republican Congress and called upon our country to meet its responsibilities of leadership. This was his warning. He said, "If we falter, we may endanger the peace of the world, and we shall surely endanger the welfare of this nation" ... Let us do what it takes to remain the indispensable nation, to keep America strong, secure and prosperous for another 50 years.[23]

Although the threats to America's security and prosperity remained, they were therefore, in Clinton's rhetoric, by no means unmanageable: "[b]y keeping our military strong, by using diplomacy where we can and force where we must, by working with others to share the risk and the cost of our efforts,"[24] America could reap all the benefits of the post–Cold War world order. The "end of history" as Fukuyama envisioned it seemed indeed within reach; nothing could shake its foundations, provided America continued to assert its "leadership" in the name of freedom and democracy worldwide. Failure to do so could mean a return to a primitive past, as implied by the images beamed into American homes of events in the still "historical" parts of the world. There was therefore no alternative but to maintain American global dominance as established by the end of the Cold War and to intervene by all necessary means to prevent any such regression. For liberal-democratic capitalism to envelop the whole of the world in its loving embrace would be only a matter of persistence and patience. The inexorable onward march of the free market, in all its boundless benevolence, seemed to promise a new golden age for America and the world alike.

Thus, there was little difference, essentially, between the Democratic and Republican approaches to posthistory, even though Clinton's rhetoric was a little more measured and his focus on human rights more pronounced. What had seemed the biggest threat to world peace – the Cold War nuclear threat – was "history," so he claimed, and America could now get around to ensuring a better future for all. The benefits of American leadership in the world were indisputable, as was the superiority of its values over those that enabled atrocities to take place elsewhere. Threats remained, but the Persian Gulf War had demonstrated America's ability to defuse them swiftly and quite nearly effortlessly, not to mention humanely; Clinton's continued commitment to the military would ensure that such problems in the future would be managed and contained with similar ease. Progress of the sort described by Fukuyama – toward a global community united in peaceful exchange – was, give or take the occasional "aberration," right on schedule. In short, an era of global peace and stability seemed assured.

SAMUEL HUNTINGTON: REMAKING THE WORLD ORDER

What Clinton continued to celebrate, in short, was what Fukuyama had called the triumph of the "liberal *idea*," a triumph that represented, for Clinton's predecessor, the dawn of a "new world order" to be established and preserved under the guidance, both moral and military, of the United States. And indeed, the enthusiasm with which the "end of history" was embraced was in no small part a response to the dismantling of the "evil empire" and the end of the Cold War nuclear threat (even if the possibility of a nuclear accident, or the sale, theft, or smuggling of nuclear weapons, remained alive and well). Yet by the middle of the 1990s, while Clinton trumpeted the virtues of American leadership, it seemed clear that the sense of security that should have followed had not materialized. Indeed, when the dust kicked up by the fall of communism and America's victory in the Gulf finally settled, the world that was revealed seemed no less precarious than the one that had cowered in the shadow of mutually assured destruction. Mutuality might have been removed from the equation, but destruction nonetheless remained a possibility.

Evidence of an enduring and escalating fear abounded in popular culture. Disaster films, widely understood during the Cold War as direct allegories of nuclear terror (and still allegorical to some extent, although within an altered context), increased in number over the 1990s; media scares multiplied exponentially, saturating popular consciousness with fear of crime, disease, social and environmental breakdown, terrorism, and so on. Despite the relatively rosy forecast implied by the "triumph" of the West in the Cold War and America's victory in the Gulf, American popular culture, as represented in blockbuster films and on many news networks and "magazine" shows, was infused by fear and fascinated by its many sources.

It was at this historical moment – which he shared with Fukuyama – that Samuel P. Huntington came out with his "clash of civilizations" thesis. While for Fukuyama and his adherents in high places, the "end of ideology" as manifested in the triumph of the "liberal *idea*" implied a truly "unipolar" world order, the future was not so clearly defined for Huntington in that the "end of ideology" meant an "end of history" of an altogether less desirable sort.

The end of ideology, for Huntington, signifies not a new world order but the onset of a new and perhaps infinitely more dangerous era in which a declining West would face the increased military and economic power of other "civilizations" and in which religious, nationalist, and ethnic conflicts in the peripheral ("historical" for Fukuyama, "disconnected" for Barnett) parts of the globe could erupt into larger, "civilizational" conflicts that could conceivably engulf the world itself. Ideology might be over, but it has been replaced as the foundation of geopolitics by *cultural identity* and its associated passions (Fukuyama calls them "pathologies"), which, for Huntington, would not give way to the "desire for comfortable self-preservation"[25] quite as readily as Fukuyama seemed to think: "In the post–Cold War world," Huntington argues, "the most important distinctions among peoples are not ideological, political, or economic. They are cultural."[26]

For Huntington, a "clash" is always imminent, and its inevitability is a matter of "human nature" at its most basic: "unless we hate what we are not, we cannot love what we are."[27] Moreover, cultural identity – like human nature – is by his logic an almost entirely static affair:

During the Cold War, a country could be nonaligned, as many were, or it could, as some did, change its alignment from one side to another. The leaders of a country could make these choices in terms of their perceptions of their security interests, their calculations of the balance of power, and their ideological preferences. In the new world, however, cultural identity is the central factor shaping a country's associations and antagonisms. While a country could avoid Cold War alignment, it cannot lack an identity. The question, "Which side are you on?" has been replaced by the much more fundamental one, "Who are you?"[28]

The implication is that identity, unlike ideology, cannot be changed and, further, that the boundaries imposed by cultural difference cannot be transcended by any single "idea," whatever its relative merits. Liberal democracy (and it is important to note that Huntington touches only tangentially on capitalism as its economic undercurrent) is not universal but rather "unique" to Western civilization, conforming to a Western perspective to which other civilizations are constitutionally incapable of adapting themselves.[29] It is, in other words, just as much a product of Western "culture" in the anthropological sense of the word as Islamic fundamentalism is a product of Islam. There can be no reconciliation between such disparate world views, no assimilation of one into any other, and the almost inevitable outcome, for Huntington, is global strife at an unprecedented level.

Huntington's initial *Foreign Affairs* article, "The Clash of Civilizations?" made its appearance shortly after Fukuyama published his "end of history" thesis in book form; Huntington's own book-length argument appeared in 1996 while Clinton was extolling the virtues of liberal-democratic capitalism and stressing the need for America to maintain its leadership in the world for the benefit of all mankind. Both Fukuyama and Huntington enjoyed, as noted, a broad critical reception and correspondingly high rankings on bestseller lists nationwide.[30] And this is precisely why neither can be dismissed outright, however unpalatable the potential consequences of their respective world views. In fact, the disavowal of ideology that both projections imply is part of the same "structure of feeling," with the "remaking of world order" and the "end of history" as only two of the possible manifestations. In other words, the same structure of feeling that made both Fukuyama's thesis and Bush Sr's "new world order" seem plausible also makes realization of Huntington's dire predictions appear disconcertingly likely.

How is it that the "end of history" and the "clash of civilizations" can be declared at one and the same time? Is this evidence of a "double plot of world history in which cultural differentiation and cultural homogenization go hand in hand,"[31] a world that, as Eagleton suggests, is "growing both more international and more tribal simultaneously?"[32] Or are we dealing with a clash of representations?

I am inclined toward the latter response, which would imply that both are symptomatic of the "structure of feeling" I have described. Fukuyama and Huntington may well represent a certain brand of intellectual – let's say the "popular intellectual" – whose audience is far more limited than that of the print or broadcast media, but the conflict between them embodies the same contradictions that apply at the level of the broader structure of feeling. It is effectively the "end of ideology" in the post–Cold War period that connects the two, and this in itself has profoundly contradictory implications that apply well beyond the realm of academics, even academics linked, especially in Fukuyama's case, to the development and execution of American foreign policy. Let us begin, then, with Huntington's idea of the transition from ideology to identity as the primary terrain of contention. This is, after all, the cornerstone of his argument, and it can be read against a broader cultural backdrop that emphasizes differentiation in equal measure to Fukuyama's standardization.

While it is tempting at first to dismiss Huntington's position on the grounds that "identity," as the product of "ideology" in a deeper sense of the word, is always subject to change, this does not affect the ranking of *Clash* among the definitive "popular intellectual" texts of the first post–Cold War decade (and the first post-9/11 decade as well). His definition of ideology, in other words, and the binary opposition he establishes between ideology and identity, found little opposition among his readers, suggesting that there was effectively already a place for his argument within the context in which it was received – that is, that his readers were already prepared to accept the idea of such a transition and that it conformed to a world view already becoming established.[33] Walter Benn Michaels, despite his opposition to the "clash" thesis more generally, makes a point that serves to locate *both* Huntington and Fukuyama within their wider historical and cultural context, suggesting in effect that neither of their outlooks concerning the end of ideology can be reduced to mere "[artifacts] of a vanished historical moment"[34] and that the debate concerning the nature of identity is in some sense hardly relevant:

> It would be a mistake to imagine that Huntington's opposition
> between the cultural and the ideological would be undone by
> the recognition that the relative fixity of the cultural is only rela-
> tive, that cultural identities are, as we say, more "mobile" than
> he recognizes ... The commitment to the idea that identities are
> not fixed in no way undermines this difference [between ideol-
> ogy and identity]; the debate over whether identities are fixed ...
> should be understood instead as a way of propping it up, as a
> way of insisting on the primacy of identity ... over ideology. To

choose between physical and cultural, fixed or mobile ... is to choose between two different accounts of identity. And to choose between two different accounts of identity is already to have chosen identity itself.[35]

In other words, one cannot escape Huntington's implicitly (and sometimes explicitly) racist logic by attacking his notion of "cultural identity"; to do so is merely to reaffirm it by asserting its primacy. His definition of civilizations as "the broadest level of cultural identity people have, short of that which distinguishes human beings from other species,"[36] illustrates for Michaels just "how powerful the notion of culture as the site of difference has become."[37] And certainly, it can hardly be denied that in whatever form, identity politics have come to the forefront in the "postmodern" era, whether as a force for liberation (inspired by the anti-colonial and civil rights movements of the 1960s) or as a force for hostile, defensive parochialism. Despite the strong case to be made for the mutual interdependence of identity and ideology (indeed, for Louis Althusser, ideology is precisely what "hails or interpellates concrete individuals as concrete subjects"[38]), the increasing prominence of identity politics can no more be denied than can the disavowal of ideology itself by both the unipolar and the multipolar world views. Even for Fukuyama, as noted, cultural identity remains an obstacle to the glorious realization of posthistory, although it is an obstacle destined to be overcome.

For Fukuyama, then, the "end of ideology" promises unity and standardization; for Huntington, it promises division, and the irreducible incommensurability of different cultures or civilizations precludes the realization of a new world order as defined by Bush or Clinton. The latter, along with Fukuyama, assume the universal applicability of liberal-democratic principles and capitalism regardless of the concrete particularities of ethnicity, nationality, and religion. By contrast, Huntington sees such particularities as moving in to fill the space left by Cold War ideologies, replacing a gridlocked global situation with a still more intractable one. If Fukuyama's declaration of the "end of history" marks the conclusion of a global "grand narrative," or what he calls the "universal history" of mankind, then what Huntington's predictions assert is that any such narrative was always impossible to begin with. Culture in the prescriptive sense, as traditionally allied with liberal-democratic capitalism, can only ever "clash" with cultures in the descriptive sense, as particular "ways of life." While for Fukuyama the latter can ultimately be subsumed by the former, for Huntington they are fundamentally irreconcilable.

The irony here is that both Fukuyama and Huntington are modernists at heart, relying on grand narratives to declare the end of narrative (in Fukuyama's case) or to predict a future narrative (in Huntington's). It is indeed an irony of postmodernism that it too relies on a supposedly "prior" narrative of fragmentation and dislocation in the history of art, capitalism, and modes of experience more generally. However, this is not how either thesis was typically received. The end of the Cold War left questions where there should have been answers, and both writers offer answers; that they are so different can be attributed to the structure of feeling that makes each equally plausible (if unpalatable, as both are for different reasons).

If Fukuyama's ideas find support in the arena of American foreign policy, then Huntington's are more readily adaptable to the tenets of postmodernist theory, although, as a historian and a de facto modernist, he might not appreciate the comparison. For the postmodern, "cultures" in the anthropological sense are impervious to "Culture" as universal civility; "[f]rom the viewpoint of Culture," Eagleton notes, cultures "perversely [seize] upon the accidental particulars of existence ... and [convert] them into the bearers of necessity."[39] Gone are the days, for Eagleton, when "high culture" in aesthetic form reconciled universal with particular and raised the individual to the plane of a "universal humanity,"[40] according to nineteenth-century imperialist doctrine and the grand narrative constructed to bolster it. Postmodernism, he claims, instead describes a universe in which there is "nothing but the particular."[41] Like the postmodern market culture that levels everything to a "host of random particulars,"[42] thereby coming into conflict with the universalizing moral justifications put forth by Culture, cultures too deny the universal, pitting fragmentation against the forces of integration, against so many "language games."[43] And it is precisely this level of "culture" that has come to fill the void left by ideology, which in the sense that Huntington and Fukuyama use it – that is, as a question of liberal democracy on the one hand and communism on the other – is indeed a category of the universal and is now, by Huntington's logic at any rate, irretrievably lost.

To put it in Michaels's words, "[t]he question of which of two social systems is *better* is intrinsically universal" so that "to prefer communism (or capitalism) is to prefer it everywhere for every-one,"[44] but differences of identity – as opposed to differences of opinion – set themselves squarely against the possibility of the uni-versal as such, appealing instead to matters of perspective or "sub-ject position" and thereby eliminating disagreement, in principle, altogether: "to see things differently because we see from different perspectives is to see the same thing differently but without contra-diction," argues Michaels, and thus, "the movement from the clash of ideologies to the clash of civilizations should be understood as movement from the universalist logic of conflict as difference of opinion to the posthistoricist logic of conflict as difference in subject position."[45] The terrain of contention is no longer one and the same as seen from each side; rather, it differs fundamentally depending on perspective. Conflict is no longer about the *same thing*, a fact that ostensibly became clear on 9/11 and in the years that followed. The mere question of whether the conflict can be seen as a "reli-gious war" should demonstrate the fundamental intractability of the "subject position" problem, because whether it is or isn't depends on which side you ask.[46]

Huntington's insistence on the incommensurability of different cultures – that, for him, a Western democrat can carry on a debate with a Marxist-Leninist but not with a nationalist Orthodox Rus-sian[47] – is to this extent thoroughly postmodern, however adamantly he would reject the label. It is, after all, consistent with the pro-nouncements of some of the foremost theorists of postmodernism. Jean-François Lyotard, for instance, sees a future configured on a "pragmatics of language particles" or a "heterogeneity of elements," giving rise to "local determinism" in place of the "grand narratives" or "metanarratives" that had assumed universal applicability.[48] This is not a position that Huntington would endorse, seeing as he does the fragmentation of society as part of a much broader historical narrative, but his emphasis on incommensurability between cul-tures meshes nicely with Lyotard's "language games," also funda-mentally incommensurable, thoroughly resistant to the imposition of consensus. The "rules" of language games are "the object of a contract, explicit or not, between players," and where "there are no rules, there is no game."[49] Disagreement, in other words, is effect-ively impossible in the absence of a common perspective from which to define the object of contention. Similarly, Richard Rorty, whose "pragmatic" epistemology rejects the possibility of any overarching

"Truth," suggests that "we cannot justify our beliefs ... to everybody but only to those whose beliefs overlap ours to some appropriate extent";[50] truth can only ever be based on an "intersubjective agreement" between members of a "community" speaking a common language and establishing a common "reality." Over and against an impotent relativism, however, Rorty suggests – unhelpfully, I would say – that we "grasp the ethnocentric horn of the dilemma" and "privilege our own group,"[51] which is, in effect, precisely what Huntington prescribes for America and the West. Indeed, in some ways Huntington is even more vocal an opponent of relativism than Rorty, blaming "multiculturalism" in large part for what he sees as "internal rot," "moral decline," "cultural suicide," and "political disunity" within the West.[52] The postmodern, then, like Huntington's "multicivilizational" world, is "characterized by a widening array of incommensurable language games ... each with its own players, rules, and ends."[53] And such a world is by definition chaotic, unpredictable, immune to rational analysis – rationality as "we" understand it being, as Huntington endeavours to show, by no means universal but exclusively a product of Western civilization and the history of Western thought. The removal of ideology from the equation is for Huntington what the removal of the "rules" is for Lyotard or Rorty: that is, it constitutes the removal of any mutually acceptable mediating framework from the "game" and therefore the termination of the game altogether. From this point on, by such a logic, the wider global configuration can only be predominantly anarchical in structure.

For Huntington, then, the end of ideology is a source of fear. In place of the "balance of terror" maintained across decades of ideological disagreement arises an infinitely more volatile global configuration, one that can be "mapped" in space but not in time. In place of a malevolent yet rational "other," possessing a different set of beliefs concerning a single system, arises a not merely culturally "different" other but an irrational, intransigent one with whom dialogue is utterly impossible. (His own Orientalist bias comes through in, among other ways, his famous description of the "bloody borders of Islam."[54]) People with different beliefs, in other words, are replaced by people with different identities, since "ideology" as rational adherence to a given, systematic world view has no place, by Huntington's logic, in the realm of cultural identity. Even religion in this account – and despite a multiplicity of cultural "others,"

Huntington does target Islam as a leading threat – is less a question of belief than of identity. As Michaels puts it,

> no one really thinks of Islam, or any other religion, as a set of beliefs in the same way that communism was. We treat religion on the model of a culture, which is to say, we treat people who belong to different religions not as if they have false beliefs, but as if they have different identities ... Religious belief *as belief*, which would require a commitment on the part of people who didn't believe in Islam to the idea that people who did believe in Islam were mistaken, is replaced by religion as a kind of identity, from which standpoint people who *believe* differently are treated as people who *are* different.[55]

It is such difference apprehended spatially or synchronically – as in Huntington's (and Barnett's) maps demarcating "the West" from "the rest"[56] – that allows for the persistence of this illusion of incommensurability, eliminating as it does any temporal axis along which any form of negotiation might unfold. The inherent universality of disagreement over the mode of socio-economic organization gives way to a fragmented world of incommensurable subject positions, whether these positions can be ultimately "assimilated" to the imperatives of liberal-democratic capitalism (Fukuyama) or not (Huntington).

It is not, then, the specific characteristics of different civilizations that Huntington sees as a cause for concern, although he seldom has anything positive to say about them and tends to focus on one or two "culprits" in particular. In general, it is more the form than the content, more incommensurability itself than the differing perspectives, that portends for Huntington the catastrophic and inevitable "clash." This insistence on incommensurability – whatever Huntington would say about postmodernism or posthistoricism in particular – makes sense against a broader backdrop in which events in the "historical" world are seen as aberrations: Huntington denies any common or mediating ground in the same way that the media deny any unifying principle between the system as "lived" in the posthistorical, privileged West and the same system as experienced elsewhere.[57] No common set of rules unites the West's experience of "the rest" with the rest itself. The global totality, as Jameson warned thirty years ago, simply cannot be apprehended.

It is here, of course, that the illusion of objectivity Huntington wishes to sustain effectively breaks down, for although he pretends to relativize Western civilization as one among many, he nonetheless "[grasps] the ethnocentric horn of the dilemma" and falls back upon a politics of exclusion. As Sandra Buckley points out, his dissection of "the core values of 'the rest'" is "presented as the source of authority for his judgment that Common Sense resides ... with 'the West'"; he confirms in this process that "the West is the master grammar which can interpret all difference but itself exceeds and resists translation."[58] In other words, his world view reconstitutes a centred, Western subject against an incompatible "rest" or set of "civilizational" others.

If this implies a politics of exclusion – and Huntington's insistence that the West reinforce its protective "walls" against this multifarious otherness would seem to suggest that it does – then it is difficult to see how his argument could appeal to any segment of society other than its rightmost extremity. Whatever the "consumption-satisfaction" afforded by the portrayal of an irrational set of "others," the focus on cultural identity is bound to raise some problems within a liberal society that tends to *value* cultural difference. If liberal "relativism," as he calls it, is anathema for Huntington, then what accounts for the widespread appeal of this book – particularly before 9/11 – beyond the question of intolerance?

The answer may lie in the book's very title, which includes two central ideas. The first part of the title, the idea of a "clash" of "civilizations," contains a hint of apocalypticism, a suggestion of fearsome, sweeping historical moments that could overwhelm and engulf humanity itself. To the extent that this image is part of the same "posthistory" that promises for Fukuyama a sameness without end – that is, that the same structure of feeling portends a "clash" of apocalyptic proportions – what may be at stake is a sense of incompletion, a sense that if life at the "end of history" is really "all there is," then the narrative of "universal history" would seem troublingly inconclusive. If what the posthistorical structure of feeling takes away from Western society is any sense of a "master" narrative – whether Huntington would admit this or not (he would not) – then what the "clash" does is reassemble posthistory's supposed "aberrations," or the "random particulars" of continuing events elsewhere in the world, into a narrative framework, one that may not promise a happy ending but that purports to make sense of a fragmented world. Thus, the second half of Huntington's title – *The Remaking of World Order* – seems to promise a solution: not, of course, a solution to the problem of cultural incommensurability or even to the apparent inevitability of a clash, but it does promise a way to restore some semblance of order on the chaos he describes.

It is this imposition of a master narrative and its constitution of the West as the narrating subject that strikes me as the most important aspect of Huntington's thesis, when considered, that is, as symptomatic of its time rather than as a viable theory in its own right. Like *The End of History*, it purports to interpret and explain an ever less "mappable" global configuration. And the appeal of such narratization lies in its application to the constitution of the Western subject not only against its cultural Others but, by extension, against a broader set of perceived dangers as well.

AN EPIDEMIC OF FEAR

Huntington's thesis, in other words, appeals to a culture at a loss for an intelligible epistemic framework and grasping for narrative coherence, and this same "narratizing impulse" is manifested in a broader range of popular cultural phenomena that respond to the "schizophrenic" experience of posthistory and its associated anxieties and paranoias. In other words, the impulse to narratize – to impose a narrative order upon – the ungraspable "sublime" of postmodern hyperspace insinuates itself within the cultural representation of a host of perceived threats. What Fukuyama calls the "pathologies" of cultural identity (an assessment implied by Huntington as well) thus applies to the "rational" West as narrating subject.

In his book *Culture of Fear*, Barry Glassner catalogues a series of panics that gripped the American popular imagination over the course of the 1990s, sparked by anything from viruses to crime waves to aviation safety (or lack thereof) and beyond. His concern is to show how such fears are amplified and disseminated well out of proportion to the actual level of danger involved as well as in whose interests all of this takes place. The media, Glassner notes, assume a central role in this respect, presenting threats biological and otherwise as forming part of a "wave" of ills engulfing American society. With television in particular, the media subsume the message, or at least any aspect of it that seems contradictory: vivid imagery and dramatic reporting such as characterizes most prime-time "news magazines" and daytime talk shows can easily override any statistics that suggest a given risk is actually much smaller than it seems. Rather than citing a host of examples, all of which obey essentially the same structural principles, it seems more useful to consider the proliferation of such "panics" as a phenomenon in itself. Much as Huntington is less concerned with the specific "subject positions" of individual civilizations than with the principle of incommensurability itself, so too is the *form* of such "panics" – as narratives and as commodities affording a certain consumption-satisfaction – more central here than their specific content. It is narrative for the sake of narrative that counts, rather than the plausibility of the narrative content itself.

The range of threats documented by Glassner includes the following, non-exhaustive list: flesh-eating disease, Gulf War Syndrome, Multiple Chemical Sensitivity, breast implant disorders, drug addiction, road rage, youth homicide, child abuse, crack babies, and plane wrecks – to name just a few. A sociologist by training, Glassner backs up his analyses with statistical evidence to demonstrate just how vastly such threats are blown out of proportion. Between 1990 and 1998, for instance, the murder rate declined by 20 per cent, while the number of murder stories on the news increased by 600 per cent;[59] similarly, while road rage accounted for less than one in a thousand road traffic deaths between 1990 and 1997, it was commonly reported as an "exploding phenomenon" or a "plague."[60] To cite another example, while only one in 114,000 stands a chance of being murdered on the job, news networks presented an "epidemic" of fatal workplace violence.[61] Finally, while homicide by children under thirteen had decreased in frequency since the 1960s, news networks manipulated statistics to show a massive increase.[62] The underlying pattern is clear. Such examples abound in Glassner's book, and although on the surface they might seem to be very different from the doomsday scenario that Huntington describes, I would suggest that they hold very much the same broad cultural appeal and are premised on a similar concept of what, to the individual or social body, is truly insidious and harmful.

For all the panic they incite, they too possess a clear narrative logic that compensates for what the "end of history" and the posthistorical structure of feeling took away while simultaneously on some level emblematizing this new state of affairs. The structural narrative aspect they share consists in the fact that despite the actual scale of the threat such dangers pose in relation to more pervasive social ills, they are *always* presented as part of a growing trend. This illusion, moreover, is de facto confirmed by the fact that once a given threat has come to light, the media seize upon each new instance of it, whereas under different circumstances it might have passed unremarked. The result is a snowball effect in which increased reporting of a given type of danger generates a still greater increase, at least until something more sensational takes its place. Hence, it is easy to see how a few isolated shooting incidents became a "disturbing trend" overtaking American schools or why a few sensational road rage deaths became evidence of a "plague" of aggressive driving. One might say, indeed, that the anomaly is exaggerated to the point where it comes to *appear* no longer anomalous. Obviously, the logic of market forces applies: if a sensational incident such as the Columbine shooting drew wide audiences, then similar events would, for some time at least, do the same – until, that is, the point at which such events appear to become a matter of routine. Overall, though, the phenomenon conforms to a sense of narrative that holds broad appeal in an age of instantaneity and random particulars.

The narrative logic here is one of decline and decay, and like Huntington's "remaking of world order," while it does not promise a happy conclusion, it nonetheless restores some semblance of order to what otherwise seems disturbingly random and contingent. Further, undoubtedly central to this logic is the terminology of progressive and fatal illness, which is invoked to categorize each new threat: they are always presented as part of a "plague" or "epidemic," less a threat in and of themselves than in the form they take, their implied *contagion.* If the amount of media attention awarded to sensational or violent incidents is any indication, then the whole of society would seem to be suffering from multiple contagious ailments, ranging from a "plague" of incivility to an "epidemic" of crack-addicted adolescent mothers. Indeed, in numerous ways, as Susan Sontag has famously pointed out, the metaphor of progressive illness so central to the phenomenon of media "scares" in general is a well-worn trope, a "mass cultural" counterpart to Huntington's "intellectual" portrait of incommensurability and increasing conflict.

Like Huntington's prediction of a "clash," these "tropes of epidemics," applied to these irrational fears, restore a sense of narrative; they present an opportunity to "diagnose" society; and, as Jameson says of certain pervasive symbols or metaphors, they succeed in "[absorbing] and [organizing a range of] quite different anxieties together," serving an "essentially polysemous function" that is "profoundly ideological, insofar as [they allow] essentially social and historical anxieties to be folded back into apparently natural ones."[63] The genuine anxieties brought about by an unstable economic system whose victims are almost invariably the most vulnerable in society are thereby displaced onto a host of threats disconnected (or apparently disconnected) from the chronic instabilities of post-industrial capitalism.

These "social and historical" anxieties are those already discussed – namely, the anxieties generated in the transition from Fordism to "flexible accumulation" and by the decline in economic security across the board. As Brian Massumi notes in *The Politics of Everyday Fear*, the 1970s and 1980s witnessed the implementation of "ruthless strategies of displacement, fluidification, and intensification," a shift in emphasis from "durables to intangibles," and the creation of a new and broader type of Marxian "permanent underclass," all of which augment an already existing, generalized sense of anxiety.[64] If, as Jameson says, the consumption-satisfaction of mass cultural products consists in the "management" of such anxieties, then the media scares – which are, after all, commodities – must hold a certain consumer appeal beyond their apparent value as "warnings" to the public or even just as sensational entertainment.

The illness metaphor best defined by Susan Sontag, whether applied to road rage, school shootings, or even illnesses themselves, is the ideal "messenger" for such anxieties, giving them expression while simultaneously containing them. In promoting a diagnosis of society and its manifold ailments, the metaphor displaces real, material concerns onto ones that are either "natural" (and therefore beyond human intervention) or "moral" (evidence of an inexorable moral decline – as suggested, especially earlier on, in the metaphor of AIDS). Further, it allows for the constitution of an observing subject that is both temporarily exempted and placed in a position to pass judgment on the situation, thereby de-implicating him- or herself. "Better them than me" alternates or combines with a sense that the world "out there" is getting sicker all the time. As Huntington's analysis tacitly reconstitutes the West against the rest as an observing and narrating central subject, so too do such media scares, on a wider scale, enable the reconstitution (or "interpellation," in Althusser's words) of a cognitive, narrating individual subject, a subject whose borders "external" threats – viruses, chemicals, criminals – must not be permitted to penetrate. The fact that such manufactured and mediated fears succeed as commodities points to their widely shared nature as well as their "reconstituting" function; if the effect is not monolithic, it is certainly broadly persuasive.

As Jameson points out, any such "degraded" form of "cognitive mapping" engendered by media scares and conspiracy theories leads inevitably to paranoia and conspiracism (ironically, given Fukuyama's diagnosis of "pathology" in regard to other cultures), since the media present their scares as a direct and personal threat. They are always presented as warnings to "you," the viewer, implicating "you" in the scare of the hour. Emphasis is placed on the sheer ordinariness of the victims, their neighbourhoods, schools, or hospitals or even of the weather on the day a given incident takes place (as we will see in accounts of 9/11). The drive-by shooting takes place outside a Starbucks just like any other Starbucks, including the one "you" frequent every day; the child victim of a school shooting could reasonably have been "your" own. Remarkable things happen to wholly unremarkable people, which is why "you," at any time, could find "yourself" in the line of fire. (Notably, this is the flip side of the "fifteen minutes of fame" that could be "your" experience should you appear on a reality show.) As a telling example, Glassner cites Oprah Winfrey during a special on road rage: "This woman's biggest offense was pulling out of her driveway ... countless millions of you have done that." Such statements "[t]ransmute familiar occurrences into a huge new danger,"[65] suggesting that it is at the most apparently ordinary of times that one should be the most afraid. Massumi, for his part, traces this back to the Kennedy assassination as the first mass-mediated or "instant" trauma: at this juncture, he claims, "[c]racks began to open all around ... The shot could come from any direction, at any time."[66] The same applies to the present-day "traumas" of mass-mediated culture: nobody is ever really safe.

Compounding the temporal *imminence* of the viewer's own victimization is an *immanence* to which the illness metaphor also readily adapts itself. Like the virus, which is invisible, internal, and strikes without warning, the threat – of whatever variety – lies concealed behind a semblance of pure normality and even innocence; the mass murderer is always described by his neighbours, after the fact, as wholly unremarkable, even likeable, soft-spoken, and polite. The "enemy," Massumi notes, "is no longer even clearly identifiable

as such";[67] behind the elements of society most emblematic of innocence and purity lie the darkest and most sinister of motives and
intentions. Hence the particular shock value of crimes committed by
children against priests or by priests against children, each in its own
way affirming the notion that society is heading to the proverbial
dogs, suffering the ripple effects of a distinctly moral crisis to which
there is no end in sight. The resulting situation, in Massumi's words,
is one in which

> [e]ver present dangers blend together, barely distinguishable
> in their sheer numbers. Or, in their proximity to pleasure and
> intertwining with the necessary functions of body, self, family,
> economy, they blur into the friendly side of life. The cold war in
> foreign policy has mutated into a state of generalized deterrence
> against an enemy without qualities. An unspecified enemy threat-
> ens to rise up at any time at any point in social or geographical
> space. From the welfare state to the warfare state: a permanent
> state of emergency against a multifarious threat as much in us
> as outside ... The content of the disaster is unimportant. Its par-
> ticulars are annulled by its plurality of possible agents and times:
> here and to come.[68]

Tom Engelhardt sees the "internal" enemy as arising after the
Second World War when communism threatened to infiltrate American society in the form of a racially indistinguishable entity,[69] but
what Massumi is saying, I would argue, is more accurate and more
endemic to our times. The communist threat was still ideologically distinct and, once identified, could be uprooted or at least geo-
graphically contained; the new threat (or host of threats) takes the
form of an amorphous, undefined, and annihilating illness that over-
takes its victims when it is already too late. What Massumi calls the
"imm(a)(i)nence of the accident"[70] makes the virus the ideal metaphor, immanent and imminent as it is in its very nature. The ordinary consumer of media scares such as those that proliferated over
the course of the 1990s is only ever exempt for the moment but
could easily experience the "extraordinary" and possibly fatal at
any time. One of the characteristics of postmodern space, after all,
is that theoretically, "anywhere can be a centre"; no single place,
institution, or ideal serves any longer to ground the entire system.
Yet a system that "threatens to evaporate entirely into its specific

instances" – that is, into a loose aggregate of particulars ungoverned by any universal – is one that is apparently "centreless,"[71] and there is no longer any mediating distance between the viewer – the direct audience for the media scare – and a "centre" that is external to this viewer. In other words, he or she is as likely to be at the "centre" of undesirable events as anybody else. "Immanence" signifies not only inherence but a certain pervasiveness as well, so the threat is "everywhere and nowhere," invisible to the eye but always about to irrupt without warning.

The sad truth of the matter, of course, is that at any time "you" really *could* find "yourself" unemployed or, in the US in particular, struggling to pay unforeseen medical bills (the fate of Obama's health care reform hangs in the balance at the time of writing). Anxiety in the present day is by no means uncalled for. Nor is the impulse to narratize – to fashion a tale of inexorable decline out of an increasingly "unmappable" situation – misguided, for indeed, these legitimate anxieties are part of a deeper, underlying narrative – namely, capitalism's ongoing self-transformation in response to changes that it generates itself. Further, many of the anti-social "plagues" *can* indeed be attributed to social ills generated and perpetuated by that economic system. There is no argument here that material reality does not legitimately intersect with the dominant "cultural imaginary," even though the latter so often obscures its material roots. That is, multiple media panics almost invariably displace legitimate causes for anxiety onto ultimately insignificant ones. Indeed, the situation becomes one of reversal, whereby the events that are in fact *not* anomalous – events in the "historical" world, for instance – are presented as aberrations, while genuine anomalies – school shootings, for instance – are presented as part of an ongoing narrative of moral decline before which the observing subject is utterly helpless. The narrative of decline functions much like conspiracism, or what Jameson calls the "poor man's cognitive mapping";[72] it rearranges "chaos into order, the contingent into the determined,"[73] assimilating a host of disparate and largely anomalous phenomena into an ongoing trajectory of societal decay.

In other words, the inclination persists to impose a narrative of moral decline in place of the narrative of "progress," now rendered meaningless by the relentless atomization of capitalism itself: in the face of the "imm(a)(i)nence," the unfathomable spatial and temporal immediacy of the late capitalist structure of feeling, the narrative imposes a mediating buffer between the subject and the external world – in effect, the mediation of the paranoid fantasy (a narrative, if not a "grand" one).

This applies to questions of *cultural* otherness as well – that is, on a collective level as much as on an individual one. The subjectivity effected by the metaphor of illness and the narrative of decline – the constitution of a centred self against an ever more decentred, amorphous, and all-pervasive threat – can be "sutured" to a broader collective identity as well. The narrative of decline, for instance, allows for the reassertion of collective, conservative "values" for which an "authentic" America now fancies itself nostalgic. But it also constitutes a collective against a set of cultural "others," bringing Huntington's own brand of "intellectual" xenophobia to a more populist level. The mass audience appeal of such "threats" is testament to their power as commodities.

Patrick O'Donnell, writing on conspiracy theory, views the narratives of paranoia as mediations that "[articulate] the 'individual's' relation to the symbolic order"; in his view, they are "narratives of identification with the cultural imaginary." They act as a way of "conceiving the relationship between individual and society"[74] at a time when, as noted, the individual has lost the capacity to "map its position in a mappable external world."[75] Paranoia is, in short, a "mediation" between the universal and the particular, inscribing disparate phenomena with the evidence of some deeper controlling mechanism; fear is what "mediates," in other words, *in the absence of ideology proper.*

O'Donnell further defines the "work of paranoia" as "that which both polices the boundaries between self and other, and like the border patrol, has more to do the more susceptible those boundaries are to transgression and erasure."[76] And susceptible they are – or seem – in an era of mass communications, mass transit, mass migration of commodities and individuals alike. It is, to this extent, like the conspiracism that Jameson sees as a "degraded" form of "cognitive mapping." Much as conspiracy theory of the more "subcultural" or oppositional sort "begins with individual self-preservation, with an attempt to defend the integrity of the self against the social order,"[77] so too does the fear of the "virus," both directly and metaphorically, seek to delineate the integrity of the body against external threats. And the same applies to the "body politic" in relation to which such threats take on precisely the same "viral" characteristics.

Susan Sontag's metaphors are particularly apt here. In her treatise on the (ab)use of illness as metaphor, Sontag writes of the predominance of the AIDS metaphor in particular, pointing out that

> [t]he AIDS epidemic serves as an ideal projection for First World political paranoia. Not only is the so-called AIDS virus the quintessential invader from the Third World. It can stand for any mythological menace ... Predictably, the public voices [in America] most committed to drawing moral lessons from the AIDS epidemic ... are those whose main theme is worry about America's will to maintain its bellicosity, its expenditures on armaments, its firm anti-communist stance, and who find everywhere evidence of the decline of American political and imperial authority.[78]

The idea, then, is to project onto a perceived "enemy" all the attributes of the virus itself. Indeed, in his discussion of 1991 "enemy images" during the Persian Gulf War, Jürgen Link draws a useful distinction between "two totally different groups of enemy image – those with and without subject status," arguing that representations centred on the latter have become increasingly prominent in recent years. For Link,

> [t]he chaos external to the system can, depending on the symbolic bodies or vehicles used, be composed of germs, viruses, poisons, floods, deserts, storms, fires, vermin, and so on. What is decisive here is that one's own system is held to possess subject status; whereby I mean "subject" in the narrow sense of an autonomous, responsible, quasi-judicial person of sound mind, as in a legal subject ... In principle ... "subject status" applies to those in the adversarial [communist] system ... but not to those representing external chaos ... A mass of rats, for example, possesses no subject status, but, on the other hand, the devil himself is accorded subject status.[79]

In other words, just as the "virus" of general moral decline reconstitutes the individual subject as autonomous and exempt, so too does the concept of the foreign *human* enemy as "viral" in nature constitute an autonomous collective subject. This is where Huntington's argument holds its greatest appeal in popular form and seems to conform most cleanly to mass cultural "common sense." The idea of the enemy as non-subjective "virus" corresponds, after all, to Eagleton's description of "non-being" as "slimy, impure, and insidious, a nameless threat to one's integrity of selfhood," a "dreadful infiltration of one's identity [having] no palpable form in itself, and thus [provoking] paranoia in its supposed victims." As Eagleton notes, this "nameless threat" has always "[bred] a desire to lend this hideous force a local name and habitation,"[80] and it therefore often underlies a politics of exclusion such as is manifested in anti-Semitism, where the imperative is usually implicitly purificatory, transferring onto the "other" all of the "non-subjective" or "chaotic" attributes that Link describes. The idea of incommensurable "subject positions" as articulated by Michaels here takes on new meaning as that very "subject position" comes to be conceived as somehow always under threat. This, too, is Huntington's America: a collective to which "multiculturalism," that undefinable, insidious trend, is anathema.

In itself, this is nothing new: America in particular, as Michael Rogin notes, has always been "fearful of primitivism, disorder and conspiracy," a "distinctive" tradition that has been articulated in varying ways throughout American history.[81] The communist threat, for instance, was not always embodied by a properly "subjective" enemy image and could indeed be represented as viral, as in the classic Cold War–era film *Invasion of the Body Snatchers*. However, much as Rogin examines the specific representations of communism in 1950s American film both as part of and against the "cumulative history of American demonology,"[82] it seems safe to suggest that the current climate will offer up some specific cultural "inflections" of its own.

Peter Knight's comparison of Siegel's film with a 1990s remake offers a case in point. The earlier film, as Knight points out, has often been read as a metaphor for communist ideology as an insidious, non-subjective, viral entity poised to take over American society. Although other readings are possible, he notes, the film "clearly operates as an admonitory allegory." By contrast, Abel Ferrara's 1990s remake of the film, *Bodysnatchers!* is virtually bereft of any allegorical value:

Ferrara's film creates a disturbing and graphic sense of the ominous presence of danger without a clear indication what the source or nature of that danger might be. The film produces in effect an impression of conspiracy without conspiring, a generalized and at times paralyzing atmosphere of undifferentiated alarm which leaves unclear who or what might be behind it.[83]

It is this sense of "conspiracy without conspiring" that characterizes the virus metaphor in general as well as the "narrative" of social decline, connecting disparate elements into an overarching pattern without necessarily attributing that decline to the workings of any one group in particular. And the same applies to the "posthistorical" enemy more broadly: for while Siegel's 1956 film may have evoked a cultural paranoia premised on the perceived threat of communist infiltration, the later film would seem to appeal to a far more generalized paranoia, a "generalized anxiety disorder" on a mass scale, which sees danger in every direction and fantasizes the self or the nation as the possible victim of every new threat. Or, one might say, Vietnam Syndrome as an allegorical "condition" describing a decline in moral certitude vis-à-vis the national sense of self has been replaced by Gulf War Syndrome as an *actual* disease, possibly transmissible and of decidedly murky origins.

If, during the Cold War era, ideology, however insidiously, threatened to take over the mind, then in the post-ideological age it is increasingly the body itself that is at stake. It is no longer mere transformation that is dreaded as much as complete annihilation, whether at the level of the individual or of society. To be sure, the Cold War nuclear threat implied total annihilation as well, bringing an "end," as Tom Engelhardt has argued, to "victory culture" in America,[84] but in that case the threat emanated from an alternative ideological system, whereas now, its source cannot be properly discerned or acknowledged as a "system" at all. Knight observes in the popular culture of recent times an "omnipresent environment of risk which is centred on the individual body," producing a "continuous but often unspecific sense of threat that is now located everywhere but nowhere in particular." For him, the link "between the rhetoric of germophobia and national politics" suggests that the "origin of the palpable threat" is no longer external but internal. "As the Manhattan Project gives way to the Human Genome Project," he writes, "the Virus displaces the Bomb as the subterranean source of popular paranoia."[85] It is not that the threat of nuclear annihilation is *gone*; on the contrary, the fear of a nuclear attack by a "rogue" state or by terrorists persists and should by no means be dismissed out of hand. However, the "non-subjective" threat of the virus is what seemed increasingly to characterize popular cultural fears in the 1990s. If, as Link suggests, "[t]he border of [our] system corresponds symbolically to the periphery of the body, for example, vis-à-vis the danger of bacteria and viruses,"[86] then it is easy to see how the threat of a cultural "other" can also come to be portrayed as essentially non-subjective – unlike the communist or any other state enemy – as the "germs, viruses, poisons, floods, deserts, storms, fires, vermin" to which he refers. What Massumi calls the "imm(a)(i)nence" of the threat may indeed be related to the fact that in a "globalized" world, the limits of "our" body as symbolically conceived now correspond to the limits of global expansion itself. That is, given the spatial immediacy as generated by televisual coverage of every part of the globe, the perceived chaos of formerly distant places appears ever more "immediate" and ever more encroaching. Moreover, such a threat is always pervasive, "everywhere and nowhere" like the very "non-being" that it portends.

FEAR AND THE VIRAL OTHER

One recent Hollywood film serves as an ideal illustration of the centrality of the virus metaphor in the portrayal of the cultural "other" as chaotic, insidious, non-subjective, and, in accordance with Huntington's view of other "civilizations," immune to rational inquiry. Ridley Scott's *Black Hawk Down*, the release of which, significantly, was pushed forward following the attacks of 11 September, perfectly exemplifies the idea of the "non-subjective Other" as described by Link. The subject of the film is a bungled American raid in Mogadishu in 1993 that cost 18 American lives, and the portrayal of the Somalis corresponds perfectly to Link's idea of the enemy as "external" chaos, the "swarming mass endlessly multiplying itself."[87] They are portrayed on the whole as primitive, barbaric, and thoroughly inhuman; while they drop like flies, their suffering entirely ignored, each American injury or death is shown in nauseating detail. It is a resurrection of the "ambush" narrative that Tom Engelhardt sees as so central to American "victory culture,"[88] except that the victory is moral rather than military. Visually, the film's entire aesthetic is informed by an opposition between order (associated with the American forces) and chaos: the Black Hawks'

sublime formation flights over stunning seascapes are accompanied by serene vocals, violins, and oboes in a glorious celebration
of technology and speed, whereas "sinister Arab techno" is used to
characterize the cluttered, dilapidated streets of Mogadishu as well
as the armed gangs that roam them as if in search of prey.[89] Sweeping aerial shots of orderly convoys and precision-planned deploy-
ments are juxtaposed with disorienting, ground-level shots of roving
Somali hordes, attacking from any and every angle and uttering
sounds that would strike most Western ears as frenzied babbling
(rarely, in any case, is there an individual Somali speaker who is not
part of a charging mob, and rarer still are any English subtitles). As
the body of an American pilot is hauled from the wreckage of one of
the downed helicopters, stripped bare, and dragged off as if by wild
beasts, the audience is invited to marvel at the senseless brutality of
it all, at the Somalis' utter lack of reason, and at their unrestrained
savagery. Why would the roving hordes hate the Americans, who
are only there, after all, to help "restore order" and feed civilians?
The enemy can be only thoroughly irrational, a quality that, like
evil, is immune to and merits no analysis. Indeed, the fact that the
war in Somalia is "their" war is emphasized repeatedly, by Somalis
and Americans alike, and for one of the very few Somalis permitted
to speak intelligibly in the film, it is a war to which democracy can
offer no solution, bearing out Huntington's description of a world of
incommensurable subject positions.

Insofar as the film presents the "other" as a threat, this is effected
primarily through what Link calls the "imaginary situation" created by visual perspective. The metaphorical "subject position" to
which Michaels alludes is translated into sensory experience, this
time aligned with a perspective that reinforces the sense of immediate danger. Link refers in his article to anti-Semitic German political cartoons, but the use of perspective to this effect is all the more
striking in *Black Hawk Down*, which on numerous occasions places
the viewer directly into the "line of fire" – into what Link calls a
"threatening situation demanding immediate action."[90] The perspective encourages a striking degree of viewer identification with the
American soldiers stranded in the urban war zone that is Mogadishu's Baraka Market; it is effectively the first-person video-game
aesthetic applied to a film, placing the viewer in the position of the
soldier. At one point, for instance, the film depicts the capture of
an American soldier by one of many groups of frenzied, shouting

Somalis; they are shown from "his" perspective, that is, from below, as a menacing, surging mass whose faces seem suddenly unaccountably darker than at other moments in the film – an "imaginary situation" of the sort that, to borrow again from Link, presents an "emergency of the highest degree involving the legitimate defense of one's own life" and "[conveys] the sense that the threat is closing in fast." This, I would argue, takes on special significance in relation to the posthistorical structure of feeling and the idea of posthistory more broadly, for "[o]nly when readers [in this case, viewers] are placed in this kind of imaginary situation can one speak ... of subjective war preparation through the media – because this situation alone can be linked to the only remaining official legitimation for war ... 'defense against a life-threatening attack.'"[91]

The threat so presented, in other words, has a legitimating function, justifying self-defence insofar as the conflict appears to present a direct threat to the viewer. The idea of a world of incommensurable subject positions as described by Huntington becomes manifest here, making "the only relevant question ... the question of survival" such that "all conflict [is] reimagined on the model of the conflict between self and other."[92]

The effect of all this, like that of the media scares discussed above, is to place the individual viewer at the "centre"; however, in so doing, it also "sutures" that viewer to a broader illusion of collective identity. Ridley Scott, in an interview, claimed to have approached his project "without politics,"[93] suggesting in effect that he had wished to put across an unbiased or neutral perspective and promoting his work on those very grounds. His proclaimed intention, in other words, was a certain degree of "im/mediacy" in the sense of a certain self-identity between representation and referent, of a greater fidelity to reality. For some critics, such as Frank J. Wetta and Martin A. Novelli, the transition in film from patriotic celebration to "exploding bullet holes, ragged amputations, vivid decapitations, and other varied traumas," as in films like *Black Hawk Down* and Spielberg's *Saving Private Ryan*, is evidence of a new "maturity" or "honesty" among filmmakers.[94] Hollywood's "new patriotism," for them, "does not revive patriotism so much as [turn] it inside out so that the private motivations and goals of the individual soldiers superscede [sic] any stated or understood national or public rationales for whatever war is being fought."[95] Certainly, as they argue, such films are "about the experience of combat at its most elemental and personal level,"[96] but while this shift indicates for them an undermining of conventional ideological strategies, it seems rather to fit into a more postmodern and only *ostensibly* post-ideological aesthetic that is far less progressive than they seem to think. After all, the absence of any decisive victory or celebration of heroism is not necessarily indicative of a new "maturity" at work. The idea that in warfare "politics and all that shit goes out the window," or that conflict is not about "politics" but "about the man next to you"[97] – as one character unambiguously states to an idealistic young recruit – abstracts the experience of war from its wider political context and presents it as a thoroughly personal and "authentic" experience, reinforcing all the more effectively a new concept of "America in the world" that implicitly demands a renewed militarism. *Black Hawk Down* in particular conveys, through identification on a level that is all the more insidious for being purely and immediately individual, a new "reality" of American vulnerability in a globalized world.

Further, to remove any overt ideological or narrative premise from such films and to involve the viewer aesthetically in the action presented as immediate is also quite simply to naturalize warfare as the choice already made. War in such films is always a given, always inevitable, and always a necessity, whether the war being represented is fiction or fact. Any ideological premise, even of the more conservative sort, can at least be said to present something to engage with intellectually, but in the absence of any such premise, there is nothing but the conflict itself and the viewer's personal experience of that conflict as dictated by his or her positioning in relation to the shots. Postmodernism's "end of grand narratives" may to this extent be little more, finally, than their displacement onto individualistic terms, entailing a greater internalization, at the level of the individual, of the interpretive framework being promoted. Propaganda is given a whole new dimension: if, as discussed in the preceding chapter, the aestheticization of politics provides a "gaze that ostensibly looks back,"[98] then what happens in such films as *Black Hawk Down* is that the viewer is made to identify on a purely individual level with the gaze itself, through the very "eyes" of those in charge. One might say that this is less an instance of a collective Lacanian "mirror stage" than of a passage "through the looking glass" into a fantasy realm, the co-ordinates of which airbrush history proper from the equation, in the process "suturing" the individual self to the nation – but *as* an individual, nonetheless, ultimately still excluded from the "whole." Such films, in other words, evoke a thoroughly individualized identification with the wider portrayal of America's role in the world that they put across, emphasizing in this case the nation's perpetual vulnerability to outside threats. The main character, Eversmann, in *Black Hawk Down* becomes "Everyman" in a displacement that is all the more insidious for its ostensible rejection of the "illusions of social harmony" projected by earlier militaristic films or even by the coverage of the first Gulf War. At the same time, the self is "sutured" to a phantom collectivity constituted defensively – that is, against the raging virus that threatens to destroy it.

Black Hawk Down, finally, shows how the pervasive sense of a "viral" threat can be used to constitute the collective subject as well as the individual one, quite simply by casting a cultural "other" in the role of an immediate threat to the body. The implied narrative of Western or American vulnerability, moreover, is the very same narrative that Huntington draws upon with his insistence on the mutual incommensurability of the West's now numerous "others," whom he sees as encroaching, immanent, insidious, inscrutable, and ultimately a threat to the West's very survival. According to the narrative of decline and decay, which can now be extended to the world as a whole, a "clash" is inevitable and always imminent. It is to the imminence of this apocalyptic showdown that this analysis now turns.

APOCALYPSE SOON: FEARS OF MASS DESTRUCTION

Complementing the fear of decay and decline, of viruses themselves, and of "viral" threats, cultural or otherwise, is another great source of morbid fascination for late twentieth-century culture – namely, mass annihilation. Whether as the catastrophic endpoint to the narrative of decline or as an unanticipated *deus ex machina* pronouncing a sudden and cataclysmic end to the whole sordid business of life on Earth, the prospect of disaster became the object of a cultural obsession in the years leading up to the millennium, repeatedly indulged in by the mainstream film industry. Although the disaster film has a fairly long history, enhanced by Cold War threats of nuclear annihilation, the posthistorical 1990s in particular witnessed a substantial increase in disaster-genre output[99] and this despite the (proclaimed) end of the Cold War nuclear threat for which many earlier disaster films served as metaphors.[100] Certainly, to some extent there is a continuity between Cold War annihilation-based disaster movies and those of the 1990s; nuclear weapons continued to feature reasonably prominently in films such as *True Lies*, *The Hunt for Red October*, and other "political" thrillers. But the threat was now imbued with an uncertainty that can most plausibly be attributed to the demise of the enemy *state* as the organizing principle of the threat. Now, the threat – whether nuclear or not – penetrated our increasingly porous geographical, social, and individual boundaries, making the object of fear a more "polysemous" stand-in for the Bomb, one that crystallized the anxieties of post-Fordist production in particular, bringing material reality into contact with the cultural imaginary in yet another way.

One might see such films as appealing to a growing apocalyptic trend in popular culture, a secular version of which has been noted by a number of scholars over the latter half of the twentieth century.[101] Apocalypticism need not have any religious basis in particular and can be characterized, as Daniel Wojcik writes, less by "faith in a redemptive new realm" than by a "sense of pessimism, absurdity and nihilism."[102] Such nihilism, which *can* be put down to the older threat of nuclear conflagration, may also stem in part from the perception of society's inexorable decline – not only are we aware, following the bombing of Hiroshima and Nagasaki as well as the subsequent acquisition of nuclear weaponry by the Soviet Union, that the fate of all humanity hangs in the balance, but layers of amorphous, undefinable fear have been added by the chronic instabilities of post-industrialism. The development and deployment of the first nuclear weapons made mass annihilation a terrifying and always imminent possibility, and this became a focal point for evangelicals and non-believers alike. If the Bomb provided fodder for preachers, Bible scholars, and prophecy writers,[103] it also "[brought] terror back to the technological object" more generally and "[erased] any illusions that science was intrinsically beneficent."[104] Indeed, for some, like Engelhardt, it brought an end to "victory culture" more broadly, since nuclear warfare could be conceived only within the co-ordinates of "deterrence" lest a global apocalypse *truly* take place.[105] Robert Jay Lifton and Greg Mitchell refer to the post-1945 mindset as one of "nuclear entrapment," characterized by a "continuous sense of crisis, of anxiety about dangers both real and fantasized, in a dynamic of threat and counterthreat bound up with ever more bizarre scenarios of the murder of hundreds of millions of human beings."[106] Hiroshima, for them,

[h]ad not only exceeded all previous limits in destruction but had, in effect, declared that *there were no limits* to destruction. Modern war – World War I, and the saturation bombings in Europe and Japan preceding Hiroshima – had long violated the limit of targeting only combatants. But Hiroshima's suggestion of *totality of destruction* – of unbounded annihilation – was of a radically different order.[107]

True, the saturation bombing claimed as many or more victims, but the annihilation of so many in a matter of seconds changed the paradigm forever. This awareness of the possibility of instantaneous "unbound annihilation" prefigures the "presentation of the unpresentable" in contemporary disaster films, as well as the secular apocalypticism to which it appeals. But it does not explain the recent increase in disaster films despite the putative – if not truly finalized – end of the nuclear "balance of terror" and the constant threat of nuclear conflagration. It seems necessary to look more closely at the mechanisms and implications of the genre in order to better connect it to the contemporary structure of feeling.

The most salient aspect of the disaster film in terms of commodity attraction would seem, on the surface at least, to be its sheer visual appeal. In "The Imagination of Disaster," Susan Sontag discusses the aesthetics of catastrophe in film, pointing to the chief strength of the disaster genre as its "immediate representation of the extraordinary" and its subsequent "sensuous elaboration." In such films, she writes, it is "by means of images and sounds, not words that have to be translated by the imagination, that one can participate in the fantasy of living through one's own death and more, the death of cities, the destruction of humanity itself."[108] Indeed, the "representation of the extraordinary" has been continually refined over the years as escalating budgets and increasing technological proficiency allow for ever more convincing catastrophic scenes that, like the televised image, successfully deny their own artificiality. To this extent, disaster films promise a consumption-satisfaction uniquely their own. The prospect of such thrills, each one outdoing the last, brings in the revenues, and on this level they arouse the consumerist thirst for novelty, the same thirst that drives the consumption of "breaking news" in the world of "instant history."

This in itself does not account, however, for the uncanny power of the "fantasy of living through one's own death and more" or for the fact that such films always indulge a fascination with our own destruction. Nor can the appeal of novelty alone account for the fact that whatever the scale and spectacular value of the catastrophe depicted, the film in itself, as a narrative, is always more or less the same, with the same stock characters, the heroic reassertion of American (at best, Western) power following the initial trauma, and so forth. The narrative, indeed, is almost secondary; what really counts – what sells, in effect – is always the disaster itself. It is the "immediate representation of the extraordinary," or what Lyotard might call the "[putting] forward [of] the unrepresentable in presentation itself,"[109] in a way ostensibly free of mediation (that is, a way fraught with im/mediacy) that constitutes what might be called the sublime dimension of cinematic catastrophe. And as Edmund Burke well knew, a certain level of terror is always central to the experience of the sublime. "[T]error," in his words, "is in all cases whatsoever, either more openly or latently the ruling principle of the sublime."[110] Similarly, what Kant calls the "dynamic" sublime (the sublime of power rather than simple magnitude) "must be represented as exciting fear."[111] For Eagleton, summarizing the modern history of the concept, the sublime is "any power which is perilous, shattering, ravishing, traumatic, excessive, exhilarating, dwarfing, astonishing, uncontainable, overwhelming, boundless, obscure, terrifying, enthralling, and uplifting."[112] This definition, while in some ways a convenient catch-all, certainly explains to some extent the ongoing appeal of cultural products that elicit such a response.

Roland Emmerich's film *Independence Day*, one of the more successful "blockbusters" of the 1990s, evokes the sublime in several ways, "[putting] forward," as Lyotard writes, "the unrepresentable in presentation itself." In both the spectacular "realism" of its scenes of destruction and in its positioning of the viewer in relation to the shots – its creation, by means of perspective, of a "subject position" under threat – it plays on an aesthetic of terror that constitutes the main "consumption-satisfaction" afforded by disaster films in general. Even prior to the scenes of destruction, the sublime in Kant's "mathematical" sense of the term, as that which is "*absolutely great*,"[113] comes into play: the sheer size of the flying saucers, said to measure some 550 kilometres in diameter, guarantees that the viewer will never have the privilege of seeing any one of the ships in its entirety. This in itself fulfils what Burke saw as one of the conditions of the sublime: "[t]o make anything very terrible," he wrote, "obscurity seems in general to be necessary," for "[w]hen we know the full extent of any danger, when we can accustom our eyes to it, a great deal of the apprehension vanishes."[114] In this respect, the positioning of the viewer is key: the spaceships are seen predominantly from below as they position themselves over urban centres such as Los Angeles, New York, and Washington, which both diminishes the viewer and enhances the terror of a dark and seemingly boundless object filling the sky.

The destruction, when it finally begins, is utterly spectacular both in scale and in the degree of realism it achieves. The film's most memorable scenes involve skyscrapers and other prominent landmarks being vaporized on the spot, with the resulting chaos and wreckage spilling onto the streets below into the sightline of the viewer. Once again, the viewer's position, as in *Black Hawk Down*, has the effect of placing him or her directly in the path of the destruction; it is predominantly from the ground level that buildings are seen exploding, and the wreckage that follows flies directly at the viewer, along with the fallout from the blasts. Such scenes alternate with aerial shots indicating the full extent of the destruction, the levelling of formerly thriving urban centres by awesome destructive forces beyond human comprehension or control.[115] Between the computerized techniques of simulation, then, which make a fictitious event as "real" as possible, and the cinematic perspective that seems to threaten the viewer directly, *Independence Day* and films like it model themselves on an aesthetics of the sublime. They do not merely hint at the existence of the unpresentable, as Lyotard writes of modern aesthetics,[116] but put it forward in what is effectively the realm of the virtual, transcending the limits of mere representation with their mastery of the techniques of simulation. The effect is a visceral one, combining pain and pleasure – terror and release, or *jouissance* – in a way that only the sublime really can.

The element of pleasure derives in part from one of the key functions of cinematic calamity, which, as Sontag notes, is to "[suggest] and [strengthen] the feeling that one is exempt."[117] Much like the virus threats and other media scares, they evoke deep-rooted anxieties while simultaneously defusing them. As Eagleton notes, for Burke and Kant alike, the "danger" involved in the sublime is one "we encounter figuratively, vicariously, in the pleasurable knowledge that we cannot actually be harmed,"[118] and this no doubt accounts for part of the disaster genre's appeal. It is in part this feeling of exemption – enhanced by the sense of "control" over one's patterns of consumption, the fact that one can choose whether and when to subject oneself to such images – that comes to constitute in its endless repetition a sort of symbolic "mastery" over the anxieties and fears such films elicit. For Eagleton,

> [t]o experience our own destruction in art rather than reality is to live out a kind of virtual death, a sort of death-in-life ... We can know the delirious pleasures of defeating death ... at the very moment that we can also feel free to embrace our own mortality. The sublime allows us to blend a joy in our own cartoon-like unkillability with the contrary pleasures of being decentred and dissolved ... The sublime thus involves a rhythm of death and resurrection, as we suffer a radical loss of identity only to have that selfhood more richly restored to us.[119]

Yet if this accounts in part for the appeal of disaster films in general, it cannot fully explain the increase in popularity that they enjoyed over the course of the 1990s. To the extent that the consumption-satisfaction they afford can be seen to combine the fantasy of destruction with a sense of exemption from it, their increasing appeal over the first posthistorical decade would seem to signal an increase in popular anxieties rather than the decrease that should logically follow the putative end of the nuclear threat as described by Clinton. Like the virus metaphor, the spectacle of disaster is essentially "polysemous," crystallizing a host of legitimate social anxieties only to defuse them temporarily in the process. It is simply another vehicle for the displacement of legitimate social anxieties onto a safely contained and controllable medium.

These legitimate anxieties are the ones already discussed, anxieties arising from the effects of "flexible accumulation" on the economic security and stability of the majority, so again, it is a question of material reality intersecting with the cultural imaginary. Such anxieties are simultaneously evoked and cathartically released in the cinematic disaster spectacle, displaced onto surrogates that are simply forgotten (aliens), amoral or immoral (aliens and "evildoers," respectively), or natural (volcanoes, earthquakes) and are in any case not "real," strictly speaking, to begin with. But the reasons that the "surrogate" must so often involve cataclysmic destruction when such anxieties could just as easily be defused by means of a less spectacular vehicle are reasons that I would link, once again, to the posthistorical structure of feeling. I refer not only to the material effects of late capitalism on its subjects but to the juncture at which the "base" of multinational capitalism (the reality) comes to infuse the "cultural imaginary" or the "structure of feeling" – that is, every-day sensory experience.

If late capitalism, as Jameson argues, represents that system's "thoroughgoing penetration" of every aspect of social life, includ-ing "Nature and the Unconscious,"[120] then its very universalization makes it a boundless totality, an unfathomable and incalculable configuration of socio-economic and spatio-temporal relations – sublime, to this extent, in itself. Indeed, one might even say that it approaches the condition of Kant's "mathematical" sublime in its boundlessness. For Jameson as for other theorists of postmodern-ity, what effectively occurs under late capitalism is a spatialization of temporality resulting in the inability to "cognitively map" one's position within the "totality of class structures in which [the subject] is situated."[121] In another sense, however, the perceived boundless-ness of this system is complemented by a sense of ultimate limita-tion, of what Paul Virilio has called the *"incarceration brought on by Progress"*: for him, "the third millennium is confronted by the geophysical limits of the only habitable planet in the solar system," and it is this that brings to the forefront of awareness the essential "finiteness of the world."[122] Indeed, only the most recent of genera-tions have been able to see the Earth in its totality as represented in photographs taken from space.

"Incarceration" is indeed an apt term, for the expansion of the late capitalist system to its planetary limits – its perceived "conquest of space and time," if the "millennial dreamers" are correct – effect-ively robs the imagination of any notion of a qualitatively different *and better* future. In this, I would argue, lies the principal differ-ence between Cold War disaster fantasies and those of today. There is no place for the "no-place" of utopia in any such spatially total-ized system. "It seems," writes Jameson, "to be easier for us today to imagine the thoroughgoing deterioration of the earth and of nature than the breakdown of late capitalism," and it is precisely this "lack of imagination"[123] to which the Hollywood disaster film (equally unimaginatively) seems to cater. In other words, we once again face an absence of alternatives, which is the defining characteris-tic of the posthistorical, post-ideological, and post-political age. The apocalyptic scenes of mass destruction in the disaster film are thus a spectacular correlative to the narrative of decline that structures virus and other media scares.

For Jameson, indeed, the postmodern condition entails a feeling that "where everything now submits to the perpetual change of fashion and the media image ... nothing can change any longer."[124] The "millennial" sense that time is moving too quickly is thus complemented by the seemingly contradictory, posthistorical sense that time is not moving at all, and both in their own ways pre-empt any apparent possibility of radical transformation. If change is *all there is*, what more can change in a genuine sense? As Jameson puts it, the end of history is "simply the old 'end of ideology' with a vengeance, and cynically plays on the waning of collective hope in a particularly conservative market climate."[125] Further,

a rhetoric of absolute change ... is, for the postmodern, no more satisfactory ... than the language of absolute identity and unchanging standardization cooked up by the great corporations, whose concept of innovation is best illustrated by the neologism and the logo and their equivalents in the real of built space, "lifestyle" corporate culture, and psychic programming. The persistence of the Same through absolute Difference ... discredits change, since henceforth the only conceivable radical change would consist in putting an end to change itself. But here the antinomy really does result in the blocking or paralysis of thought, since the impossibility of thinking another system except by way of the cancellation of this one ends up discrediting the utopian imagination itself, which is fantasized as the loss of everything we know experientially, from our libidinal investments to our psychic habits, and in particular the artificial excitements of consumption and fashion ... A kind of absolute violence, then, the abstraction of violent death, is something like the dialectical correlative to this world without time or history.[126]

The secular apocalypticism arising from the threat of nuclear conflagration over the course of the Cold War – the pessimistic vision of the destruction of humanity at the touch of a button – has given way, then, in the post–Cold War era to a situation in which the only conceivable future that might be said to be qualitatively different consists in the very absence of one. This differs from the older allegories of nuclear terror in that in this case, another enemy to defeat is the "unremitting banality" that Susan Sontag presents as one of only two options, the other being "inconceivable terror."[127] In other words, it may well be in relation to "unremitting banality," or interminable sameness, that the fantasy of mass destruction – the only other possibility – holds such fascination. The two, then, are only "seemingly," not ultimately, opposed.

Further, the same "immanence" that enhances the terror of the virus metaphor also applies to scenes of mass destruction. For Virilio, indeed, much as "[t]he ship or ocean liner *invents* its shipwreck at the same time as its launch,"[128] so too is apocalyptic destruction always inherent within, and implied by, the very totality it threatens to tear apart. Other than threats to the world such as an enormous asteroid or extraterrestrials with almost unimaginable destructive capabilities, the seeds of destruction of such a totality can only come from an internal source.

The function that contemporary disaster films serve, then, might be explained in relation to this aspect of posthistory – that is, the part of it premised on a binary opposition between the system and non-being or between, as Michaels puts it, "what is and its negation."[129] Consider that if the consumption-satisfaction of mass cultural products consists, as Jameson writes, in an always potentially "utopian" dimension, then what the fascination with disaster films suggests is that in the age of no alternatives, the utopian impulse has been displaced onto mass annihilation itself. If what distinguishes the utopian is its radical otherness, the fact that, as Jameson says elsewhere, "it is most authentic when we cannot imagine it,"[130] then it is hard to see how anything "radically other" operates within the "illusions of social harmony"[131] projected by Hollywood films. Even the "classnessness" implied by such illusions, which would indeed be radical were it ever achieved in reality, does not, within a consumer culture that disavows the existence of social class anyway, apply to anything unimaginably "other." What *is* "radically other" in disaster films is, rather, disaster itself: the complete and inconceivable annihilation of buildings, entire cities, the sustaining symbols of liberal-capitalist rule – and this time not by a competing ideological system but as an incomprehensibly meaningless, pointless exercise. And part of its "otherness" derives perhaps from its correspondence to the unconscious wishes that it fulfills (the Freudian or Lacanian unconscious, after all, being fundamentally "other" in its own right).

Disaster in films can thus be conceived of as a form of release insofar as it evokes anarchic drives that must then be recontained (in the illusions of harmony that follow).

Even in the absence of such illusions, the presentation of the unpresentable itself serves a containing function; if the utopian is structurally similar to the sublime in its radical otherness, then the presentation of the sublime onscreen effectively defuses the utopian impulse itself.

That impulse, then, can be said to remain intact despite the "demise" of socialism, or at least to have left some traces; it is just that, with the triumph of capitalism over its alternatives, the very last of this potential has been transferred onto a still more unthinkable order, that of no order at all. The desire for radical transformation still exists, but it has now been so thoroughly repressed, driven so deep into the collective unconscious, that it can manifest itself only in its opposite, in elaborate spectacles of total catastrophe. The systematic closing off of alternatives, in other words, results in an increase in intolerable, anarchic drives, and the ever-expanding catalogue of Hollywood catastrophes might be seen as symptomatic of that increase.

One final aspect of the structure of feeling that complements the immanence and spatial immediacy in relation to the aesthetics of disaster is temporality – the same aspect that was implied by "instant history" in the presentation of the Persian Gulf War and that projected in that instance the illusion of a future already known. If on the one hand the presentation did suggest a known future, then on the other, when combined with many of the fears and anxieties particular to the age, it also reinforced the idea that disaster of any sort and of unknown proportions is always imminent, that it could take place at any given time. The compulsion to know "what happens next" that informs the consumption of real-time war coverage or "breaking news" simultaneously appeals to a chronic sense of anxious anticipation for which instant history serves as the ideal medium. After all, much as media scares are premised on the notion that "you" could be next – that the more ordinary "you" are, the more likely "you" are to become the victim of the next disease, crime wave, or disaster – so too the threat of cataclysm is presented as always about to take place. In other words, just as any "place" in a totalized system can become a centre, so too can any moment in a spatialized temporality became *a*, or *the*, defining one.

In this regard, a central narrative feature in disaster films is the countdown, a race against time. The sense of counting down speaks to a more general cultural condition to which much of the imaginative power of contemporary fear can be attributed. As the narrative of disaster film progresses forward through time, it is nonetheless always a race backwards against the clock – the timer on a nuclear or other device counting down toward zero – that moves the narrative along while simultaneously appealing to a sensibility for which counting "up" is no longer an option. The countdown is always a countdown toward the zero of apocalypse, a Ground Zero if you will, the point of extinction of all "civilization" and all of its achievements up to the present day. The idea, in other words, has nothing to do with "progress" in the sense of achieving a state of affairs that is qualitatively better. Rather, it is to bring the clock to a standstill before it reaches zero, to freeze the clock and with it the progression of time itself. The idea, as with the posthistoricist agenda more broadly, is very much to preserve things as they are. That is, if any sort of "progress" is to be envisioned for future generations, it consists less in the improvement of current conditions than in their preservation against the "threats" facing civilized, Western modernity today. In short, the "ticking clock" that must be beaten in a range of disaster films emphasizes imminent destruction over and above positive progress toward a desirable goal, which in the Cold War era might have been expressed as the suppression of the "evil empire" by the other or the reconciliation of each to each. This lack of a desirable goal contributes to the sense of anxious anticipation and ultimate powerlessness that not only informs the consumption of media scares and news coverage more broadly but also characterizes the experience of post-industrial capitalism. The perpetual imminence of instant history, the "series of pure and unrelated presents in time"[132] that it offers, therefore constitutes the temporal dimension of the structure of feeling that drives the increasing consumption of spectacles of disaster, in film and in news coverage alike.

NESSUN DORMA

The posthistorical structure of feeling therefore generates fear and anxiety as well as a sense of security and permanence, with the absence of alternatives to the present social order resulting in a generalized sense of death and disaster as both imminent and immanent, or a sense of amorphous "otherness" encroaching from every direction. Many of these aspects are crystallized in Phil Alden Robinson's film *The Sum of All Fears*, produced prior to the terrorist attacks of 11 September but, unlike *Black Hawk Down*, delayed in its release as a result of them.

The first source of fear invoked in the film is an episode from "history" itself – an incident during the October 1973 war between Israel, Egypt, and Syria in which a downed Israeli fighter leaves an unexploded nuclear bomb buried in the sands of (borrowed) time. The person who unearths this hidden treasure some twenty-eight years later is an Arab gravedigger. An already tense atmosphere is subsequently intensified in the uncontextualized presentation of a "routine" nuclear drill at CIA headquarters in Langley, Virginia, involving a scenario in which rogue elements in the former Soviet Union have launched nuclear missiles at the United States (establishing a continuity with the disaster scenarios that came before; the Tom Clancy novel on which the film is based was written in 1991 as the Soviet Union was only just beginning to crumble). In due time, it becomes clear, however, that the enemy is neither Arabs nor the current Russian government but European neo-fascism. Liberal discomfort with the portrayal of Islam as the "stock" villain (as in the novel) is largely avoided in the film by making the villain a clandestine affiliation of sinister Europeans with a substantial global following. Whatever the shifting object of fear, however, it seems clear that the film deliberately generates a host of anxieties from the outset: embittered communists, a weakened Russian state unable to control dissenting elements, wealthy neo-fascists, swarthy Arabs, rogue arms dealers, and even a white American military dropout with an apparent axe to grind. The race against the clock begins when it becomes apparent to the hero that a nuclear weapon has made its way from the former USSR into Baltimore. He fails to prevent its spectacular detonation beneath a Baltimore football stadium but nonetheless succeeds in a subsequent race against time, this one to prevent a nuclear war between the US and Russia.

Despite the selection of a more distinctly "political" enemy, neofascism, against which to define the virtuous West, the film still manages to evoke, in both form and content, the sense of an amorphous and conspiratorial threat to America and the world, as well as a sense of threat to the individual body. In a classic villain's monologue delivered as a webcast to his faithful adherents, the neo-fascist leader Dressler reminds us that history is far from over – that, on the contrary, America's Second World War enemy is alive and well. "Hitler was not crazy," he tells us, "Hitler was stupid." Fascism – "like a virus, like the AIDS virus" – needed a "strong host" in order to survive, but Germany had ultimately failed in this role because at that time, "the world was too big." Now, on the other hand, "the world has changed," with communications technologies, cable TV and the Internet, making it much smaller. Now, he concludes ominously, "the virus is airborne." As if to illustrate his point, the scene switches periodically during his monologue to a location in Baltimore where the bomb, having passed through a shadowy network of dealers, is being delivered to its destination beneath the football stadium. The story is in some ways an attempt to resurrect the "victory" narratives associated with the Second World War, but it bears traces of posthistory. Not only do such clips illustrate the "virus" metaphor itself, the porousness of the American border, and the fact that something so small yet so potent can slip past the authorities undetected, but the juxtaposition of images – the suggested simultaneity – evokes the sense of a "real-time" threat, a threat enhanced, no less, by their mediation through the grainy, black-and-white gaze of surveillance cameras. The threat may be nuclear, but its vehicle is more clearly associated with the "viral."

At the same time, Dressler himself presents a direct spatial threat to the viewer, bringing the notion of "subject position" into play. The pretext of the webcast is an effective plot device allowing Dressler to address the film's audience directly; we have here what Jochen and Linda Schulte-Sasse call "the overpowering superdimensional presence of a face that ... meets the gaze of the viewer," creating "the illusion of a personal threat."[133] And if there is any degree of "subject status" implied by this image of the demonic, criminal mastermind – and therefore some conflict between the "non-subjective" metaphor of the virus and the more properly "political" enemy with a plan to take over the world – then it is the very content of Dressler's monologue that undoes his subjectivity at a stroke. Fascism in this case is not really "political" at all but quite simply evil (not in the obvious way that it engenders *acts* of unspeakable evil, which clearly it does, but "evil" rather in the sense of being utterly immune to analysis). Further, the very way in which Dressler describes his own political ideology ensures that it will not ultimately be seen as "ideological" at all. One does not, for instance, compare one's own set of political beliefs to a virus and simultaneously hold them to be legitimate or true. Dressler speaks the language not of his convictions but of "our" fears and directs them at "us," the real audience. Indeed, the substantive content of these convictions need never be addressed in the film. What Dressler proposes, ultimately, is mass destruction on an unprecedented scale, and the battle against evil is nothing less than a matter of survival. The fact that it takes a "rogue" agent such as Tom Clancy's usual hero, Jack Ryan (although in this film, Ben Affleck plays the Ryan role instead of the older Harrison Ford), suggests that the usual structures of bureaucracy are inefficient and cannot prevent a war and that it is up to the lone male protagonist to set things right.

Further, in a departure from the James Bond–era films in which the hero and the villain typically confront each other directly at one or another decisive point in the action, the American protagonist and Dressler never come face to face. Dressler is instead assassinated by means of a bomb planted in his car, showing, in effect, that the representation of the enemy as an amorphous, "non-subjective" threat to "our" body restricts "'our' reaction to purely technical behaviour"[134] – that is, to actions similar to "surgical" strikes on rogue elements in which the victim is never directly confronted by his killers. The peculiar characteristic of post-ideological conflict that makes it, according to Michaels, a conflict "between what is and its negation"[135] allows for no negotiation, no resolution by political means. If the "global police" can also be seen symbolically as "equivalent to a doctor, especially a surgeon, who protects our body from cancer or similar insidious illnesses,"[136] then the targeted assassination of Dressler becomes directly analogous to the "surgical," purely technological (i.e., sanitized) strikes carried out on Iraq in 1991 and occasionally in subsequent years, as well as in the Balkans and other "hot spots" over the course of the 1990s. In the film, the function of combining "virus" anxieties with unmitigated evil, with a representationally more "stable" enemy – and of crystallizing a host of anxieties in a spectacular nuclear explosion on American soil – is to legitimate exactly the sort of military strategies increasingly pursued by the US following the end of the Cold War. The film's conclusion is a case in point: while on the surface it would seem to downplay the typical thirst for spectacular vengeance that both Hollywood and the news networks normally elicit, the way in which it is structured suggests that a new world order enforced "surgically" is the way of the future. Shots of the Russian and American presidents signing peace agreements are interspersed with several targeted CIA assassinations, all to the dulcet strains of Puccini's *Nessun Dorma*: they are, in other words, harmoniously united in a happy ending that suggests not only that peace has been restored and the criminals brought to justice but, more significant, that peace and this type of hunt-and-kill justice are finally inseparable – that this new "style" of warfare is entirely beyond reproach. Indeed, the fictional president's concluding speech, in which he argues for the importance of uprooting terrorism and stopping the proliferation of weapons of mass destruction, could have been written for George W. Bush himself. The fear, however, has by no means entirely dissipated: *nessun dorma*, after all, means "none shall sleep."

Such was the cultural and ideological backdrop against which, on 11 September 2001, three commercial jetliners commandeered by terrorists sliced into the World Trade Center towers and the Pentagon while a fourth went down in rural Pennsylvania, wreaking havoc on the American sense of security and setting in motion a whole new "victory" narrative – indeed a new epoch, premised more than any before on the politics of fear: namely, the narrative of the War on Terror.

4

"History's Call" and America's Response

The preceding chapters described and accounted for a "posthistorical structure of feeling" commensurate with third-stage, multinational, or consumer capitalism and comprising two contradictory but not incompatible elements: first, a sense that qualitative change is no longer possible, and second, a sense that things might change altogether too quickly – an apocalyptic sense of impending and unpredictable transformation for the worse. The triumphant equation of the end of the Cold War with the end of history, played out to its fullest in the media spectacle of Gulf War I, gave way not to a new sense of confidence and security but rather to a structure of feeling permeated by fear. This was not so much a fear with a specific, definable object like the Cold War fear of nuclear annihilation (although it had not yet faded from popular memory); rather, it was decidedly amorphous in nature, generalized and all-pervasive, shifting endlessly across a broad spectrum of perceived dangers, often from one day to the next. It also possessed a distinctly apocalyptic sensibility, with each new threat portending not only individual death but often destruction on a mass scale as well. The neo-conservative sense of the "end of history" was thus complemented by the sense of an "end of history" of a different and less desirable sort altogether. Yet the perceived imminence of mass destruction spoke to the same posthistorical sensibility arising from the same structure of feeling already described, while its apparent immanence – adding a new dimension to an earlier generation of fears – suggested a world system that had reached the limits of expansion and for which the only imaginably different future entailed its implosion from within, or, in other words, the absence of any system whatsoever.

It was against this cultural backdrop that the 11 September terrorist attacks were labelled "the end of 'the end of history,'" the "end of America's holiday from history," and "the day that changed the world," all of which are meant to suggest a truly radical break in the course of events, a cataclysm the "before" and "after" of which would remain forever distinct in cultural memory. Whether the commentators who spoke of the "end of the 'end of history'" were lamenting posthistory's demise or taking the angle that history had never actually ended, there can be no doubt that, for them as for countless other writers, critics, and spectators, the events of 11 September had shaken America to its foundations and therefore had irrevocably transformed the proverbial "world as we know it."

Certainly, the collapse of the World Trade Center towers in succession, floor upon floor, on live television marked the flip side of live coverage, turning the euphoria of triumphant warfare as seen in the Persian Gulf War to the shock of ambush on American soil. The narrative unfolding onscreen that morning seemed to defy all expectations, all logic, all comfortable assumptions concerning what could conceivably take place "here," in America itself. The attacks took on the essence of Paul Virilio's catastrophic "accident," which "[snaps] the chain of causality that so perfectly characterises everyday reality,"[1] and thereafter they took on what Couze Venn calls the "patina of myth," made to "play the part of a new beginning and origin."[2] Codified as "9/11," its wreckage dubbed "Ground Zero," the event came to serve as the index of a new and terrifying era.

Part of the shock value of the attacks can no doubt be attributed to the simple fact that after the "end of history," such an event could be seen to occur only "out of a clear blue sky," not only without warning or precedent but also outside the sequence of causality that structures what we might call "intelligible" reality. Amplified through the media, they came to represent in effect a sort of large-scale psychological trauma, an occurrence so profoundly destabilizing as to defy all comprehension. Like the psychoanalytic Real, which for Lacan "subsists outside of symbolization" – in other words, for which a discursive framework (a language, a terminology) has not been developed – and is "thereby withdrawn from the possibilities of speech,"[3] it was initially incomprehensible, inassimilable within the symbolic order or the ordinary framework of language and logic.

Hence, CNN correspondent Aaron Brown's remark following the collapse of the second tower: *"there are no words."*[4]

Indeed, in the absence of a ready-made discourse proper to the event itself, it was none other than the vocabulary of nuclear conflagration that was invoked during and after the attacks. For CNN producer Rose Arce, the immediate aftermath was comparable to a "nuclear winter"; similarly, Brown described the collapse of the first tower as producing a "mushroom cloud."[5] And above and beyond these assorted remarks, of which there were undoubtedly many others in the same vein, nothing connects the spectacle of 11 September so vividly with nuclear apocalypse as the widespread and by now fully assimilated (if profoundly ironic) use of the term "Ground Zero" to designate the site of the attacks, since Ground Zero signifies not only the site of a nuclear explosion but also "the center or origin of rapid, intense, or violent activity or change" and "the very beginning: square one."[6] The term is now in fact inseparable, in America, from the memory of the attacks, from the images of the fallen towers and the site itself; it no longer resonates with any memory of Hiroshima, Nagasaki, or any of the desert nuclear testing sites to which the term had traditionally been applied. In a situation for which "there [were] no words," only the language of nuclear holocaust seemed adequate to the task.

This is certainly in part because, against the cultural backdrop described in the preceding chapters, the footage of the 11 September attacks was too easily seen through the lens of apocalypticism. The monster clouds of dust and ash that engulfed entire buildings, cascading down the city's streets and blocking out both sun and skyline; the survivors, in the immediate aftermath, covered in a chalky residue and walking spellbound, like the living dead; the charred and mangled wreckage of the towers themselves: all of these images were resonant with intimations of millennial doom such as had crowded both the silver screen and the TV set in the previous decade. Further, the media themselves, precisely in their social function *as* media, amplified the images to make the events an instant national phenomenon, with an instant, levelling impact on their audience. Whereas the terrorists were unable to achieve a nuclear explosion in the literal sense, the media, by their sheer presence and with the lightning speed of real-time, international coverage, made it nuclear psychologically. The real-time disaster spectacle of 11 September effectively hijacked the major networks and with them the attention of the nation.

The media also took on a more direct role in the presentation of the event as an inassimilable shock. For Fritz Breithaupt, "the media themselves responded to the attack by creating that which they perceived as the outcome of the attacks: 'a trauma.'"[7] To some extent, this was inevitable, given that the networks were no more prepared for the event than were the public at large; however, it did not take them long to regain control. Framing, arresting graphics, and slow-motion repeats were part of the media event even before the president knew what was going on, as was speculation concerning the identity of the hijackers. And the figure of trauma remained central to their representations of the attacks, played over and over as if in an attempt to exorcise from them some intractable quality, their inescapable uncanniness, perhaps – or as if to verify that they were indeed "real." Whatever the motive, as Breithaupt notes, the repeated presentation served a clear ideological function: "The most prominent and ... appealing aspect of the ideology of 'trauma,'" he writes, "is, of course, the innocence of the victim."[8] Certainly, the event was traumatic for those directly affected, including thousands of bereaved families, but the concept was vastly manipulated and deployed in such a way as to draw in the entire nation (and even the world) as one large, collective victim. Here was the perfect opportunity for the revival of Tom Engelhardt's "victory culture," built on a narrative of ambush by "savages" and brutal (but justified) retaliation.[9]

Indeed, had it not been for posthistory as the "age of innocence" – that is, in particular, if violent events around the world had not been presented as aberrations, as incidental to the deep-structural configuration of the times – the terrorist attacks might not have come as such a shock. It was not, after all, the first time that al-Qaeda had struck. Yet had America's effortless performance in the Persian Gulf War, followed by Clinton's reassurances that American leadership would keep America itself safe from harm, not perpetuated the illusion that "history" would no longer have any bearing on the American "way of life," the media might have had recourse to a framework other than that of "trauma" in which to present the attacks. This argument is not meant to justify the attacks, or to suggest that they should have been anticipated, but rather to highlight the networks' role in projecting a very *real* trauma – that of the actual victims and their families – onto the broader level of the cultural imaginary as experienced by the majority of the viewing public and in such a way as to suggest that the nation itself (and, by implication, the state) had been brutally victimized for no imaginable reason. As Baudrillard notes, "the media are part of the event, they are part of the terror, and they work in both directions."[10] The ceaseless repetition of the event in its immediate aftermath in effect took it "out of time," fixing it *as* trauma in what Ruth Leys calls a "painful, disassociated, traumatic present"[11] destined to be relived without end. To this extent, indeed, the media were complicit with the terrorists' goals: a central condition of terrorism's effectiveness as a psychological weapon is that it be spectacular, and the framing and memorialization of the event as a national trauma ensured that it would remain so for years to come.

9/11 AND THE FREUDIAN UNCANNY

CNN and CBS issued two commemorative DVDs that seemed to be aimed at satisfying a Freudian "compulsion to repeat" occasioned by the "trauma" that the networks themselves had helped to generate in the first place (for Freud, the principle of repetition-compulsion arises from a situation inassimilable into "reality," or Lacan's "symbolic order" – essentially, language – which therefore leads to repeated attempts to resolve it). CNN's *America Remembers: The Events of September 11 and America's Response* and CBS's *What We Saw: The Events of September 11, 2001 – in Words, Pictures, and Video* reassert the event's "traumatic" significance while at the same time re-indulging in repetition-compulsion. Both releases emphasize the shock value of the event, alluding first and foremost to the sheer ordinariness of the morning prior to the first strike on the North Tower. CBS anchor Dan Rather begins his introduction to *What We Saw* with the most banal of observations concerning the circumstances of that morning – namely, the weather: "September 11th, 2001," he intones, "The sky over New York that morning was crystal clear."[12] Similarly, CNN, in its rather more dramatic and high-budget re-encapsulation of events, begins with a view of the curvature of the Earth from space, at the edge of which gleams the first light of day, in the process making the event a global rather than simply a national trauma. Following some opening remarks by an assortment of prominent reporters and news anchors about what they had been doing or covering that morning, on that "most routine day,"[13] dated footage shot from inside a passenger plane shows the Twin Towers intact on the New York skyline – an attempt, it seems, to lull viewers into remembering exactly how "normal" things once were. The emphasis on ordinariness – of the weather, of a working day for tens of thousands of people, of the victims and survivors themselves – serves the same function that it does in the media scares already discussed, placing the viewer at the centre of the next "event" while simultaneously maintaining the status of the attacks as a shattering, inassimilable shock to the system. Also stressed is the theme of innocence lost that accompanies the presentation of a trauma: CNN's *America Remembers* lingers on a shot of a deserted school playground strewn with debris from the towers, even though no children from the school were injured or killed in the attacks.

Each network, while commemorating the attacks in its own way, does so with fetishistic overtones. While CNN "reconstructs" the morning by inserting file footage of the New York skyline and adorns its account of the events with a sentimental soundtrack, CBS presents the events as they were seen for the very first time – that is, without the musical score, without the input of assorted pundits and "experts," without the stars-and-stripes motif that would come to dominate the memorialization of 11 September from that day onward. Absent from the CBS film are any omens of the sort that portend disaster in Hollywood films, nor are there any clear protagonists, no "heroes" as such, only ordinary people, bewildered and shaken, many of whom had escaped death by chance alone. In seeing it presented this way, one is reminded of an important fact: only in retrospect did the attacks come to mean what they do now; only through a significance retroactively (though quite promptly) imposed did they come to mark a dividing line between a "before" and an "after," that they came to be known as "the day the world changed." To see it as it was at the time – the newsrooms of the nation as yet untouched by disbelief, the reluctance of the anchors to describe the ongoing events with any certainty, indeed their dependence on early reports from random witnesses at the scene – is as close as one can get to the initial viewing experience. A prominent building had been struck by a plane. Whether the plane was small, large, civilian, military, in distress – none of this, viewers were repeatedly reminded, could be ascertained. For Dan Rather on that morning, it was "important to say that there is much that is not known," and it was "very difficult to draw many conclusions"; further, "there will be rumours all day," and part of CBS's responsibility consisted in "[separating] the rumours from the facts."[14] It was only when the role of that image in a far greater spectacle became clear that the media were able to construct and frame it as a "trauma" in the full psychoanalytic sense of the word. The sight of the North Tower in flames was unusual and disturbing, of course, but the "end of history" had not at that point ended.

While *What We Saw* implies, in its very title, an attempt to recapture the event "as we saw it," CNN's *America Remembers* – first broadcast on the anniversary of the event and then distributed as a commemorative DVD – takes place strictly in the "after." A solemn retrospective, it bypasses the initial uncertainty memorialized in CBS's account in favour of a presentation that affirms from the outset the event's status as a "defining moment." The element of disbelief that came to infuse the coverage only over time on the day itself is already implied in *America Remembers*. The idea of a world "before" 9/11 – last seen in the unadorned, as yet uncontextualized footage of the North Tower in flames – is nowhere present (it haunts the footage, as Žižek might put it – and as I will explain – as something that "*insists*"). The event is thus treated with the unquestioning reverence that the architects of the subsequent and ongoing War on Terror would have us believe it merits. There is something chillingly uncanny in CNN's precision-edited footage of the second plane striking the South Tower, and not only as a result of the slow-motion replay, the shocked screams of onlookers, and the sentimental soundtrack.

Both releases seem to evoke the Freudian "compulsion to repeat," that post-traumatic mechanism that, according to Freud, attempts to enact a "symbolic mastery" – some measure of control by representation – over the trauma in question. By re-presenting it time and again, it seems, those in charge of the representation can gain some purchase over the unforeseen. Yet given that the trauma was a construct of the media coverage in the first place, it is hard to see how either network could thereafter genuinely neutralize it, either by replaying the incident as it appeared at the time or by incorporating it into a highly structured dramatic framework complete with skilfully edited footage and an evocative soundtrack. It could be, indeed, that to focus on the event as "traumatic" involves a sort of category mistake, that in fact the inability to "domesticate" the event places it instead in the realm of the Freudian Uncanny.

For Freud, the uncanny (*unheimlich*) – which we tend to associate with something external, aberrant – signifies only *in part* what is "unknown and unfamiliar." In his elaboration of the concept, it embraces considerably more than this alone, such that "[s]omething must be added to the novel and the unfamiliar if it is to become uncanny."[15] This is because a second definition of *heimlich*, he astutely points out, suggests secrecy, concealment, and deceit, such that

> what is called *heimlich* soon becomes *unheimlich* ... This reminds us that the word *heimlich* is not unambiguous, but belongs to *two sets of ideas*, which are not mutually contradictory, but very different from each other – the one relating to what is familiar and comfortable, the other to what is concealed and kept hidden ... The term "uncanny" (*unheimlich*) [thus] applies to everything that was intended to remain secret, hidden away, and has come into the open.[16]

Thus does the commonly accepted notion of "uncanniness" as denoting something strange or mysterious come to be complemented by its apparent opposite – namely, something that is altogether too familiar, as in an "uncanny resemblance," and the same, I believe, can be applied to the spectacle of the attacks of 11 September, both shockingly unfamiliar (to the extent that such a disaster could ever take place "here") and yet possessing, at the same time, an eerie familiarity that goes even beyond its similarity to the spectacles of destruction in Hollywood film. And it is more a result of the latter than the former that on the day itself "there [were] no words." The attacks may well have been framed and projected as a trauma in and of themselves, but this does not account for their uncanniness as a spectacle; the footage is indeed imbued with something beyond itself, something that even the images of the burning and collapsing towers cannot adequately represent, and it is this that points to the existence of something repressed, something that was "intended to remain secret, hidden away, and has come into the open."[17] "Existence," however, is not quite the appropriate word, for, as Slavoj Žižek writes of the "symptom," as noted, the "opposite of existence is not non-existence but *insistence*: that which does not exist, continues to *insist*, striving towards existence."[18] In other words, there was more to the shock value of the events than the "trauma effect" as amplified by the national networks.

What, then, was repressed that might have *recurred* in the media event of 11 September? "At a pinch," writes Jean Baudrillard of the attacks, "we can say that they *did* it, but we *wished* for it ... Even those who share in the advantages of [the global order] have this malicious desire in their hearts," to which "countless disaster movies bear witness."[19] Seeing the images on television indeed gave rise to an undecidable reality arising from its similarity to previous spectacles of destruction on the cinematic screen, an intellectual uncertainty to which the sense of the uncanny can no doubt be partly attributed. Baudrillard, however, fails to account satisfactorily for the provenance of what he calls this "malicious desire," attributing it somewhat implausibly (or perhaps just incompletely) to an "[a]llergy to any definitive order, to any definitive power."[20] Nor does even Žižek quite resolve the matter: "[a]s poor people around the world dream about being American," he writes, so too do Americans dream "about a global catastrophe that would shatter their lives,"[21] but again, it is hard to see exactly why this might be the case, unless one considers the possibility that, as posited in the preceding chapter, the obsession with total destruction is in part a manifestation, however distorted, of what remains of the utopian impulse under posthistory.

The "compulsion to repeat" in this case might then be reconceived: it is not an index of trauma but rather evokes a form of what Lacan would call *jouissance* or "obscene enjoyment." If this is unconvincing, consider the advertisement aired on CNN for the *America Remembers* retrospective prior to its first broadcast on 11 September 2002: the advertisement concluded with a sequence from CNN's spectacular footage of the second airplane approaching the South Tower, abruptly cut short by a blackout. The similarity to trailers for Hollywood blockbusters is undeniable: the overall implication is that the viewer must tune in so as not to "miss out" on the thrill of mass destruction. Similarly, in the DVD version the viewer is treated to a slow-motion replay of the same spectacular footage, accompanied by a melodramatic soundtrack and edited in such a way as to present the approach and collision from multiple angles, first from a distance and then up close, almost directly beneath the point of impact, as the plane slices into the concrete and steel framework of the second tower. The media, to this extent, are indeed complicit with the terror, as Baudrillard noted in his initial response to the event: in their presentation of the attacks according to the spectacular logic of the Hollywood disaster film, they advance an aesthetic of the sublime, which, as discussed in the preceding chapter and taking into account Burke's inflection on the concept, is never too far from terror itself.

The fact that the endless repetition did not neutralize the media spectacle in any way is therefore more than a question of the attacks "really" happening whereas Hollywood disasters remain safely fictional. The element of uncanniness that heightens the impact of this particular media event above all others arises instead from a degree of excess that threatens to betray the presence of what ought to have remained "secret" and "hidden away." The attacks of 11 September, in other words, "changed" nothing at all but rather were *uncanny* for a betrayal that they threatened – for their uncanny fulfillment of a powerful unconscious fantasy, a fantasy structured in large part on the experiential co-ordinates of posthistory. If disaster films both manage and contain anxieties and fantasies, evoking and defusing them simultaneously, and if these fantasies at the "end of history" come ever more to embrace visions of mass destruction as the only conceivable alternative to contemporary "reality" (or to "unremitting banality," in Sontag's words), then what the media spectacle of 11 September seemed to embody was the intolerable realization of this fantasy and, by association, the equally intolerable complicity of its spectator-victims. Žižek, then, is surely correct to "invert the standard reading according to which the World Trade Center explosions were the intrusion of the Real which shattered our illusory Sphere," arguing rather that "[i]t is not that reality entered our image: the image entered and shattered our reality," or rather, the symbolic (representational) order that structures lived experience. For Žižek,

> the dialectic of semblance and Real cannot be reduced to the rather elementary fact that the virtualization of our daily lives, the experience that we are living more and more in an artificially constructed universe, gives rise to an irresistible urge to "return to the Real," to regain firm ground in some "real reality." The Real which returns has the status of a(nother) semblance: *precisely because it is real, that is, on account of its traumatic/ excessive character, we are unable to integrate it into (what we experience as) our reality, and are therefore compelled to experience it as a nightmarish apparition.*[22]

Fantasy, for Žižek, is *both* "pacifying, disarming ... *and* shattering, disturbing, inassimilable into our reality": hence, the perception of the attacks as a "nightmarish unreal spectre,"[23] the "uncanny satisfaction" of which constituted "*jouissance* at its purest."[24] That is, the intolerable and inassimilable, or traumatic, realization of the fantasy becomes the object of an obscene enjoyment "beyond the pleasure principle."[25] Its inversion into the realm of un-reality is a necessary defence mechanism in the absence of what is normally supplied in cinematic disaster – namely, that degree of containment required to protect the fragile psyche from actual trauma. In the initial (if later more assimilated by narrative) presentation of the terrorist attacks, there could be no such mechanism; the media, in their "traumatic" presentation of the event, offered no neutralizing framework. The unconscious desires evoked by disaster films are impossibly and intolerably "realized" in the spectacle of the attacks such that, on sight, they become the "nightmarish apparition" of Žižek's interpretation, inassimilable into the realm of the symbolic and thus destined to be revisited repeatedly and in vain. The Ground Zero of the twenty-first century is the endpoint of the countdown to apocalypse as played out time and again in film, but it is now a Ground Zero from which escape is impossible: a visible absence on the New York skyline, or what cartoonist Art Spiegelman has aptly termed "the shadow of no towers."[26] What the attacks thereby exposed, among other things normally hidden or repressed, is that apocalyptic thinking is anything but confined to the religious fringe. On the contrary, the very same popular cultural structure of feeling that compels the mass consumption of disaster films accounted at least in part for the impact of the terrorist attacks. In a posthistorical context of interminable sameness, of "unremitting banality," an event as sudden and spectacular as the 11 September attacks lends itself instantly to the language of apocalypse; anything so radically "different" from the ordinary course of events, after all, can be interpreted only as the beginning of the "end."

In the final analysis, however, the attacks did not constitute the "end of the 'end of history,'" and it is in part their inversion into the "nightmarish apparition" that was responsible for posthistory's continuation. Certainly, they were incorporated into a new "master" narrative, as we will see, but the American response to the events has represented more of a preservation of posthistory than a radical break from it. Posthistory's "logic," that is, has continued to inform

America's actions in the world, along with the "politics of fear" that the administration engenders, emphasizing total annihilation of all things worthwhile as the only alternative to the survival of the "new world order."

AMERICA'S "NEW WAR"

It was indeed in the "shadow of no towers" that George W. Bush, on 14 September 2001, told a cheering crowd and television viewers nationwide that "I can hear you. The rest of the world hears you. And the people who knocked down these buildings will hear all of us soon."[27]

The administration's response – like that of the media – entrenched the status of the event as national trauma. For Bush too it was the "end of the 'end of history,'" if not quite the end of the world. Policy decisions made thereafter took root in this popular cultural understanding of events, or at least were well suited to it – as indeed major policy decisions have to be. The necessary healing, for the administration, would take place in a "different" world, a world "where freedom itself is under attack."[28] And this healing would, inevitably (inevitably, that is, in line with the cultural narratives already under construction as opposed to any alternatives), take the form of "war," with its promise of ultimate triumph over the forces of fear. As Stuart Croft points out, there were always alternatives, but once a single narrative framework had taken centre stage, it relegated all other options to the shadows.[29] It was only a matter of days before what Bush described as "evil, despicable acts of terror"[30] became an "act of war,"[31] determining, as Alain Badiou writes, "a [narrative] sequence – the entire sequence is from now on considered as 'the war on terrorism.'"[32] The "end of the 'end of history'" reintroduces the notion of a narrative, a future against which all of "our" actions will be measured; for Bush, indeed, "[h]istory will judge harshly" those who fail to take advantage of this "historical opportunity to preserve the peace."[33]

Thus, for the administration too, "Ground Zero" marked a new beginning, setting in motion a "new type of war" involving a "new thought process" and destined to "take a long time to win."[34] A "different world," after all, demands quite plausibly a "different type of war":

This war will not be like the war against Iraq a decade ago, with a decisive liberation of territory and a swift conclusion ... [It will] not look like the air war above Kosovo two years ago, where no ground troops were used and not a single American was lost in combat. Our response involves far more than instant retaliation and isolated strikes. Americans should not expect one battle, but a lengthy campaign unlike any other we have ever seen. It may include dramatic strikes visible on TV and covert operations secret even in success.[35]

In other words, Bush here declares an end to "posthistorical" war of the sort that ensured swift victories in the Gulf and in other interventions throughout the 1990s. But in fact this too would be a posthistorical war, from the initial "act of war" itself as a media event through to what increasingly appears to be a new "quagmire" in Iraq. If anything is truly "different" now, it is that nobody – despite the 2008 change in administration – seems to be in a position to truly determine how or when this "war" will end to the satisfaction of all parties.

But the ostensible reinstatement of history as the onset of a healing process is really a continuation of posthistory, at least in terms of its corresponding structure of feeling. It is essentially a narrative that emerges in order to determine how the crisis will be handled, a narrative among numerous possible others but one that also merges seamlessly with the dominant structure of feeling and its popular cultural manifestations as they have been described throughout this book. If the subject's negotiation with the lived reality of late capitalism reinforces the posthistorical structure of feeling both as interminable sameness and as the threat of always imminent annihilation, then barring a change in the deep-structural configuration of global power relations itself – a virtual impossibility given the momentum of capitalist globalization – the structure of feeling so defined must remain. Just as Fukuyama's "end of history" thesis, Bush Sr's "new world order," and Samuel Huntington's "clash of civilizations" appeared plausible in equal measure against the backdrop of this structure of feeling, so too would Bush Jr's new War on Terror need to conform to the same sensibility in order to "sell" it to the public, just as the first Gulf War had been "sold" ten years before.

ONE NATION UNDER GOLD: THE HEALING COMMODITY

If, as I have argued, universal commodification has resulted in a thoroughgoing "aestheticization of politics," making both war and its justifications the object of an aestheticized consumption, then the initial response and the representations of this "new type of war" must afford, on the scale of any Hollywood film, a substantial degree of "consumption-satisfaction." And this, I will argue, took the form of a real-life "containing" mechanism following the initial (if constructed) trauma of 11 September, a trauma folded back into the appearance of a nightmare and thereby framed as trauma at the expense of any more fruitful revelations about America in the world, revelations that might have led to an alternative narrative framework.[36] Further, in a manner consistent with the structure of feeling of posthistory, this mechanism is one that continues to evoke the very fears that it simultaneously contains.

If a central aspect of "containment" takes the form of an illusion of collectivity, then in this case the illusion was largely premised on outrage, grief, and a desire for revenge. Indeed, as Stuart Croft points out, the "meaning" of the "terrible events of [11 September]" was "the product of social interaction, not of some kind of 'normal' or 'commonsense' response."[37] A "crisis discourse," he points out, "is truly a social one – one that is shared throughout the body politic, and not just its leadership," and "can be understood from its cultural representations" such that "the interpretation of [11 September] that came to discursively dominate was one that was co-produced and reproduced in many different aspects of American cultural life." It came from a

> particular set of understandings about the world that had been as much produced in and by the media, by churchleaders and by television, radio and novelists as by politicians. There was a mutual constitution between ... these groups, who form an American elite. Second, in reproducing the meanings of [11 September] subsequent to the event, very little discursive space was allowed for alternatives.[38]

The spectacle of terror, fetishized like the disaster scenes in Hollywood movies as the moment at which good and evil become clearly delineated and military retaliation an undisputed necessity, set the stage for the necessary illusion of social harmony, encoded both in the mass displays of public mourning and in the buildup to America's "new war." That is, the "coming together" of Americans *as Americans* in their collective outpouring of grief and subsequent demand for revenge is socially constructed, functioning at the level of the cultural imaginary in much the same way as the narrative paradigm in films such as *Independence Day*: all structurally inherent differences and divisions are ostensibly overcome in a collective assertion of superiority, freedom, and independence. In Croft's analysis, imagery and discourse combined to produce the dominant "common-sense" narrative, according to which the events of 11 September changed America and the world, in a "decisive intervention":

> Such a crisis – politically and socially deep, culturally profound in all popular terms – demanded a response ... On 11 September 2001, the window for decisive intervention was short. It was not clear which narrative would be developed at that moment. Did [the events] represent failure by the American state's security apparatus? Was this the onset of more attacks? Was the government to blame? Should the response be low key, and engaged with conflicts abroad? ... Many different narratives could have come into play ... But ... it was at the heart of the American state that the decisive intervention came to be played out.[39]

This "decisive intervention" comprised a number of key narrative elements – four, according to Croft – "the construction of an enemy image; the avoidance of blame on any other than the enemy; a definition of core values that were at risk; and a claim to global leadership, that these values were global as well as American, and that the world accepted American leadership in projecting them."[40] As noted above, alternatives were always at hand, but the speed of televised transmission demanded that a dominant explanatory framework be embraced within a very short time horizon, and the one so adopted, while seeming to reinstate history along the narrative lines of "victory culture" as described by Tom Engelhardt,[41] also depended on the "end" of history as envisioned by the neo-conservative paradigm. Even Croft agrees that the "absence of 'history' due to affluence is precisely one of the reasons why the discursive conditions for a socially constructed crisis ... were so propitious"[42] – in other words, why the idea of an "ambush"[43] on an innocent nation out of a "clear blue sky" and the subsequent justification for revenge were discursively so compelling.

The War on Terror was effectively underway, after all, well before it officially began. Even though the bombing campaign in Afghanistan did not begin until 7 October, the assimilative or "containing" function of the war took hold on the network news considerably earlier than that. By 15 September, CNN's banner headline "America Under Attack" had given way to "America At War"; subsequently, "America Strikes Back" was deployed to give the euphoric impression that America was somehow avenging the victims of the terrorist attacks, and "America's New War" promised a dramatic spectacle on the scale of Gulf War I, a staggering novelty and a source of euphoria as that earlier conflict had been in its time. As Baudrillard writes, the effect is "to substitute, for a real and formidable, unique and unforeseeable event, a repetitive, rehearsed pseudo-event. The terrorist attack corresponded to a precedence of the event over all interpretative models; whereas this mindlessly military, technological war corresponds, conversely, to the model's precedence over the event."[44]

Further, its sheer novelty following a period of "posthistory" promised a commodified spectacle with which an eager majority could collectively identify. If the Afghan war was on the one hand "new," it was also intended to be therapeutic in its reassuring familiarity, entailing as it did a swift and decisive demonstration of America's military might, accompanied by its representation in real time. Yet for this very reason it was also posthistorical in nature. The imposition of narrative form in real time by the networks, even before Bush had formally declared a war or specified its target, was a reassertion of the "choice already made." The story system was already effectively in place, and it was one according to which an innocent people wronged would set things right, thereby reaffirming a set of "values" desperately, it seemed, in need of renewal. As Croft puts it, "The 'war on terror,' that which emerged as the meta-narrative after the attacks, constructed an image of a third world war dominating international relations for a long time: not a vision of potential global conflagration, as had been imagined during the cold war, but one in which there was no choice other than to take the fight to the enemy.[45]

The "foundational myth" created by the attacks did not *have* to lead to this particular narrative construction, but alternatives – even those that questioned America's role in the Middle East prior to 11 September – were powerfully silenced in the aftermath and for several years to come. They were "institutionalized," according to Croft, in light of a "shared meaning" proliferating through all aspects of American popular culture, not just at the administrative level.[46] Whatever alternative discourses might emerge to challenge the dominant narrative yielded, for the moment, to the mainstream response. Once the perpetrators had been identified with "evil" – which did not take very long – there could be "only that one acceptable interpretation," leading to "the naming of one perspective as legitimate, reasonable, common sense, and all others as weak, foolish and underhand. Failure to share the meta-narrative ... is equated with appeasement; that vile crime of sacrificing others to avoid confrontation is equated with the Nazi evil."[47]

The restoration of a collective identity at the national level – embodied in the proliferation of American flags, the memorialization of the attacks in countless forms, and so forth – rather than at a regional, religious, or racial level (although, of course, religion and race hung at the edges of the mainstream) was indeed a key element of the healing process following 11 September. By fashioning a national trauma from a local one, the media had already to some extent set the stage for such an assertion of solidarity. And implicit in this was a reassertion of "traditional American values"[48] in the face of a palpable threat to them. Indeed, for Bush, "the evil ones have sparked an interesting change in America," leading Americans to "[reassess] what's important in life,"[49] namely, "service and citizenship and compassion"[50] combined with a "renewed spirit of pride and patriotism."[51] So effective was this "containing" interpretive model that by the time of his State of the Union Address in January 2002, Bush was able to claim that "the state of our union has never been stronger,"[52] appealing to the essential decency of American men and women:

[n]one of us would ever wish the evil that was done on September 11, yet after America was attacked, it was as if our entire country looked into a mirror and saw our better selves. We are reminded that we are citizens, with obligations to each other, to our country and to history. We began to think less of the goods we can accumulate and more about the good we can do. For too long our culture said, "If it feels good, do it." Now America is embracing a new ethic and a new creed: "Let's roll." In the

sacrifice of soldiers, the fierce brotherhood of fighters, and the
bravery and generosity of ordinary citizens, we have glimpsed
what a new culture of responsibility could look like. We want
to be a Nation that serves goals larger than self ... The time of
adversity offers a unique moment of opportunity, a moment we
must seize to change our culture. Through the gathering momentum of millions of acts of service and decency and kindness, I
know: We can overcome evil with greater good.[53]

Bush's emphasis here, ironically enough, is on a sense of unity
and collectivity increasingly lacking in posthistorical consumer society. Like the containment mechanisms of Hollywood film, then, his
words constitute an imaginary resolution to real needs – namely, the
need for genuine community in a world that is ever more atomized
by the imperatives of capital. If rampant consumerism and individualism erode the bonds that hold society together, then "traditional"
principles of generosity and self-sacrifice are here made to replace
greed and self-interest in a displacement of material concerns onto
essentially moral ones. Bush's words, indeed, sidestep the fact that
it is capitalism itself that atomizes and fragments society and that
poses by far the greatest threat to the established social values pre-
scribed by modern, liberal morality. Indeed, for Bush, "[w]e cannot
let the terrorists achieve the objective of ... frightening our nation
to the point where we don't ... conduct business, or people don't
shop."[54] And as in Hollywood film, such a spurious, aestheticized
conformity, reinforced by the stars-and-stripes motifs of frames,
banners, and graphics on the news networks as well as in the proliferation of American flags on homes, cars, and apparel, is achieved
at the expense of any authentic solidarity; it is, in effect, a form of
consumption-satisfaction in itself, masking profound social alienation with an illusion of social harmony. In the process, it perpetu-
ates the very disavowal of ideology that sustains the posthistorical
structure of feeling and that will come to define the rhetoric of the
War on Terror as well. The rallying-cry "Let's roll," a long-standing
catch phrase in action films and crime dramas, became, following 11
September, an assertion of collective duty and collective agency, of
unified purpose and unyielding resolution, and the social cohesion
so implied knows no vulnerability (although, ironically, the societal
infrastructure sustaining it would remain vulnerable throughout
the narrative and particularly as it intensified). As with Hollywood,

however, such a collective amounts to very little in the absence of a suitable "other" against which it can be defined – hence the need for a new variation on an old "enemy-image."

DEFINING THE ENEMY

The construction of this enemy-image following the 11 September attacks was informed by precisely the same logic that governs the portrayal of the cultural "other" in Hollywood films, an "other" with values utterly antithetical to those defined as "American." Indeed, it might be said that the enemy so conceived is bereft of anything that could be defined as a value system in the first place. If ideology, as Huntington argues in his *Clash*, has given way to identity as the "fault line" of the future – to a question, that is, of incommensurable subject positions over "merely" antithetical belief systems – then the representations of the War on Terror would seem to confirm, at least initially, the central premise of his thesis. It should come as no surprise, then, that the attacks were immediately followed by a dramatic increase in the sales of Huntington's 1996 book.[55] The enemy, it appeared to many, was Islam – political Islam, perhaps, or fundamentalist Islam, but Islam nonetheless. Yet the fact that English translations of the Qu'ran and other books about the Islamic faith became bestsellers[56] alongside Huntington's *Clash* suggests that the direct identification of Islam with the "enemy" remains problematic in relation to the very liberal precepts of tolerance that the "War" was supposed to defend – a contradiction not lost on the administration, if not exactly promoted by Fox News. Thus, despite President Bush's initial (and quickly retracted) reference to the new War on Terror as a "crusade," the administration was soon at pains to convince America and the world that the "war" was not a war against Islam. To allow it to be perceived as such would clearly inflame further anti-American sentiment in the Islamic world. Further, in order to remain relatively immune to alternative discourses, the ideological justification of the American mission depended in part on the putative universality of the desire for (American) "freedom" regardless of religion or culture. Indeed, among the American "values" repeatedly invoked following the attacks was tolerance for "people of all faiths."[57] As Croft points out, "the enemy was, in a biblical sense, 'evil,' and evil cannot be accommodated: it can only be destroyed."[58] As Bush asserted,

the American people were appalled and outraged at last Tues-
day's attacks. And so were Muslims all across the world. Both
Americans and Muslim friends and citizens, tax-paying citizens,
and Muslims in nations were just appalled and could not believe
what we saw on our TV screen ... The face of terror is not the
true faith of Islam. That's not what Islam is all about. Islam is
peace. These terrorists ... represent evil and war.[59]

Vice-President Dick Cheney, too, was keen to describe the campaign
as intended "to save the civilized world and values common to the
West, to Asia and to Islam. This is a struggle against evil, against an
enemy that rejoices in the murder of innocent, unsuspecting human
beings."[60]

In other words, a "perversion" of Islam was required to justify
what might otherwise be perceived as an unacceptable assault on
the Muslim world. Indeed, the terrorists had to be stripped of everything that might define them as "human." For Bush, accordingly, the
terrorists have "no true home in any country, or culture, or faith."[61]
They have "no religion, no conscience, and no mercy."[62] They "pro-
fane a great religion by committing murder in its name."[63] The new
enemy thus becomes terrorism as such – defined by Bush, at the
time, as "premeditated ... violence perpetrated against innocents,"
no longer "a single political regime or person or religion or ideology"[64] but rather a certain type of violence, a particular type of
crime. "[I]t is certainly true," notes Walter Benn Michaels, "that our
so-called war on terrorism remains rigorously indifferent ... to the
reasons terrorists might give for their acts," making "the question of
what terrorists believe ... as irrelevant as the question of what nation
they come from."[65] And the criminals who perpetrate this crime are
"evil-doers" and "barbaric people"[66] who have "chosen to live on
the hunted margin of mankind" and, in so doing, "divorced themselves from the values that define civilization itself."[67] There is thus
no belief or value system that can possibly sustain them, nor is there
any legitimacy to their cause: they "hate what they see right here in
this chamber: a democratically elected government," Bush told Congress and the nation on 20 September. They "hate our freedoms:
our freedoms of religion, our freedom of speech, our freedom to
vote and assemble and disagree with each other";[68] even more out-
rageous, America in particular was targeted for being "the bright-
est beacon for freedom and opportunity in the world."[69] These are

enemies who hate "not our policies but our existence, the tolerance of openness and creative culture that defines us."[70] In other words, such an enemy is wholly apolitical and cannot lay claim to any ideology: it opposes the United States on the basis of its very existence. This narrative flew in the face of several interviews of bin Laden conducted prior to 11 September in which his focus was clearly on American actions rather than on American values.[71] For instance, bin Laden claimed in 1997 that

> [w]e declared jihad against the US government, because the US government is unjust, criminal and tyrannical. It has committed acts that are extremely unjust, hideous and criminal whether directly or through its support of the Israeli occupation of the Prophet's Night Travel Land [Palestine]. And we believe the US is directly responsible for those who were killed in Palestine, Lebanon and Iraq.[72]

Politics, however, has no place in a fight against "evil" pure and simple; the War on Terror as it began – as the "decisive intervention" developed between the morning of 11 September and early 2002 – was not a matter of politics proper but of life against death, or between being and its negation.

It was also a struggle between humanity and inhumanity, for in making the "choice" to live on the "hunted margins of mankind," the terrorists effectively forfeited their subject status. Indeed, for Bush, they are "an enemy that likes to hide and burrow in";[73] they are "an enemy who can only survive in darkness";[74] they "dwell in dark corners of earth";[75] they "hide in caves" and must be "[smoked] out of their holes."[76] The enemy is thus portrayed as fundamentally inhuman, as a bestial manifestation of a "perverted" faith. And this is indeed the ideal enemy for a "new," posthistorical war, for it takes on some of the attributes of the virus, devoid of "subject status" and representing the "chaos external to the system"[77] or the unsymbolized gulf of "non-being."[78] And the effect of such an enemy image, as is the case in the broader cultural context, is to confirm the proposition that the system admits of no alternatives – that the only alternative to life "as we know it" is, in fact, non-being. Hence Bush's famous declaration that "you're either with us or you're with the terrorists."[79] This is, as Žižek says of the choice between "democracy and fundamentalism" more broadly, a "forced choice"[80] – that is, not merely a choice between allegiances with only one "acceptable" answer but rather a choice in which the "wrong" answer annuls the capacity to have chosen in the first place. Lacan's "forced choice" in psychoanalysis, after all, is the choice the child makes to submit to the "big Other" of language in exchange for subjectivity, the alternative being psychosis and, accordingly, the forfeiture of subjectivity. Bruce Fink explains this well: "the choice of submission is necessary if one is to come to be as a subject, but it maintains its status as a choice since it is nevertheless possible to refuse subjectivity."[81] Subjectivity, however, is a privilege only of those who go "with us"; subhuman status is conferred upon the "rest," a group that includes not only terrorists but, certainly in the initial stages of the War on Terror, those who protested or questioned the aggression in America's foreign policy. In other words, the "choice already made," here as in posthistory more broadly, continues to prevail.

At the same time, however, the construction of an enemy concealed in darkness can be disabling within a culture so thoroughly dependent for its self-reproduction on images. A single, identifiable enemy had to be named, and this was the elusive terrorist mastermind Osama bin Laden. Throughout the war in Afghanistan and for quite some time afterwards, his periodic reappearance on the airwaves served a function similar to that of the villain in Hollywood films, reminding Western viewers that he was alive and well and still needed to be "smoked out" according to the frontier-justice rhetoric of the Bush administration. Bin Laden was the "evil one,"[82] the "prime suspect" who was "Wanted, Dead or Alive"[83] – a throwback to the victory narratives Tom Engelhardt rightly associates with the genre of the western.[84] Thus did the grainy, America's-Most-Wanted image of Osama bin Laden's face come to stand in for the essential and unrepresentable inhumanity of his adherents, providing a stable "identifier" onto which America's outrage could be properly projected, a visible index for an otherwise dispersed and invisible enemy.

The construction of the enemy-image in these terms too is fully consistent with the "logic" of posthistory. On the one hand, there is bin Laden himself, the Hollywood master-villain; this imposes the "normalizing" framework of law and order, the culturally anchored model that determined the representation of Saddam Hussein during the Persian Gulf War some ten years earlier. The framework, that is, continues to give the impression of an interaction between

Bush the policeman and bin Laden the criminal, notwithstanding the rich irony of the Bush administration's dismissal of the conventions of international law in its enterprise abroad. Further, it automatically invalidates the grievances bin Laden lists on behalf of the Arab world, which, being the words of the Hollywood villain par excellence, warrant neither discussion nor elaboration. To this extent, therefore, what is offered is a "choice" between the status quo and criminal anarchy, between order and disorder, with the first term in each binary always the privileged one.

Even the image of bin Laden, however, poses a problem, for in portraying him as a Hollywood villain, there may well be some risk of imbuing him with a degree of subjectivity that the terrorist, through the logic of the "forced choice" described above, is necessarily denied. Because the image of the criminal can easily be granted "subject status," the nature of both the hunt for bin Laden and its object – bin Laden himself – subsequently changed. In a matter of mere months, bin Laden, "wanted dead or alive," was both dead *and* alive as rumours of his death proliferated alongside new "releases," video and audio, of his calls to jihad, the precise spatial and temporal origins of which could apparently never be determined. As Secretary of Defense Donald Rumsfeld noted on 20 January 2002, "he could be dead, he could be alive, he could be in Afghanistan, he could be somewhere else."[85] Bin Laden, in other words, was no longer presumed to have a fixed location in time and space – a condition, surely, for "subjectivity" in the sense of a bodily unity. He went from being a subject who could be tracked down and captured to a spectral and indeterminable presence, simultaneously "everywhere and nowhere" like the "non-being" that the terrorist threat can be said to represent. For a decade, he remained essentially "spectral," his periodic if increasingly rare appearances alternating with outdated footage that condemned him to repeat, ghost-like, the same actions in perpetuity whenever his image was called upon to serve its ideological purpose.

The terrorist enemy so constructed thus embraces two contradictory aspects of posthistory: it is on the one hand the "criminal" element that can be easily captured or killed in the process of law enforcement, however technically illegal a form such enforcement should take, and on the other hand it is the spectral or "viral" enemy that constitutes a source of unending fear. It is the "bad guy" who will be captured "dead or alive" according to the conventions of the

Hollywood western and the "swarming mass endlessly multiplying itself"[86] and that cannot be contained. Its "network is extensive," according to Bush, and it has "no borders."[87]

To summarize, then, the American collective subject (at least at the mainstream level) defines itself all the more effectively against a spectral, undefinable entity that threatens to undo it. The constitution of this "social order" as effected by the displacement of internal chaos outwards continues to apply, at least to some extent, despite the growing force of alternative discourses, which will be further examined in chapter 5. Against "shadowy networks" defined by hatred without reason is an America that, for Bush, is "united" and "strong," an America bound by "our faith, our love of family and friends, our commitment to our country and to our freedoms and our principles."[88] The more ominous, amorphous and diffuse the threat, the more seamless and totalizing the corresponding illusion of collectivity. The "politics" of fear, in other words, taps into the more generalized "culture" of fear already described to produce an illusion of identity and agency, of a collective subject for whom the slogan "Let's roll" takes on the overtones of the sacred.

POLITICS OF FEAR (REPRISE)

Central to the maintenance of the enemy image described above is the maintenance of an appropriate level of fear, and this more than anything is the function of the enemy depicted as a non-subjective, viral entity with "cells" hidden throughout the "civilized" world. If the idea of a war between being and its negation has to some extent always played an implicit role in demonology and dehumanization for the purposes of sustaining the fantasy of collectivity, then what differs under the terrorist threat at the "end of history" is the coincidence between the non-subjective, spectral nature of the enemy and the ostensible absence of alternatives to the current order. Terrorism and its spectral weapons – chemical, biological, nuclear, even "our" own technologies turned against "us" – stand in at the representational level for the spectre of non-being that haunts all the more effectively as the mediating levels between existence and non-existence are progressively eliminated. Because what terrorism ostensibly proposes, according to the politics of fear, is not another system but rather an end to systems as such, the "war" upon it can be represented only in such absolute terms. The construction of the terrorist enemy thus effects an ideological foreclosure fully consistent with the posthistorical claim that ideology itself is at an end.

This is not to suggest that there are not in fact terrorist "cells" in the Western world or that there is no reason to fear further attacks in North America and Europe. The bombings in Madrid and London constitute ample evidence that such "cells" remain in operation throughout the world. Nor is it to claim that there was not an alternative discourse under development throughout this early period and particularly leading up to, and throughout, the war on Iraq. However, in the cultural mainstream, legitimate fears were routinely manipulated by the administration and the media to serve their own particular purposes. Rather than advance a perspective taking into account the historical conditions of possibility for such a threat, the architects of and adherents to the ideological strategies of the War on Terror fabricated an enemy-image along the lines favoured by Hollywood films, projecting real social anxieties onto an enemy that might indeed in some cases be equally "real" but that did not, in fact, constitute an embodiment of these fears. And this projection outwards diverted attention that should instead have been directed at the broader historical context (as indeed it was in the emerging counter-discourse) if any of these "real" anxieties were ever to be resolved. Further, it enforced a thoroughly ahistorical, even anti-historical, understanding of an enemy that would likely not have had access to the resources it did had it not been for the covert actions of America itself during the long, "cold" war against the Soviet Union. The creation of an enemy image that represents pure negation did a greater disservice to the American public than to the terrorists themselves in that it substituted mindless fear for productive analysis. It was thus not just terrorists who made "a philosophy out of frightening people"[89] but the administration and the media themselves.

Indeed, one might say that the Bush administration and bin Laden himself, in his periodic videotaped calls to jihad, advanced the very same "philosophy" of fear. Much as bin Laden insisted on the imminence of another terrorist attack while never specifying a time or location, so too did Bush insist that the next mass attack, likely to dwarf the attacks of 11 September, was a matter of "when, not if." Bush thus replicated the logic of imminence as discussed in the preceding chapter – that is, the notion that the threat exists in "real time" and might be only a matter of seconds away. "When, not if" refers to the perpetual imminence of another act of mass destruction and terror, and its logic infused the official rhetoric as well as the news, entertainment, and "infotainment." If on the one hand "instant history," as manifested in the first Gulf War and the war in Afghanistan, promised the security of a future already known, then on the other it presented the public with a constant menace, the imminent threat of total destruction, a catastrophe that could take place anywhere and at any time. The "terrorism of the spectacle,"[90] as Baudrillard calls it, is thus undercut by the spectacle of terrorism that suggests an "end of history" of an altogether different sort from that proposed by Fukuyama. If on the one hand it appeared to herald the fulfillment of capitalism's "millennial dream," then on the other it held this dream just out of reach, imposing between the capitalist world and its ultimate self-realization as a harmonious totality the ever-present threat of annihilation at the hands of its enemies. It was in "real time," after all, that the 11 September attacks had their devastating psychological impact, and it is in "real time" too that the next act of mass destruction will irrupt into everyday reality, a fact that was never lost on Bush. "Thousands of dangerous killers," he claimed, "schooled in the methods of murder, often supported by outlaw regimes, are now spread throughout the world like ticking time bombs, set to go off without warning."[91] The "ticking clock" that had already once reached zero had been re-set, and America could not delay in its "war to save civilization itself"[92] from imminent apocalypse.

In popular culture and infotainment too, the logic of "when, not if," of perpetual imminence and the "ticking clock," continued to apply. Indeed, it came to serve as a primary narrative motivator in one of the more popular television series of the post–11 September era – namely, 24.[93] Each season comprised twenty-four episodes, each one representing, in sequence, a real-time hour in the lives of its protagonists. The "real-time" aesthetic of the series thus mimicked live coverage in its presentation of "up-to-the-minute" action, and in the second season this "live action" narrative form was brought to bear on the issue of nuclear terrorism. The first episode launches the action with the revelation that a nuclear bomb is scheduled to detonate in Los Angeles at a predetermined time, and subsequent episodes involve a veritable race against the clock, during the course of which the protagonist manages to locate the bomb and transport it to the desert before its timer runs out. 24 is thus in many ways a fictional parallel to "instant history," appealing to some of the same impulses and anxieties that drive the consumption of real-time, all-the-time news, particularly as they did in the days following the 11 September attacks when, as Spiegelman aptly describes it, everyone was "waiting for the other shoe to drop."[94] The "race against time" informs the show's entire aesthetic, from its digital ticking-clock "identifier" to, in narrative terms, the implausible twists and turns that complicate the development of the plot. It sets up impossible deadlines for a character whose heroic efforts are continually thwarted in the most improbable ways. Yet it is ultimately not the quality of the series that matters so much as the unique way in which real-time network news, format, aesthetics, subject matter, and current events converge, and it is the "real-time" form, combined with fear of mass destruction, that constitutes in my opinion the most revealing aspect of the series, at least in relation to the contemporary structure of feeling as already described. As a case in point, the CNN documentary *Nuclear Terror*,[95] produced long after the second season of 24, deals with almost exactly the same premise: the smuggling of a nuclear weapon into Los Angeles. Throughout the documentary, a host of "experts" insist that America has been living on "borrowed time" and that preventing catastrophe is first and foremost a matter of "beating not a ticking bomb, but a ticking clock."[96] If a documentary can so readily "imitate" a televised work of fiction, then the best that can be hoped for is that reality does not come along and imitate both, yet the politics of fear, relayed through the real-time medium, is premised on precisely this possibility. The threat is "real" and exists in "real time," and television is fully complicit with its terrors. On CNN as on 24, anything is possible; the idea is that disaster could strike from any angle and at any time and that nobody is exempt from fear or suspicion.

The third season of 24, moreover, pulls together all the strands of conspiracism, paranoia, and apocalypticism that together comprise the mindset of the contemporary culture of fear, none of which can be isolated or "contained" but instead are diffuse, amorphous, omnipresent, and insidious: foreign nationals (in this case, at least in the first instance, Mexicans); the drug trade (the fallout of which has in this case come to involve the protagonist himself, who undertakes to rescue the world even in the throes of heroin withdrawal); the virus (its potency and mass transmissibility confirmed by epidemiologists, pathologists, and other experts in the field); and last but not least, the terrorist imperative behind the anticipated release of the virus, predicted to infect hundreds of thousands within the space of a week. As in the preceding season, nobody can be trusted, and unforeseeable plot twists thwart viewer expectations while fulfilling the structural imperative of drawing the series out across twenty-four episodes. All the while, the "countdown," the sense of time running out, continues to motivate the action. In short, the producers of the series had hit upon the perfect combination of narrative elements to perpetuate the "hyper-fear" that informed the series' consumption.

Crucially, the centrality of the "ticking bomb" scenario to entertainment and infotainment alike, when combined with the spectacle of 11 September as seared into popular memory, has had some terrifying material consequences, fusing fact with fiction in such a way as to open up what is now an ongoing debate on the legitimacy of torture. In other words, torture – prohibited by numerous international conventions – has been reintroduced into the realm of public debate as, in some people's eyes, a "justified" means of garnering information from sources deemed affiliated with terrorism. Indeed, so pernicious and insidious has this discourse become that at a 2007 conference in Ottawa aimed at addressing the balance (or lack thereof) between civil rights and national security, US Supreme Court Justice Antonin Scalia rose to the defense of 24's protagonist, insisting that the fictional Jack Bauer had "saved LA" from a nuclear bomb by means of extreme interrogation techniques.[97]

Further, the practice of "rendition" – the transportation of suspected terrorists to countries that sanction torture – has also come under scrutiny in recent years, fuelling a debate the very persistence of which attests to the capacity of fear *as politics*, or *in place of politics*, to override some erstwhile quite fundamental perceptual norms. Fortunately, there *is* a debate and a reasonably strong political will to end the practice – a will that did not always prevail in the early years of the War on Terror. However, a hypothetical situation in which an imminent terrorist attack might be prevented through the extraction of information under duress poses a problem to which even the more liberal elements in society are unable to advance a solution.[98] And despite the fact that such a situation is hardly likely to arise in "real life," the reopening of the debate is in and of itself cause for serious concern, for in debating the legitimation of torture at all, the US seems to differ from its enemies only in degree.[99]

Complementing the temporal immediacy of the terrorist threat, moreover, is a spatial immediacy the logic of which, like any "viral" threat, implicates everybody as a potential victim. In the context of a War on Terror, as in the context of the media scares of the 1990s, anything or anyone can be at the "centre" of an event. The idea of terrorism, like any other "media scare" or mediated scare, is that it can happen anywhere, that anyone can be the next victim, that the individual's own life is always somehow at risk. It can happen to the most ordinary people, as our commemorative DVDs remind us, on the most routine of days. Indeed, this is true of terrorism in general, but the manipulation of such a threat by the Bush administration immediately adopted a paralyzing function. The colour-coded danger scale, graded from green ("low risk of terrorist attacks") to red ("severe risks of terrorist attacks") and comprising "general," "significant," and "high" levels of risk in between, presents terrorism as always and invariably a clear and present danger. Yet Bush denied that the scale was a means of perpetuating unnecessary fear: questioned about it by a reporter, he replied that Americans should "take comfort in the fact that their government is doing everything we possibly can to run down every possible lead and take threats ... seriously."[100]

Further informing the logic of fear as promoted by the Bush administration was a form of conspiracism – not of a subcultural type, although conspiracy theories concerning who was truly responsible for the attacks of 11 September abound, but rather of a sort that portrays the terrorist threat as one far better co-ordinated and integrated, on a global level, than it surely ever has been. According to the conspiracist rhetoric of the Bush administration, "shadowy networks of individuals" were poised to "bring great chaos and suffering to our shores"[101] and conspiring to develop the means to do so. The Bush administration, capitalizing on the currency of conspiracy theory both as pathology and as commodity, mobilized it toward the creation and perpetuation of a generalized, national paranoia that could then be tapped in support of the War. Much as conspiracy narratives involve the "[rearrangement of] chaos into order, the contingent into the determined" in a comprehensive "(re)writing of history,"[102] so too did the narratives of the Bush administration link disparate phenomena into a global plot orchestrated by a conspiratorial "axis of evil."[103] Not surprisingly, the Associated Press reported on 6 August 2003 that nearly 70 per cent of Americans believed in a link between Saddam Hussein and the

terrorist attacks of 11 September, despite an utter lack of evidence
to this effect.[104] Even by March 2008 – the year that Barack Obama
would topple the Republican administration – 28 per cent still
believed in such a connection, according to a CBS poll – a significant
decline but a disturbing figure nonetheless.[105] Although such "officially sanctioned" paranoia has a lengthy history in American politics, the legitimating discourses of the War on Terror employed the
"paranoid style" in certain ways unique to the posthistorical structure of feeling, constituting an American collective subject in a manner fully consistent with it. The "poor man's cognitive mapping," as
Jameson famously called it, was displaced from the incomprehensible
networks of global capital to fantasized networks of fanatical terror.

THE HOMELAND: PARANOIA AND NATIONAL COHESION

In Patrick O'Donnell's account of the relationship between paranoia and national identity, he explains that paranoia as a "narrative
process" relies on "cultural mnemonics" that "enable the buttoning
down ... of discrete traumatic events as moments in which cultural
identity-narratives reveal their shape and horizon as a kind of destiny."[106] The rhetoric of the War on Terror brings together a number
of such mnemonics: the phrase "axis of evil," transparent to critics
as it may be, is indeed a remarkable condensation of them, uniting
the Axis forces of the Second World War with the "evil empire" of
the 1980s.[107] Hitler's dehistoricized, iconic status merges with that
of the insidious communist threat in a manner consistent with the
portrayal of terrorism more generally, with its evil, human face (bin
Laden) and its subhuman agents who "burrow in" and "live in darkness." The media spectacle of the terrorist attacks links America's
current "mission" to rid the world of evil with similar "missions"
carried out in the past; the terrorists become "the heirs of all the
murderous ideologies of the twentieth century," following "fascism,
Nazism, and totalitarianism" into "history's unmarked grave of discarded lies."[108] Dehistoricization and the erasure of temporality are
related: as O'Donnell notes,

> history under paranoia is latent destiny, or history spatial-
> ized and stripped of its temporality. Such history is constructed
> through a process of interpretation that compresses contingent
> events, memories, or traumas into a singular story that manifests

the real of self or nation as organized around a central paranoid
"truth": that it is always, and has always been, at the focal point
of historical processes rather than on their periphery.[109]

The power of combining these "cultural mnemonics" into an ever-
present "now" – enhanced, in this case, by the spectacular violence
of "the day that changed the world," 9/11 – reinforced the paranoid
nature of "nationhood" as linked to "self" that was evoked in the
first Gulf War and over the first posthistorical decade more generally, continuing to apply in the unfolding of the War on Terror,
with America destined to lead the way to a brighter future for all.
Or, one might say, the real narrative of American power since the
end of the Second World War is displaced onto a constructed narrative whereby America, victimized unfairly yet again – as in the gen-
eric Western trope of ambush[110] – must now realize its "manifest
destiny" by civilizing the world at large. "Let's roll," then, implies
the dutiful assumption of what might now be called the "American
man's burden": in O'Donnell's words,

> now alone at the center of a global history ... "we" have taken
> on the encumbrances of the historical superego who must define
> and sublimate or destroy the evil others who would foul up his-
> tory, and who simply can't understand that their narrative is, in
> a sense, a historical lie because it does not fit ours. In short, the
> "we" here, itself a paranoid projection ... positions "us" as the
> schizoid arbiters of history: both its authors (the ones who make
> history) and readers (the ones who organize its signs into the sig-
> nificant patterns of historical destiny).[111]

As George Gerbner said of Gulf War I, "the boiling point is
reached when the power to create a crisis merges with the power
to direct the movie about it,"[112] and this has been America's modus
operandi since the neo-conservative "end of history" placed it in a
unique position, a position long desired yet paradoxically undesirable to the extent that its "grand narratives" were now under threat.
The paranoid, national "self" constructed by the conflation of "cultural mnemonics" must act, and act *now*, to direct the course of history, to write it, and subsequently to interpret it, all at once.

Much as Huntington's thesis constitutes a rational, subjective
"West" against a generally inferior "rest," then, so too does the

official grand narrative position "America" as the primary agent of
"history," whose actions over the coming decades will determine
both its own fate and that of the world. In much the same way that
clinical paranoia "centres" the self, what Richard Hofstadter called
the "paranoid style" in politics[113] places America "at the focal point"
rather than on the periphery. Much as paranoia and conspiracism
of the more subcultural or oppositional kind often "[begin] with
individual self-protection, with an attempt to define the integrity of
the self against the social order,"[114] so too did the Bush administration's conspiracist rhetoric seek to delineate a freedom-loving "we-
group" against an insidious and omnipresent threat to its integrity.
And much as the former in its paranoia sees the self as potentially
already controlled by "powerful external agents,"[115] so too did the
latter obsess about an "enemy within" – about the quasi-viral "cells"
in various cities and towns across the United States and about the
secret transfers of funding and information going on between them.

This logic in itself is by no means new, but in the context of the
War on Terror it became all the more effective as a result of the
immediacy and imm(i)(a)nence of the threat, which in its direct
appeal to individual security "sutured" the believing subject to the
destiny of the nation. In other words, the conspiracist logic of the
"axis of evil" paradigm, in the context of the terrorist threat, managed to bring, through mainstream cultural production and official
rhetoric, the individual in line with the imagined community of a
nation in danger. Just as the trauma of the World Trade Center victims was construed as a blow to "national" innocence, so too did
Bush's invisible, omnipresent network of doom place the self at the
"centre of intersecting social and historical plots,"[116] its perpetual
imminence and immediacy transcending the "real" barriers between
the individual and the American "imagined community." Where anyone can be a "centre," as in the media panics discussed in the previous chapter, the individual consumer of mainstream ideology is
united with the narratives of the nation much as the rituals of religion link the believer to the faith; the subject who checks the colour-
coded terror scale before leaving home each day – assuming such a
subject exists – is also the distinctly *American* subject, "sutured" to
the homeland by means of a common fate.

Hence the establishment, on 25 November 2002, of the Department of Homeland Security, charged with protecting the United
States against terrorist attacks and responding to natural disasters.

Indeed, Bush began to speak of the "homeland" a mere nine days after the 11 September attacks, creating an Office of Homeland Security directed by "a true patriot," Tom Ridge.[117] As Amy Kaplan notes, the word "homeland" has not been "historically a part of the traditional arsenal of patriotic idioms [in America]," and it has "an exclusionary effect that underwrites a resurgent nativism and anti-immigrant sentiment and policy." Indeed "[t]he notion of a nation as a home, as a domestic space, relies structurally on its intimate opposition to the notion of the foreign,"[118] putting into play "a history of multiple meanings, connotations and associations"[119] – one of which, I would suggest, is the connection between *das Unheimliche* and *die Heimat*, with the latter restoring a spatialized, aestheticized sense of the "home" where what "was intended to remain secret, hidden away"[120] has unexpectedly come to light. It is, in other words, a sealing off of the space of the "home," defensively, in the wake of a spectacular defeat (a defeat, that is, at the level of the image). In any case, the use of the word "homeland" confirmed a process already underway – the constitution of a "purified" American collective identity in the face of a viral, insidious, and thoroughly foreign threat.

It was also in defence of the "homeland" that America (it must be noted, in outright defiance of the international community and the norms of international law) sought to justify a pre-emptive strike on Iraq (exposing, of course, the irony of the policeman/criminal binary as applied to Bush and bin Laden). Again, the climate of fear was mobilized toward these ends and to quite remarkable effect.

Following the swift and decisive "victory" in Afghanistan – a questionable victory, given what has transpired over the years since then – the logic of the politics of fear was deployed to legitimate a second war in Iraq. Indeed, even before the conclusion of the first "battle" in the War on Terror, Bush was busily highlighting the dangers posed by "rogue states" in an attempt to justify his (illegal) abandonment of Cold War–era treaties:

I'm going to ask my friend [Vladimir Putin] to imagine a world in which a terrorist thug or a host nation might have the ability to develop, to deliver a weapon of mass destruction via ... rocket. And wouldn't it be in our nation's advantage to be able to shoot it down? At the very least, it should be in our nation's advantage to determine whether we can shoot it down, and we're restricted from doing that because of an ABM treaty that was signed during a totally different era ... ABM is outmoded, outdated, reflects a different time.[121]

"Our war against terror is only beginning," stated Bush in January 2002, and the "gravest danger in the war on terror, the gravest danger facing America and the world, is outlaw regimes that seek and possess nuclear, chemical and biological weapons."[122] According to Bush,

> [b]efore September the 11th, many in the world believed that Saddam Hussein could be contained. But chemical agents, lethal viruses and shadowy terrorist networks are not easily contained ... Imagine those nineteen hijackers with other weapons and other plans, this time armed by Saddam Hussein. It would take one vial, one canister, one crate slipped into this country to bring a day of horror like none we have ever known.[123]

This is the act of "writing" history and then "reading" or "interpreting" it – constructing a narrative linking the Ba'athist regime to terrorism and therefore to the attacks of 11 September so effectively that, as noted, 70 per cent of Americans believed at that time in a connection between the two. In making a case for war on Iraq, the Bush administration placed increasing emphasis on the rhetoric of fear, invoking the 11 September attacks as a "cultural mnemonic" compounding those contained within the "axis of evil" paradigm. The "choice already made" was therefore reasserted in a reversal of the logic of cause and effect, with a hypothetical scenario – "those nineteen hijackers" *could* have been armed by Saddam Hussein – made to compensate for the lack of any actual evidence against him. By this logic, 11 September itself became the "smoking gun," incriminating any nation upon which the administration should choose to wage "pre-emptive" war. By this logic, the "trauma" of 11 September, dissociated as it is from time and frozen in a perpetual present of terror, can be invoked to justify anything. As a media event, it inaugurated a "new world" in which the "old rules" – such as the Geneva Convention and anti-ballistic missile treaties – would no longer apply and could be disregarded (despite the violation of international law this would entail) and in which vague suspicions about a nation's ability to pose a threat would constitute grounds for waging war upon it. That the terrorist attacks took place at all served as "proof" that they will take place again; for Bush, therefore, "we cannot wait for the final proof – the smoking gun – that could come in the form of a mushroom cloud."[124]

Saddam Hussein, the "Hitler" of Gulf War I, now became a terrorist Hitler surrounded by "nuclear mujahedeen" or "nuclear holy warriors,"[125] a phrase combining fears of mass annihilation with fears of a depraved and fanatical other impervious to rational analysis and therefore fit only for pre-emptive eradication. Saddam Hussein "must not be permitted to threaten America and the world with horrible poisons and diseases and gases and atomic weapons,"[126] weapons that coincide with the "viral" threats evoked by the media during the posthistorical 1990s. In a fascinating turn of phrase, Bush accused Saddam Hussein of being a "homicidal dictator *addicted* to weapons of mass destruction,"[127] undermining whatever subject status he might have possessed as a head of state by characterizing him as suffering from a pathological obsession. The rhetoric of "addiction" applied to the "rogue state" was designed to project middle-American fears of drug-fuelled crime onto a global scale, portraying the enemy leader as highly unstable and apt to resort to extremes to sustain his "habit."

Further, the "spectral" nature of Osama bin Laden, dead and alive at one and the same time, was transferred onto Saddam Hussein as the "master of deception"[128] as if he were somehow possessed of supernatural abilities. Indeed, just prior to the fall of Baghdad he became something of a spectral presence in his own right, his bodily unity sacrificed to the debate as to whether it was indeed him on television or one of his "body doubles" and whether the broadcasts were live or taped before the war. To some extent, Hussein as an enemy figure could indeed be schematized according to an older set of "rules"; he could be clearly identified, that is, with a specific nation-state and even with a certain "ideology" insofar as the fascist-style "cult of the leader" was manifested in statues and giant murals bearing his likeness. But it was ultimately the fear of negation in one sense (the "viral" threat of his alleged arsenal of WMDs) that was invoked to justify a second, illegal war against him. Accordingly, the images of his capture in Tikrit represented a monumental triumph: the public humiliation of having his medical exam, a violation of his bodily space, viewed by millions worldwide, marked a defining moment of the suppression of the other, a genuine, if short-lived, triumph at every ideological level. In a war of images, Saddam Hussein went from being "larger than life," in the enormous, imposing murals and in the threat he ostensibly posed, to a helpless captive, dragged "like a rat"[129] from an underground "hole" and subjected to all manner of indignities before the global media. Yet despite this euphoric victory and the narrative resolution it implied, the second war in Iraq would unfold in directions unanticipated by either its architects or the guardians of its spectacular representation. Its failure to advance "according to plan" will be explored in more detail in the next chapter.

"NOT THAT SHOCKING AND AWESOME": SPECTACULAR FAILURE IN IRAQ

The failure of the spectacle that was to be followed, in short order, by spectacular failure began on the first night of the invasion. Ironically, this failure is evident in CNN's packaged narrative, *War in Iraq: The Road to Baghdad*, released even before Saddam Hussein's capture in December 2003. This release, like its earlier *War in the Gulf* collection, was clearly meant to suggest that victory was already assured and came complete with soundtrack, dramatic visual effects, and a clear narrative structure marked by "chapters" and by the defining or iconic images of the war, such as the first night of "shock and awe," the fall of Saddam Hussein's statue in Baghdad, and the "rescue" of Private Jessica Lynch. Toward the beginning of the retrospective, correspondent Nic Robertson describes the spectacle of "shock and awe": "this was the beginning essentially of the war that we'd heard about, the shock and awe. [There were] huge fireballs erupting ... all in the same area ... huge clouds of black smoke coming up ... the lights were still on [in the city], which was strange ... [there was] almost this backlit effect ..."

This is followed, however, by a voice-over that qualifies the description: "for all the hype," it begins, "there was a lingering sense that shock and awe had fallen short." Followed again by Robertson: "I thought that it would be *so* horrendously intense, that there would be *so* many more places hit, that I think ... well, I've seen it, and I've witnessed it, and yes it was shocking and awesome, but it wasn't *that* shocking and awesome."

The purpose of "shock and awe," according to CNN Senior Pentagon Correspondent Jamie McIntyre, was to "create the perception at the beginning that the result is inevitable"; it was directed, ostensibly, at the Iraqi people and at the Ba'ath regime in particular. Yet Robertson's remarks unintentionally betray a secret truth: that it was never meant to be directed exclusively at the Iraqis but also, and perhaps more importantly, at "us," the viewers and consumers of the network news. The phrase "shock and awe" set up expectations that ultimately could not be met; if the spectacle of bombs over Baghdad was "shocking" and "awesome" in 1991, then now – according to the logic of the spectacle by which each "event" must outdo the one that precedes it – it would have to be considerably more "explosive" to achieve the desired result. If the "familiar spectacle" was meant to have a therapeutic effect on a population warned, day in and day out, of the imminence of a large-scale terrorist attack, it fell far short of its target.

Partially making up for this, over time, was the Pentagon's new strategy of "embedded reporting" – an intensification and tightening of the "pool" system – according to which approximately 600 pre-approved journalists were stationed with American and British troops to provide coverage of the war. In contrast to the "pool" system of old, as well as to the networks' limited access to the action in Afghanistan, the "embedded" system seemed to promise greater access to information. According to the Project for Excellence in Journalism (PEJ) and the Committee of Concerned Journalists (CCJ), two organizations committed to "[raising] the standards of American journalism,"[130] 58 per cent of Americans considered embedded journalism a "good" thing, and of the 34 per cent who disapproved, most were concerned that it would provide too much information to the enemy.[131] In the first days of the war, according to PEJ and CCJ, 61 per cent of reports were "live and unedited"[132] such that "[i]n an age when the press is often criticized for being too interpretive, the overwhelming majority of the embedded stories studied, 94%, were primarily factual in nature," providing information directly from reporters as opposed to "soldiers or other sources."[133] The idea, as presented to the viewer, was to provide an "up close and personal"[134] account of the war, which, with only 6 per cent of the coverage consisting of analysis and commentary, could consequently be seen as "free" of ideology.

And yet, as Fredric Jameson notes, "ideology is not necessarily a matter of false consciousness, or of the incorrect and distorted representation of historical 'fact,' but can rather be quite consistent with a 'realistic' faithfulness to the latter."[135] In other words, the same ideological effects examined earlier in relation to the supposedly "realistic" *Black Hawk Down* pertain to embedded coverage as well.

That is, the new "realism" of network war reporting is ultimately no less ideological than what Wetta and Novelli call "Hollywood's new patriotism." In the same sort of development from the "mirror stage" into a fantasy realm "through the looking glass," as discussed in the previous chapter, the viewer of embedded reports is brought into an implicit first-person alliance with the journalist, who is now effectively inseparable from the troops with whom he or she is stationed. The direct involvement of the journalist in the military action pre-empts any "mediating" perspective he or she could otherwise offer, while the visual effect of the first-person camera comes to implicate the viewer in a "video-game" presentation of the war. The new "realism" is therefore both tightly controlled and compelling to a still greater extent because of the "self-replications" it affords. The spectator-consumer becomes *involved* in the action in a different way, implicated in a different way, as a result of a new degree of "im/mediacy" as ostensible *non-mediation*. What appears initially as an absence of ideology thus takes the form of an ever more insidious ideology; it replaces context with the promise of the thrill of shock and awe, of the unpredictable and the immediate, combining triumph (the "wave of steel"[136]) with dread (the periodic donning of gas masks by reporters and troops). It also presents a fragmentary account of the war in Iraq, offering microscopic "slices" as immediate experience rather than any broader political perspective with which the viewer might be able to engage on a more intellectual, or at least on a more detached, level.

Further, "retrospective" compilations such as CNN's *War in Iraq* present the illusion of neutrality, exemplifying the paradox whereby what might be apprehended as "random" or unscripted and therefore "free" of ideology – an inescapable characteristic, one would *think*, of live, twenty-four-hour "coverage" – is in fact micromanaged to its very smallest detail. While to some extent it might seem surprising that *War on Iraq* does not overtly "take sides," highlighting among other things the plight of civilian casualties and the debate as to the veracity of the Jessica Lynch story, there is another way in which this ostensible lack of bias is precisely what reinstates bias on a deeper, more "structural" level. This is the case particularly in CNN's assessment of the coverage on Al Jazeera and other

Arab networks, much of which was rebroadcast on CNN itself. CNN's footage of civilian casualties – accompanied, notably, by the exact same sentimental soundtrack used in *America Remembers* – is followed abruptly by the accusation that the Arab networks focused exclusively on the civilian victims at the expense of a more detached objectivity. To reinforce the point, virtually everything broadcast on Al Jazeera during the war is subjected either to doubt or to ridicule, from the footage of Saddam Hussein (or his "body double") to the cavalier pronouncements of Mohammed Saeed al-Sahaf, his Information Minister cum Western cult hero. Meanwhile, micronarratives or subplots such as the Jessica Lynch "rescue" (courtesy of the Department of Defense, which filmed its execution from beginning to end) were presented without a trace of scepticism, coming into question only well after the intended impression had already been made.

The "icons" of the war in Iraq, however – Bush's "Mission Accomplished" landing on the USS *Abraham Lincoln* (off the coast of California), the fall of Saddam Hussein's statue, the capture of Saddam Hussein himself – were never, at the time, subject to questioning; instead, they served until more recently as "logos" or "identifiers," spatializing history into a series of iconic images intended to promote "Brand America" as a force for good in the world. And above them all looms the "shadow of no towers," the master-signifier of the "new normal," the Lacanian *point de capiton* that "buttons down" the entire enterprise in its suggestion of mass annihilation as the only alternative to a global War on Terror.

Whatever the compensatory value of such images, and of the first-person perspective generated by embedded coverage, they grew increasingly inadequate in the face of a war that persists in varying degrees into the present day, some nine years after Bush appeared on the deck of the USS *Abraham Lincoln* to declare its triumphant end. Although the Obama administration declared "combat operations" "over" on 1 September 2010 – in a bid to end the war "responsibly" – thousands of troops remain in the region if not the country at the time of writing, and a hefty American presence will likely be required for many years to come.

Whatever the future holds, it is important to remember that the aesthetic of realism deployed in militaristic films and in network news coverage of the war is always liable to backfire. Indeed, as the authors of *Afflicted Powers* remind us, "[a]t the level of the image

... the state is vulnerable."[137] In the "battle for the control of appear-ances,"[138] as they aptly put it, the state has come to appear increas-ingly desperate over what is now a considerable period of time, and this sense of desperation is reflected in a number of fiction films of the era as well as documentaries. An already convoluted logic – the shifting justifications for the war in Iraq – took a further impro-visational turn as Bush, confronted with actual terrorism in a state that had previously had only minimal, if any, connection to terror-ist organizations, attempted to frame the situation as evidence of freedom's imminent victory. Prior to the official government "hand-over" on 30 June 2004 – an event marked, at the level of the image, by Bush's handwritten note "Let Freedom Reign" – Bush attributed the increase in violence to the terrorists' "desperation": "As June 30 approaches, the enemies of freedom grow even more desperate to prevent the rise of democracy in Iraq. That's what you're seeing on your TV screens. The desperate tactics of a hateful few. People who cannot stand the thought of free societies in their midst."[139]

Bush's eagerness to interpret for his public "what you're seeing on your TV screens" speaks all too clearly to "the state's *anxiety* as it [tries] to micromanage the means of symbolic production," to its fears that "every last detail of the derealized décor it [has] built for its citizens [has] the potential ... to turn utterly against it."[140] The same attempt at micromanagement informed the official response to the shocking images from Abu Ghraib, images of an instance of "aberrant" behaviour, we were told, on the part of individual sol-diers or "bad apples." Indeed, six days after his diagnosis of the "hateful few," Bush brought the "battle for the control of appear-ances" to bear on that scandal as well. "[W]ith the approval of the Iraqi government," he announced on 24 May 2004, "we will demol-ish the Abu Ghraib prison, as a fitting symbol of Iraq's new begin-ning."[141] (US military judge Colonel James Pohl later ruled that the prison was a crime scene and could not be demolished[142]). That the battle was one over images was barely concealed at this point, with Bush proposing a purely symbolic measure to exorcise this ghastly "aberration." Indeed, the battle over images proved so central to the war effort that Bush is reputed to have considered a strike on Al Jazeera's headquarters in Qatar, a Western ally.[143]

Never mind that US strategy created the impression of an "occu-pation" rather than a "liberation"; never mind other mistakes, such as disbanding the army, which had left thousands jobless and ready to take up arms against the invaders as well as other ethnic groups: by the administration's logic, the enemy, for the insurgents, was "freedom" itself. With insurgent attacks showing a slight increase leading up to the "real" handover of 1 September 2010, and with the situation in Afghanistan still nowhere near resolution (a crippling insurgent attack had just taken place at the time of writing, and NATO troops are reviewing their plans for withdrawal), it is very difficult to predict the turn events may take.

Even a year after that first official "handover," Bush's increasingly convoluted logic continued to apply: "the terrorists have chosen to wage a war against a future of freedom," he announced in August 2005, but "[a]s democracy in Iraq takes root, the enemies of freedom, the terrorists, will become more desperate, more despicable, and more vicious."[144] Not only was this a response to the persistence of violence in Iraq, it was also an admission that the violence was likely to intensify and a warning to expect more of the same. Nonetheless, he reassured his public,

> [w]e will stand with the Iraqi people. It's in our interest to stand with the Iraqi people. It's in our interest to lay the foundation of peace. We'll help them confront this barbarism, and we will triumph over the terrorist's dark ideology of hatred and fear.[145]

Yet ultimately, Bush's faith in the justness of his cause has failed to compensate for the approximately 5,500 deaths of Americans in the War on Terror[146] (not to mention innumerable life-altering injuries), for the all-too-familiar footage of Western hostages pleading in vain for their lives, and for the abhorrent images of physical abuse emanating from American-run detention centres. Most decisively, it does not compensate for the spectacular, and still haunting, image-defeat of 11 September 2001. "The Towers keep falling," note the authors of *Afflicted Powers*, "and now they are joined by the imagery of Abu Ghraib." For them, "the present madness is singular: the dimension of spectacle has never before interfered so palpably, so insistently, with the business of keeping one's satrapies in order." Further, they note, "never before have spectacular politics been conducted in the shadow – the 'historical knowledge' – of *defeat*."[147] Yet the battle at the level of the image persisted, propelling the Republicans' convoluted logic in ever more unanticipated directions. At the time of writing, following the withdrawal of troops from Iraq at the end of 2011

and somewhat understated precautions being taken for a conflict
with Iran, with 15,000 troops recently deployed to Kuwait, it seems
that only the future will tell how the battle of images will play out.

That the power of the "forced choice" in a war between what
"is" and its negation, between "freedom" and "terror" – between, in
other words, the one viable alternative and the absence of alternatives – continued to work in President Bush's favour was evident
during the 2004 presidential election campaign when Democratic
candidate John Kerry, asked why he had advocated pulling out of
Vietnam but would stay the course in Iraq, was forced to adopt
the same line as his opponent. "[The two situations] are very different," he told his interviewer. "This is a war on terror. That was
a civil war, an ideological war."¹⁴⁸ Implicit in his response was the
shift from ideology to ideological foreclosure, from "communism"
to an "ism" that demanded no further elucidation and indeed pre-
cluded it; his campaign was conducted within the same paradigm as
his opponent's. "Most 'isms,'" notes Eagleton, "are abstract, but this
one is alarmingly concrete. It is as though you can convert rage into
an agenda, or build a programme out of pure resentment."¹⁴⁹ If the
"ism" in "terrorism" can be said to represent an ideology at all, it is,
as Bush has it, a "dark" ideology of "hatred and fear" rather than
a rational system of belief or a strategy (however illegitimate) arising from a list of legitimate grievances. Indeed, the foreclosure so
effected became so established that the "ism" was largely dropped
from official rhetoric, according to which the war became a "war"
on "terror" as such. Resistance to the American global enterprise
became by this logic a form of "terror" in itself, with Iraqi insurgents
branded as "terrorists" even when their targets were military rather
than civilian.

Further, a war of what "is" against its negation required no consistent mediating narrative. The failure to find any arsenal of WMDs
simply shifted the focus onto the admittedly brutal nature of his dic-
tatorship as sufficient justification for the war. The "liberation" of
the Iraqi people took precedence over the threat allegedly posed to
the West as Iraqis queued up to take part in their first "free and fair"
elections, another iconic moment overriding, if only temporarily, the
reign of chaos in the country. Although the moment would fade soon
enough in the continuing insurgency and American atrocities in Iraq,
it was nonetheless part of a strategy placing the American nation at
the spearhead of a "human rights"–based intervention, which had

become increasingly familiar and acceptable over the course of the posthistorical 1990s.

Thus, one might conclude that for the most part, the War on Terror, despite having begun with the "end of the 'end of history,'" has been mainly represented in fully posthistorical terms. Despite its ostensible reinstatement of "history," "narrative," and "victory culture" (as Tom Engelhardt calls it), it has been in many ways an enhanced means of framing the posthistorical project as defined by the "new world order" and the Persian Gulf War. The "comprehensive doctrine" identified by Perry Anderson and alluded to in previous chapters – linking free markets to free elections to human rights – now incorporated a further dimension, linking all three to the critical issue of "homeland" security. In the logic of the Bush administration, it was oppression and poverty that "bred" terror, as if the latter were a disease emanating from the slums of the world and only the extension of "free markets and free trade" to those parts of the world still "stuck in history"[150] could prevent it from striking once more on American soil. The element of fear that was lacking in the Clinton administration's rationale for American global leadership thus moved to the fore following 11 September, emphasizing a clear link between those who "resist" the benefits of "modernity" and those who hate and kill without reason. Restraint on the part of America was seen, even at the time of the 2004 election, as tantamount to "false comfort in a dangerous world"; indeed, there was "no going back to the era before September the 11th, 2001"[151] – that is, to the context of international cooperation in which America's actions abroad were subject to the approval of the world community. It thus combined the elements of posthistory as described in the preceding chapters, stressing the necessity of a neo-conservative free-market utopia and linking it to the ever-present threat of imminent mass destruction on a scale likely to dwarf the 11 September attacks.

Further, the war's undefined spatial and temporal boundaries coincide both with the undefined spatial and temporal boundaries of the terrorist threat *and* with those of the late-capitalist structure of feeling as an "unmappable," boundless totality. The ubiquity of the threat, the scope of the war, and the "totality" of social and power relations all resist conceptualization, if to slightly different effect. In other words, they are all immediate both spatially and temporally, all virtual and "unmappable" and structured on the logic of a "molecularized" temporality. That the Obama administration in

2009 dropped the term "War on Terror," replacing it with "overseas contingency operations," did not, in effect, *end* the war.[152]

For the duration of Bush's presidency, we were led to suspect that into this boundless and unrepresentable totality a shattering "event" of apocalyptic proportions threatened to irrupt, at any point in space and time, the precise nature of which would not be known until after the fact. And certainly, this was – and remains – to some extent more than just a matter of perception or representation. The element of surprise is after all part of the terrorist strategy, not only for purely tactical reasons but also for its sheer psychological impact that, to date at least, surpasses the physical impact in long-term effects. The bombings in Madrid and London in 2004 and 2005, respectively, were directed more at a broad Western audience than at the population immediately at risk. However, it is the administration's deployment of the same psychological strategies to a mainstream American audience that is of concern in this book. "When, not if" was the strategy shared by Bush and bin Laden, and it was predicated purely on fear, on the notion that total destruction was always at hand. The constant threat facing one and all was repeatedly invoked in a way that made Bush's logic as impervious to reason as he saw bin Laden's to be. It closed down avenues for rational debate in the same way as did his dehumanization of the terrorists, his characterization of them as embodying pure, unmitigated hatred and evil. If spectacular acts of terror create a void in "meaning" itself, placing themselves beyond the grasp of language, then the "forced choice" implied by the official response was ultimately equally devoid of meaning, removing as it did any "mediating" levels between being and non-being: the "options," in other words, spoke for themselves. The legitimating rhetoric of the War on Terror was thus designed to hold sway in an age for which boundless totality prefigures boundless annihilation. The "new normal" of late capitalism, post-9/11, essentially comprised utter alienation and disorientation in a boundless, "unmappable" system, the sustained terror of the colour-coded alert scale, gauging (by whatever mysterious means) the relative proximity of an omnipresent but invisible threat, and finally, an isolated and senseless death as the only conceivable escape.

Another way of putting this might be to say that the posthistorical system, in order to remain conceivable as a system at all, depends precisely on its conceptual limit, which, given the apparent boundlessness of that system itself, takes only the form of its own negation.

In the same paradoxical way that, for Lacan, the Symbolic (language, meaning, "reality") depends on the limit imposed by the Real (the unrepresentable), or the Freudian ego upon that imposed by the Unconscious, the only way to maintain a sense of place in an increasingly "unmappable" totality is with reference to the ultimate horizon of that system – to what Alain Badiou might call the *site événementiel* or "evental site,"[153] the last rampart between existence and the void. The boundlessness of the system continually generates the boundlessness of annihilation as its own immanent and imminent undoing. Indeed, in a very real sense the American global project under the Bush administration "justified" itself in relation to the need to eliminate the terrorist threat before it could strike again, however senseless such a "mission" increasingly appeared over the course of the decade. And indeed, at the level of the structure of feeling, the "mathematical" sublime of an ever less "mappable" world system seems to generate the "dynamic" sublime of destruction, a perverse fascination that explains both the overwhelming popularity of the disaster genre throughout the 1990s and the uncanny impact of the 11 September media spectacle. The catastrophic "accident," as Virilio might call it, is always imminent; the system's own negation inheres within it as its structurally enabling limit.

It was by this very same logic, I would argue, that the architects of the War on Terror came increasingly to resemble what they pretended to oppose. When the enemy comes to be represented in terms of being versus its negation (that is, between life itself and chaos, disease, non-being, or an obscure, ever-encroaching and unnameable threat), what happens is the constitution of a collective "bodily unity" on increasingly parochial, exclusive, and jingoistic grounds. That domestic opposition grew in the later years of the war on Iraq, enough to help bring a new administration into office, came as an exhilarating relief to millions of more moderate Americans after nearly eight years of the War on Terror. But up to that point, the incorporation of the struggle between "what is and its negation" into the very techniques of representation itself (that is, not only as a metaphor or manifest content but within the very form, as in the subject perspective created by embedded reporting or by films like *Black Hawk Down*) ended up betraying precisely what it was attempting to displace. If the enemy is constituted by a projection outwards of internal negativity or antagonism, then what these representations of the "new" enemy as pure negation or non-being should tell us is that now, more than ever, the "West," "America," the "liberal democracies" face a representational crisis in terms of their own constitution as societies and subjects.[154] That is, behind the illusion of collectivity and cohesiveness, shared identity and culture, is an anomie so pervasive – an absence so fundamental – that its external projection can only take on the various guises of nothingness. As Kaplan notes, the word "homeland" betrays a "sense of loss, longing and nostalgia," evoking not so much "stability and security" as "uprootedness, deracination and desire." It possesses a "kind of anxious redundancy, home and land, as though trying to pin down an uneasy connection between the two that threatens to fly apart."[155] The "end of history" – in particular, the perceived elimination of the possibilities of a qualitatively different future – ultimately leaves the West increasingly unable to legitimate itself culturally. "[V]otes and videos," as Perry Anderson puts it, are not nearly enough to fill the "lurking vacuum within the value-order of liberal capitalism" that the end of communism left behind,[156] and this is especially true in the face of increasing poverty, economic insecurity, dispossession, and disempowerment. Along with a growing sense of a loss of control, of being at the mercy of a system too vast and powerful to comprehend, these factors amount to a troubling "lack" at the centre of the social order itself. And when this lack is projected outwards onto an external enemy, the inherently universalist patriotism into which America was "born," a patriotism that was essentially political and that "assumed the basic harmony between the interests of civilized nations,"[157] is replaced by a more chauvinistic nationalism that is less political and more cultural, insisting upon its sovereign exceptionality and its mission to cleanse the world through war. An "authentic America," in other words – an America committed to liberty, democracy, and the possibility of a global just society – is increasingly in danger of being supplanted by a "fervent cult of the homeland,"[158] by the crude language (blood, guts, and soil) of nationalist passion. This may change, but it is clear that the US, projecting its inner tensions outwards and constituting itself ideologically as the "homeland," became ever less liberal and democratic, transforming itself instead into an image of its antagonists. The Tea Party, for instance – incoherent though its agenda may be – seems a frightening remnant of Bush's conservative America.

"Today," announced Bush in 2001, "the sun comes up on a vastly different world," a "dangerous" and a "less certain, less predictable one," consisting of "less responsible" states for whom "terror and blackmail are a way of life" and harbouring an "implacable hatred of the United States of America," including its "friends," its "values," its "democracy," its "freedom," and its "individual liberty." For Bush, it was time to "move beyond the constraints of the thirty-year-old ABM Treaty," which "does not recognize the present or point us to the future" but instead "enshrines the past," ignoring the "fundamental breakthroughs in technology during the last thirty years." What was needed was a "new framework that reflects a clear and clean break from the past" and especially from the "adversarial legacy of the Cold War"; Americans needed to "look at the world in a new, realistic way."[159]

These words might have been uttered at any point following the 11 September terrorist attacks; however, they were delivered some five months before, in a carefully scripted rationale for a new missile defence system. Bush's speech proclaimed a "new world" while stressing the constant proliferation of threats to its integrity; his description of these threats, as well as his emphasis on the obsolescence or irrelevance of Cold War–era treaties, corresponded precisely to his later rationale for the War on Terror and the need for America to assert its independence from the will of the international community. There was no longer any need for "history" as "enshrined" by earlier non-proliferation treaties; the new "reality" demanded a better-defended America, one that could respond to threats without the permission of the outmoded United Nations.

The world, in other words, did not "change" on 11 September 2001; on the contrary, it remained too much the same. And nine years later, as the United States ended the war "responsibly" by leaving 50,000 troops stationed in Iraq while ramping up activity in Afghanistan – after what can properly be described as a "quagmire," with further uncertainty ahead – the world appeared more "the same" than ever. The ever-present risk, however, is that the more violently America lashes out in blind pursuit of its imperial objectives, the more likely the nightmarish reality of a strike on American soil. The Obama administration's "overseas contingency operations" may lessen the risk, but "if" (or "when," according to Bush) such a strike were to occur, it would indeed come "out of a clear blue sky" on an otherwise perfectly ordinary, posthistorical day, and it could be on a scale that would dwarf the attacks of 11 September: it could usurp that day's status as the "day that changed the world."

In his introduction to the book accompanying CBS's *What We Saw*, Dan Rather writes, "[w]hen big events occur, they always loom large in the present. And there are times when the television screen enlarges what the perspective of years will show to be stories of only passing importance." The "historical implications" of 11 September, however, are "reckoned with accuracy": "[w]hen the event happened, while it happened, we knew we were watching history unfold. We saw a line – a shadow – fall over the newsreel of our lives, one that would forever mark the days after as separate from the days before. We understood that we would remember, would someday tell our grandchildren, where we had been and what we had been doing when we heard the news."[160]

Rather's prediction was by no means uncommon; indeed, for many, the "shadow of no towers" continues to loom large. But a decade later, with even the Obama administration cautiously assessing the potential of a nuclear Iran, it may prove to have been rather optimistic.

5

A Cultural "Climate Change"?

This book set out, in essence, to answer the question of how America, in the seven or so years following 9/11, became what it did – how torture became a "legitimate" subject of debate, how the majority were led to support, or at least not oppose, an invasion of Iraq on highly dubious grounds, how that same majority came to re-elect the administration that had dragged its young men and women into what looked increasingly like a quagmire, despite all the evidence emerging from that country. In an attempt to answer this question, it has traced the evolution of the "structure of feeling" back to the end of the Cold War, a structure of feeling of which Fukuyama's "end of history" and Huntington's "clash of civilizations," though ostensibly opposed, were both distinctly symptomatic, and I maintain that this structure of feeling and all that generates it can be held to account for the general consensus that formed around the War on Terror.

Thus, the preceding chapters set out to depict a near-monolithic structure of feeling that brought the media, the administration, and the military-industrial complex more broadly into an apparently seamless and undefeatable entity impervious to resistance and free of contradictions. This, at least, was the administration's intention: to tap into the spirit of the times by constructing a new metanarrative, a victory narrative, that would place the Bush administration at the helm of a new global order in which "terror" would become a thing of the past. This final chapter, therefore, addresses the gradual unravelling of the victory narrative – an unravelling that, I will argue, is just as much an outcome of its meticulously constructed nature as its initial plausibility was. How else to explain the administration's need for impeccable micromanagement – of news coverage, of image dissemination, of damage control? If the narrative, indeed, was that dominant from beginning to end, why did Bush have to reinterpret, for "us," what we saw on our own television screens – images of torture and violence, of a quagmire increasingly reminiscent of the Vietnam War?

Of course, as Croft and Halloway correctly insist, there had always been an undercurrent of debate and dissent, even if, by and large, it had been silenced by a dominant narrative that at times even suggested that dissent amounted to treason. As the years dragged on, however, the question of whether a "war" on "terror" could ever achieve its objectives gained traction outside the academy and became increasingly evident in popular cultural production, prompting an increasingly widespread demand for an explanation, a manifestation perhaps of a new Vietnam Syndrome at a different time and in a different guise. The latter years of the War on Terror proved the twilight of the Bush era, with the transformation of righteous vengeance into profound unease, of moral certitude into embarrassment and shame, of assured victory into chaos and defeat – or at best, in the case of Iraq, neither victory nor defeat as of 1 September 2010, the date of the official American "withdrawal," or rather, Obama's attempt to "end the war responsibly." By this point, the integrity of the narrative had long been in question. Certainly, the fundamental structural instability of post-industrial "frontier capitalism" was increasingly apparent, despite the "structure of feeling" it generated, one that converged, for some time, with popular culture and the victory narrative, as well as the politics of fear. The "cultural climate change" evident in more recent developments is thus the subject of this final chapter.

VIETNAM SYNDROME, REVISITED?

In keeping with the overall theoretical paradigm informing the rest of this book, I will argue that the new Vietnam Syndrome cannot be explained as merely a response to the deterioration of the "war" and its supporting narrative. To explain it as such would go against this book's overall contention that a "structure of feeling" accompanying late capitalism has been integral to the politics of fear exploited by the administration following the attacks of 9/11. That structure of feeling, after all, cannot simply have disappeared along with the legitimacy of the administration's narrative. Rather, it remains as strong as or stronger than ever and continues to manifest itself in cultural production, the presiding aesthetic of which remains the elimination of a "mediating" barrier between subject and object. This chapter will show, however, that while on the one hand popular opinion can be manipulated, and consensus formed, against the backdrop of this structure of feeling, it can also be the site of dissent and resistance by exposing, at some level, the contradictions of the system that sustains it. The combination of *zeitgeist*, media, and geopolitics that enabled, in the cultural imaginary, the "kicking" of Vietnam Syndrome through the spectacle of Gulf War I was the same combination that gave rise to insoluble moral chaos and confusion, finger-pointing, evasion, and "horror" of a distinctly "Kurtzian" nature – a horror invoked first by Joseph Conrad and later by Francis Ford Coppola, as well as by other Vietnam-era directors, and was apparent once again in various cinematic interpretations of Bush's War on Terror. Paul Haggis's *In the Valley of Elah*, Gavin Hood's *Rendition*, Nick Broomfield's *Battle for Haditha*, Kimberly Peirce's *Stop-Loss*, Kathryn Bigelow's *The Hurt Locker*, and a host of documentaries, including Errol Morris's *Standard Operating Procedure*, not all of which can be given full attention in this chapter, are only a few examples of how what I have called the "aesthetics of hegemony" can be turned against the prevailing ideology, just as images – in what has been, more than any other, a battle of images – can backfire against those who would control their dissemination.

SOME BACKGROUND: THE IRAQ STUDY GROUP REPORT

Before launching into a theoretical discussion, it is perhaps useful to briefly reiterate the historical context in which dissent took on a more "acceptable" public role.

Indeed, the tide had begun to turn before 6 December 2006, some five years into America's War on Terror and approximately three and a half years following the invasion of Iraq,[1] when a group commissioned by Congress made public its assessment of the "situation" along with a number of recommendations for improving it. The Iraq Study Group (ISG), funded by a $1.3-million grant from the United States Institute of Peace, comprised ten prominent Americans, both Democrats and Republicans, all of whom had had illustrious careers in the public service. Led by former Secretary of State James Baker and former Democratic Congressman Lee Hamilton, the group travelled to Iraq to assess the escalating crisis in both political and military terms and to consider its implications for security and reconstruction.

The results of the study were somewhat less than heartening to the administration. The situation in Iraq, they reported, was "grave and deteriorating," and "[n]o one [could] guarantee that any course of action in Iraq at [that] point [would] stop sectarian warfare, growing violence, or a slide towards chaos." What had already become a "lengthy and costly war" seemed destined, "if current trends [continued]," to drag on indefinitely with scant chance of success, and many Americans, in the ISG's words, were growing "dissatisfied" with the progress of the enterprise. In the report's executive summary, the "situation" is characterized thus:

> The challenges in Iraq are complex. Violence is increasing in scope and lethality. It is fed by a Sunni Arab insurgency, Shiite militias and death squads, al Qaeda, and widespread criminality. Sectarian conflict is the principal challenge to stability. The Iraqi people have a democratically elected government, yet it is not adequately advancing national reconciliation, providing basic security, or delivering essential services. Pessimism is pervasive. If the situation continues to deteriorate, the consequences would be severe. A slide toward chaos could trigger the collapse of Iraq's government and a humanitarian catastrophe. Neighboring countries could intervene. Sunni–Shia clashes could spread. Al Qaeda could win a propaganda victory and expand its base of operations. The global standing of the United States could be diminished. Americans could become more polarized.[2]

This was a far cry from the hopes and promises issued repeatedly by the Bush administration leading up to the invasion and over the course of its first three years. Already mired in Afghanistan, where the military had toppled the autocratic Taliban regime and now faced escalating internecine conflict, the Bush administration had sent its troops into Iraq ostensibly to dismantle Saddam Hussein's putative WMD infrastructure and remove the dictator from power. Drawing on the generalized anxiety produced by the 11 September terrorist attacks, as well as the liberal sympathies of its more dovish opponents, the administration justified, planned for, and executed an invasion against the explicit wishes of the international community and in outright defiance of international law, giving the lie to the cop/

criminal scenario encoded in popular culture. Time and again, the rhetoric of presidential statements strove to orchestrate a consensus based both on fear and, ironically though logically, on the precepts of liberal-democratic tolerance: Hussein's Iraq was, according to Bush, one of a number of "outlaw regimes" that "seek and possess nuclear, chemical and biological weapons,"[3] and despite assertions to the contrary from not only the United Nations but even American agencies charged with assessing the threat, the only means of defusing the dictator's threat to world peace was to forcibly remove the Ba'athists from power and replace them with a democratic government. But when by 2004 it became clear that the alleged WMDs were nowhere to be found, the failure to legitimate the enterprise on the grounds of pre-emptive self-defence prompted a shift in focus, foregrounding instead the imperative of democratization and the spread of American values to parts of the world accustomed to oppression and tyranny. Imagery of cheering crowds, falling statues, and "free" elections was manipulated to evoke and satisfy distinctly liberal sympathies.[4] Yet over time it became increasingly apparent that the removal of the notorious dictator from power had failed to yield the promised benefits for the people of Iraq.

Indeed, by the summer of 2007, following the "surge" in US military and "diplomatic" activity,[5] the situation "on the ground" was being described as essentially hopeless. According to Republican Senator Chuck Hagel, erstwhile proponent of the war in Iraq, the country was "coming undone," with a regime that was "weaker by the day": "The police are corrupt, top to bottom. The oil problem is a huge problem. They still can't get anything through the parliament – no hydrocarbon law, no de-Baathification law, no provincial elections (needed to bring Sunnis into the governing process)."[6]

What the facts were suggesting was the unsurprising conclusion that the US administration had led its troops into a war on false premises at best and with minimal strategic consideration of the long-term consequences for the Middle East and the world at large. By that point, the false premises (WMDs) and increasingly convoluted logic (shifting justifications) were being discussed across an increasingly broad spectrum of critical commentary, journalistic, academic, and otherwise, both within the US and beyond.

What remains surprising – and indeed what the bulk of this book has attempted to address – is that a workable "consensus" on the invasion of Iraq was ever reached in the first place, not only at the upper levels of the administration but among the American people as well. Yet to claim that the American people had been "brainwashed" or "duped" into supporting (or tolerating) a military invasion is ultimately an inadequate explanation and certainly oversimplifies the issue. While the corporate news networks indeed overwhelmingly supported – at least initially – the administration's justifications for war, concealing facts that were inconvenient and distorting others to fit the prevailing viewpoint, they were by no means the only sources of information available to the American public. The Internet gave them access to a wide variety of critical commentary, including journalism from Britain, Canada, and the rest of the world. Moreover, if the important questions were not necessarily being raised on Fox News, they were at least present in some American print journalism, such as the *New York Times*, and central to the international response to American sabre-rattling during the build-up to war.

More troubling still, evidence of grievous human rights abuses (such as the 2004 images from Abu Ghraib), which were largely explained away at the time as evidence of the deviant behaviour of a few "bad apples," failed to raise enough questions to prevent the Bush administration from winning a second term in office that same year. And the re-election occurred despite the fact that the "bad apples" narrative could not be reconciled with the increasingly frequent practice of "rendition" whereby terror suspects were secretly transferred for "questioning" to countries not known for respecting human rights.

Yet if it wasn't mere "brainwashing" that accounted for the consensus developed around the war in Iraq, what was it? To be sure, the narrative was persuasive and totalizing, similar in scope to the classic detective form: a crime had been committed, and the Bush administration took charge of first "hunting down" the terrorists responsible for 9/11 and then of linking "rogue" regimes such as Saddam Hussein's to terror more generally in a "war" that could take decades to complete. Yet the "mastermind" of 9/11 had not yet been captured, the weapons of mass destruction were never found, fundamental American values (alongside domestic and international law) were flagrantly violated, and now thousands of troops in their twenties were returning from the wars to serve an extended sentence of post-traumatic stress and unemployment in a severely battered economy. And just as Bush's narrative eventually broke down, so too does the monolith described in the preceding chapters fail to account for the changes that led to the Republican defeat in 2008 and to more widespread opposition to the imperial endeavour in general.

To put it another way, the crisis in legitimation, only temporarily resolved by the revival of the victory narrative and backed by a politics of fear, had returned. Whereas that narrative had satisfied a demand for meaning arising out of the vertiginous experience of post-industrialism, a desire for a solid metaphysical ground from which to orient one's world view, it was nonetheless vulnerable to what psychoanalysis sees as the "return of the repressed," of that persistent hollowness that gives the lie to America's idea of itself as global saviour in an era that simply cannot be reduced to one of "good" versus "evil," as the Bush administration endeavoured to convince the public, with the corporate news networks in tandem.

This in itself shows that the "brainwashing" diagnosis is misleading, that if popular cultural production began to turn against the war, along with mainstream networks such as MSNBC, it had to be at least in part because there was a growing *demand* for dissent. And this demand could not have been spontaneous or imposed by the same forces that had tirelessly promoted the war for some six years. Communication is a two-way street, and even if one narrative succeeds in dominating for a substantial period, a counter-narrative (always present, as noted, although silenced) will eventually emerge. And since the postmodern "structure of feeling" had not changed in any way, one might say that this embodies the same sort of paradox that allowed both Fukuyama and Huntington to co-exist (both a "unipolar" and a "multipolar" world) or that merged a post–Cold War era (and the ostensible end it brought to nuclear war) with a rising tide of amorphous, undefinable fear. I have already explored the "aesthetics" associated with the postmodern or late-capitalist "structure of feeling" – an "aesthetics of hegemony" that is "im/mediate" in the sense of striving for non-mediation, for placing the subject in a first-person position against any number of threats, all of them conducive to vigilantism and/or militarism. I have noted that because nothing is more ideological than the "end of ideology," so too nothing is more mediated than the "end of mediation" (the ostensible elimination of the detached perspective from which the subject can observe and contextually interpret a historical sequence of events). *Black Hawk Down*, as I have shown, is a prime example of this "aesthetics of hegemony," with embedded reporting a close cousin. But what if Walter Benn Michaels's idea of "subject position" can be every bit as paradoxical as the structure of feeling of which it is a part – what if, that is, the first-person gaming aesthetic, the quality of im/mediacy can be exploited precisely to push back against the hegemony?

This chapter will further explore that possibility by examining some of the films that have emerged in recent years – the ones that exploit that very aesthetic to counter the dominant narrative – and detect what differentiates these products from films like *Black Hawk Down*. Clearly, such differences would not be sufficient to provoke any sort of popular revolution, but it is important to determine how the aesthetics of popular culture can be less a Benjaminian "aestheticization of politics" than a "politicization of the aesthetic" and thus contain, if only in microcosmic form, the critical force necessary for change.

THE UNITED STATES DOES NOT TORTURE

One thing that became increasingly apparent over the course of the War on Terror, particularly as it migrated from Afghanistan to Iraq, was a puzzling disconnect between the approved, official rhetoric and the indisputable facts that were appearing "on our screens" – facts that, as noted, Bush was at pains to interpret as evidence of impending victory. It was through these aporias that the fallacy structuring the totalizing narrative became evident, the contradiction underlying any constructed "totality" – namely, that pure boundlessness cannot of itself function recognizably as a system. If "frontier capitalism," by whatever means, continues to push its boundaries further and further outwards, it continuously destroys what constitutes its limits, or, in other words, what defines it. This is, of course, an abstraction that can serve no immediate, practical purpose in itself, but at the same time, it is an abstraction that finds concrete instantiation in recent Hollywood film, exposing in its own way the hollowness of the myth, and for this reason, if only for this reason, it is worth keeping in mind as fundamental to the following analyses.

"The United States does not torture," claims Meryl Streep's character in Gavin Hood's *Rendition*, echoing earlier claims by the Bush administration that its detention and interrogation policies were necessary and effective and fell within the boundaries of domestic and international law.[7] There is nothing terribly radical or even surprising about a senior government official uttering a lie in such blatant contradiction of the facts while "extraordinary rendition" (also referred to as "torture by proxy") became increasingly common under Bush's regime, if also increasingly subject to scrutiny. *Rendition* is, after all, a fairly conventional film with a range of stock characters, including the conscientious American agent who ultimately sets the victim free, reaffirming the triumph of Western liberalism over barbarity of any sort, even the kind abetted and sanctioned by the US government. Yet the film is not conventional in *every* respect and not just because it is one of the earlier critiques of the practices of the US government during the War on Terror. The crux of its critique, I would argue, lies in its narrative *form* – its breakdown of chronology – which we are not initially aware of and which reaffirms on a structural level the disconnect between what Streep's character says and what those working under her auspices are authorized to do. Content takes a back seat to form at the end of the film when the viewer is made aware of the power of suspension of belief, forced to reconstruct and re-evaluate all that he or she has understood to be the case throughout the film. Without, of course, undermining the horrors of torture – especially given the viewer's awareness that there are limits to what can be screened – *Rendition* nonetheless demonstrates that what we see is not necessarily what *is*, that the apodictic or ostensibly self-identical nature of the image does not necessarily correspond to reality. The master narrative of the war does not allow us any such opportunity, given its necessary adherence to convention and its corresponding teleology. The film suggests that it might not be the first time the viewer has bought into representation at the expense of reality. *Rendition* offers a moment – a jolt of detachment or estrangement – that recreates a space for objective reflection on what has been seen rather than, like *Black Hawk Down*, total, credulous immersion. I suppose it is less a matter of aesthetics here (the aesthetics of hegemony/counter-hegemony that I have described in relation to "im/mediacy") than a matter of narrative form, but the film's implicit critique of ostensibly "faithful" representation emerges in its narrative self-awareness, a critique that recurs in even more challenging films that bring the official 9/11 narrative (with narrative itself) into question.

Indeed, I would argue that this is the implicit critique built into nearly all of the Iraq war films of the latter years of the Bush administration (and the early years of Obama's): namely, that amid the sheer absurdity of a war in which, as Bush once put it, "[there are] no rules," representation and reality need no longer coincide. Sometimes this critique appears more at the recognizable level of plot than within the narrative form and/or in the very aesthetics of the film itself, but in all cases it points to a re-emergent Vietnam Syndrome, arising to destabilize the putative moral certitude deployed to legitimate the "just war" triggered in 2001.

THE AESTHETIC STRIKES BACK

As noted, the aesthetics of hegemony crystallizes around a number of distinct but related phenomena: the removal of a mediating "narrative" permitting a detached critical or political perspective; the ostensible "im/mediacy" of the visual media themselves; the positioning of the viewer/consumer in relation to the events depicted; and the "suturing" of this viewer to an imagined community, itself under perpetual threat. Such elements, I have argued, are symptomatic of a "structure of feeling" for which, indeed, "grand narratives" have come to an end, badly needed though they are, and under the right convergence of circumstances these elements can be, and have been, deployed in place of that missing narrative in the construction of a politics of fear. Again, take *Black Hawk Down*, perhaps the most striking instantiation of such a convergence and perhaps the most timely as well, although *Saving Private Ryan*, released in 1998, shows that this hegemonic aesthetics was already helping to shape the "cultural imaginary" well before 9/11. Both do away with the larger historical/geopolitical narrative in favour of an individualized perspective limited to personal survival and loyalty to one's brothers in arms. As noted in the earlier analysis of *Black Hawk Down*, however, this disavowal of ideology relies for its plausibility on the very absence of a larger narrative, allowing no detachment that might enable the viewer to step back and re-compute. A "grand narrative" explicitly stated is not a prerequisite for a politics of fear; within the aesthetics of hegemony, the latter may be manifested entirely in the gritty details of face-to-face combat, the chaotic camerawork, the placement of the viewing subject in a subject position that is in continuous, imminent danger. It is "biopolitics" (of a certain, strictly aesthetic sort)[8] rather than politics proper.

This is also the aesthetics of Paul Greengrass's *United 93*, praised by some as relatively "neutral" in its representation of events. Again, any wider political context would only be cumbersome and unnecessary, particularly given that we already know the outcome. But the *aesthetic* pressure, throughout, is uncompromising. The already claustrophobic space of an airplane – the all-too-familiar bustle of commuter travel, which reminds us that any ordinary place can be a centre – is transformed seamlessly into the setting for what follows, with an aesthetic of time and space that confines the viewer as well as the actors onscreen. Even when the action shifts to other settings, it retains the sense of panic and proximity that dominates the scene in the airplane itself and that is central to the politics of fear. Whatever Greengrass's intentions, the film's "faithfulness" to reality does little for politics proper but rather serves the politics of fear, the involvement of the viewer, the suturing of the subject to a nation under attack. It reaffirms what *Black Hawk Down* reaffirmed but in the context of 9/11 itself: the vulnerability of the victims and the nation, the inevitability of a military response, and the sense that there are no alternatives.

To analyze other films in a similar vein, such as Oliver Stone's *World Trade Center*, would be to belabour the point. However, such analysis would be in line with a fairly commonplace critical perspective that the mainstream film industry churns out, with the help of the Pentagon, the CIA, and other sympathetic bodies, film after film aimed at reinforcing the goals, implicit or explicit, of the American global enterprise. Certainly there is some truth to this critique, but it also underestimates the critical potential of Hollywood audiences as well as the persistence of what Jameson famously called the "political unconscious,"[9] that socio-economic undercurrent that is attuned to the injustices of the present and that strives for a genuine sense of community (as opposed to the "deadly simulacrum" described by the authors of *Afflicted Powers*). In other words, it is not true that Hollywood commands a mass audience of muppets *or* that it is the "liberal" establishment its neo-conservative enemies so stridently claim it to be. As a producer of commodities, it will respond, quite naturally, to what the audience seems to want, and granted, in many cases these commodities are the simplified, often regressive (and mostly inherently conservative) narratives, novel only in terms of their technology and special effects. To be sure, when it comes to films that deal expressly with political subject matter (such as *Rendition* or *Redacted*, the latter of which was screened at only fifteen theatres nationwide[10]), the system of production and distribution is usually manipulated so that the box-office returns garnered by wide-release blockbusters far exceed the humble revenues of more critical films. There is no doubt, in other words, that the industry caters by and large to the production and distribution of films that are at best not progressive in their approach to American foreign policy, either falling back upon the dehistoricized "few bad apples" scenario or a context in which America enters a situation with good intentions but insufficient information to restore real "order" to the "failed" states in question (real or fictional).[11] And this is quite apart from the countless films unrelated to the war in any way – the myriad films that are pure diversions from the truth and that rely for their revenues on the escapist fantasies of an audience wearied by anxiety and loss.

Even so, the situation is not, nor will it ever be, hopelessly monolithic. A political unconscious responsive to and productive of fissures within the given social order is always and already a threat to the micromanagement of imagery both real and fictitious that the ruling orders conspire to sustain. In fact, such micromanagement is necessary: if the "monolith" were firmly in place, such efforts to this end would not be needed. Bush would not need to interpret for us "what we are seeing on our screens." The fissure between representation and reality – no matter how ostensibly "faithful" to reality that representation strives to be – can indeed sustain a politics of fear, but it can also be turned against the dominant ideology. While this is obviously not the *solution* to the present crisis, it is important and will be the subject of analysis in the following pages: the very fact that it points to such a political unconscious is what offers a glimmer of hope.

A NEW VIETNAM SYNDROME? *THE HEART OF DARKNESS* TROPE IN IRAQ WAR FILMS

As noted, the mainstream representation of events in American culture involves a way of transmitting and perceiving that elicits the complicity of the viewing public in a way that has proved, to date, more in line with what could be called the "aesthetics of hegemony" than an "aesthetics of resistance." It is indeed what Benjamin would call the "aestheticization of politics" to the stultification of "the masses" and their unconscious anarchic or revolutionary drives, but such a strategy, *pace* Adorno, is a double-edged sword: what can make it so effective – in favour of the imperial endeavour – can also undercut it at a stroke. And in recent years, it seems that films like *Redacted*, *The Battle for Haditha*, and *The Hurt Locker*, which captured the award for Best Picture in 2010 over its far more populist (if to some extent still critical) rival *Avatar*, have succeeded in eliciting viewer complicity to give the lie to the dominant narrative rather than to bolster it. Eliciting complicity, in other words, may be a dangerous game, especially if you happen to be trying to win the sympathy of a mainstream American audience; there is no guarantee that the same techniques that work in some films will also work, even if intelligently exploited, in others.

It may seem odd or out of place, then, to refer back to late-nineteenth-century literature, to Joseph Conrad's *Heart of Darkness* and what I call the "*Heart of Darkness* trope," to explain my approach to the aesthetics of these films. Yet *Heart of Darkness* offers an ideal paradigm for narrative theory, for the study of representation, modernity, and modernism, as well as for what it says about an imperial civilization in decline. In some ways, it is a literary version of that drive for complicity I have tried to describe, eliciting as it does, in its compelling narrative form, a desire for meaning that merges with the (unreliable) narrator's, all the while revealing *and questioning* the power of linear narrative form in relation to the events and the spirit of its time. The relationship Conrad identifies between narrative form and geopolitical realities remains dispiritingly (if usefully) pertinent today: the setting has undoubtedly changed, as has the imperial powerhouse, but one has only to look beyond these surface details to see how its "trope" continues to apply.

In this chapter, my use of "trope" relates generally to theories of what constitutes a "conventional" narrative – an epistemologically satisfactory sort, indeed the most satisfactory in this sense, as Peter Brooks has said (following Todorov) of the detective story.[12] Indeed Brooks's reading of *Heart of Darkness* reveals it as a deliberate and troubling distortion of this otherwise heavily codified and totalizing form. As Todorov noted, detective fiction – of the type Victorian Britain most relished at the height of its economic and imperial power – distinguishes two layers of narrative in the genre, one (the story) "[telling] 'what really happened'" and the other "[explaining] 'how the reader (or the narrator) has come to know about it,'"[13] leading Brooks to declare it the "narrative of narratives, its classical structure a laying bare of the structure of all narrative in that it dramatizes the role of *szujet* and *fabula* and the nature of their relation."[14]

Not only does it provide, then, the requisite, satisfactory closure, a closure that in its retelling sheds light on the beginning and the middle (it is inherently satisfying in its form – a crime is committed, one question leads to another until the crime is solved beyond all doubt and all questions have been laid to rest), but it also reveals the logic of *retelling*, of narration, within its very structure. The detective follows, often quite literally, in the footsteps of the criminal in order to reach the solution; his actions, in other words, *retell* the story of the crime. The form exposes the workings of narrative not merely by bestowing order on seemingly disparate events but by revealing *how* these events are placed in order. For Brooks, this literary aesthetic reached its peak with that of British imperialism and a Western faith in linear narrative more generally as the principal means of comprehending mankind's origin, present, and destiny. Crime and inquest run parallel to the structuralist paradigm of story (the events themselves) and plot (the "common thread upon which [such events] might all hang," according to the master of plot, Sherlock Holmes);[15] elements that seem unrelated are brought together by the detective in such a way as to reinforce an unerring faith in the power of the scientific method and deductive logic to explain the world. It was thus a fitting form for what Brooks calls the "great nineteenth-century narrative tradition that in history, philosophy, and a host of other fields as well as literature, conceived certain kinds of knowledge and truth to be inherently narrative, understandable (and expoundable) only by way of sequence, in a temporal unfolding," marking an era in which "authors and their public apparently [shared] the conviction that plots were a viable and necessary way of organizing and interpreting the world, and that in working out and working through plots ... they were engaged in a prime, irreducible act of how human life acquires meaning."[16] We *expect* the end to shed light on a cryptic beginning and middle; we become drawn into the narrative in a search for resolution, for the imposition of order upon chaos.

Heart of Darkness, Brooks convincingly argues, is a significant and revealing variation on that theme: a crime of murky implications has been committed, and Marlow, framed by the narration of a member of his audience, tells the story of his mission to find the rogue Colonel Kurtz. As Marlow journeys upriver, he is drawn ever closer to the mystery of Kurtz's mindset as he progressively distances himself from the hallmarks of "civilization" and approaches what he finally declares his "answer": Kurtz's wholesale repudiation of "civilization" itself, his having (in the terminology of the time) "gone native," turned his back on the signifiers of European society, and looked directly into the abyss, the unrepresentable, or to state it in quite obvious terms, the heart of darkness itself. As Marlow progresses toward the ending that ought – according to the conventions of the genre on which the text is modelled – to confer meaning onto the beginning and the middle, his tone takes on a reverence, a desire, that strongly inflects the act of reading itself. Yet finally, Brooks argues, Marlow is at pains to impose meaning on what appears, disconcertingly, to possess none at all;[17] Kurtz's famous dying words, "the horror, the horror," fail to indulge the reader's craving for resolution. Marlow insists that Kurtz "had summed up – he had judged ... it was an affirmation, a moral victory paid for by innumerable defeats, by abominable terrors, by abominable satisfactions. It *was* a victory,"[18] yet the horror, curiously, remains beyond the reach of what can be signified. Despite the explanations Marlow fabricates to justify the telling of the tale, Conrad reveals the emptiness at its core, at the "heart of darkness" that gives the novella its name. Narrative resolution had already been undermined by the discovery of Kurtz's paper for the "International Society for the Suppression of Savage Customs," which gave Marlow "the notion of an exotic Immensity ruled by an august Benevolence ... unless a kind of note at the foot of the page, scrawled evidently much later in an unsteady hand, may be regarded as the exposition of the method ... at the end of that moving appeal to every altruistic sentiment it blazed at you luminous and terrifying like a flash of lightning in a serene sky: 'Exterminate all the brutes!'"[19] The sense of ostensible altruism undermined by "method," of "the idea" betrayed for what it is, foreshadows what is to come and explains, if in hindsight, the sense of unease with which Marlow's tale concludes.

Thus are Marlow, his listener (the framing narrator), and the reader drawn into the enigmatic "horror" that Kurtz describes, drawing his last breath at a place as far from "civilization" as can be imagined. To the extent that Marlow's narration follows the pattern of a detective story, the reader *wants* the ending to shed light on the cryptic beginning and the middle but is given a conclusion that, infuriatingly, provides no such illumination. It seems, then, that Conrad had his finger on the pulse of the era – on the genuine horror of imperial capitalism and the imminent breakdown of an overstretched system – and he gave us Brooks's "detective story gone modernist," a story displaying "an acute self-consciousness about the organizing features of traditional narrative, working with them still, but suspiciously, with constant reference to the inadequacy of the inherited orders of meaning."[20]

If America has a formal equivalent to the model of the Victorian detective narrative – and this is not to deny that the latter genre was quite seamlessly integrated into American cultural production in all media as well – it is the form of the western, which, while it does not reveal the functions of plot in the same way that the detective story does, nonetheless incorporates some of its elements into what is retroactively constructed as a uniquely American foundational myth. The "Wild West" and its manifold unknowns stand in for the mystery the detective must solve; the "frontier" marks the ever-moving threshold of westward expansion, separating the known and the orderly from the unknown and disorderly. Like the detective, the western protagonist must bring order to disorder, law to law-lessness, and in so doing to render darkness into light. The equivalent of the crime, as Engelhardt describes it, usually consists in the ambush of westward-bound protagonists by Native Americans, followed by a "justified" retaliatory slaughter that at once confirms the moral superiority of the "victims" and confers intelligibility upon a land hitherto unknown. It is this foundational narrative more than any other that bolstered the American sense of "victory culture"[21] at least until, for Engelhardt, the dropping of the atomic bombs in Japan, followed by the wars in Korea and Vietnam, and its hybrid-ization with the conventions of the detective tale may be seen in the imposition of order upon chaos that naturally ensues. Victorian England's quintessential narrative form reinforced ideologically what the Western came to reinforce at the outset of the American Century – a notion of manifest destiny, of law and order, crime and retribu-tion, self and other, reaffirming the monopoly of violence granted the state over its "enemies," internal or external. And there is surely a link to be found between European imperialism and American westward expansion, between colonial occupation and the American crossing into "untamed" or "hostile" territory with all its inher-ent savagery.

But the insularity of the form, the identification between the protagonist's journey and that of the Self into a great unknown domin-ated by the Other, came into question following the Second World

War in the same way that the detective genre did in Conrad's proto-modernist masterpiece. The link between it and the current geopolitical situation first became apparent in Francis Ford Coppola's adaptation of Conrad in the 1979 film *Apocalypse Now*, which brought the "*Heart of Darkness* trope" into the present in its cinematic portrayal of an imperialistic war.

Of course, as a modern adaptation of Conrad's tale, the film could not help but incorporate this trope, but in doing so, I will argue, it bridges the imperialism of Conrad's era with that of our own while subtly merging the detective paradigm with that of the western. The periodic voice-overs alone could not provide the presumed insularity of Marlow's first-person narration, but the camera-as-narrator, and Coppola's deft exploitation of the cinematic medium, revealed the aporia inherent in the act of representation, the unavoidable fact that whatever is being narrated – cinematically or otherwise – can never achieve self-identity with its referent. The "trope" is transposed into the representation of the Vietnam War, with the "official" narrative – that communist China sought "the domination of Southeast Asia, and indeed ... the domination of the great world beyond," with Ho Chi Minh's "reign of terror" encroaching upon the "peace and security" of the Vietnamese[22] – undermined by a foreign venture essentially imperialistic in nature, seeking to preserve that nebulous phenomenon known as "American interests" abroad. The ostensible altruism that underwrote Kurtz's "benevolence" in bringing Western civilization to the "savages" of Africa is brought to bear on America's "defence" of South Vietnam and simultaneously merged with the threat to America posed by the "domino effect" of communism, a spurious conflation that would be seen later in Iraq. But as the critics of the war were more than well aware, the rhetoric concealed certain pockets of darkness that, despite the greater freedom allowed to journalists at the time, were often not exposed until well after the fact.

Coppola's Kurtz, despite criticisms of the final third of the movie as overly "metaphysical" and "pompous,"[23] is in fact quite true to Marlow's, articulating (if more clearly, to meet the demands of the medium) a "philosophy" premised on unspeakable horror, on an unfathomable emptiness: "You have to have men who are moral ... and at the same time who are able to utilize their primordial instincts to kill without feeling ... without passion ... without judgment ... Because it's judgment that defeats us."[24] Here, though, the unsettling complicity that draws the reader into Marlow's triumphant affirmation of "the horror" as an "answer" of sorts is integrated into cinematic perspective, into the act of *viewing* – into the *subject position* and perspective of the viewer in relation to the action. Both texts display an awareness of their own narrativity and the impossibility of "faithful" narrative as such, exposing the inadequacy of representation while at the same time incriminating, to some extent, the viewer. This is particularly the case in Coppola's deployment of the cinematic medium – not only is the viewer drawn by verisimilitude to *believe* more thoroughly in the story, but more important, he or she is drawn to participate: the viewer cannot help but be complicit in the sublimity of the famous "Ride of the Valkyries" scene, which depicts the indiscriminate slaughter of Vietnamese, some armed, some not, from the first-person vantage point of a soldier aboard a Huey, even more than the reader of Conrad's text is complicit in the desire propelling the narrative forward. The scene approaches the Kantian sublime in its magnitude and the Burkean sublime in the terror it evokes (terror being a necessary condition of the sublime, according to Burke), and in so doing it puts the viewer into Willard's position when we finally come face to face with Kurtz, who has seen and committed unimaginable atrocities: we can *kill* him, we are told, but we *cannot judge*. And how can the viewer judge – objectively – having participated in that brutal, unforgiving spectacle early in the film with that degree of *jouissance* only the cinematic sublime can afford?

Coppola had a keen sense, in other words, for what his predecessor was attempting to demonstrate – the futility of representation (at least in the sense of a "grand" or "victory" narrative) in a world beset by imperial atrocities. The ironic, unsettling awareness of narrativity that Conrad brought to his text is enhanced by the capacity of Coppola's medium; the blurring of boundaries between audience and spectacle in the Valkyries scene is complemented by a cameo appearance of Coppola himself, actively directing the soldiers and in so doing foregrounding the ambiguity between cinematic direction, newsreel direction, and reality, bringing into question the objective frameworks of mediation, rational selection and combination, linear narrative, and resolution as a whole. The spectator, in the no-man's-land that Coppola creates, is drawn into the madness of a "philosophy" determined by an excess of power, a madness without bounds that underlies the will to power itself. The massacre at My

Lai, initially hailed as an American victory, is perhaps an iconic, real-life equivalent to this trope of excessive power taken to unthinkable extremes: *Apocalypse Now*, then, is the detective story/frontier narrative, the ending of which, like that of the novel that inspired it, sheds not light but darkness on the story that precedes it. The profound unease with which the viewer is left is precisely what underlies Vietnam Syndrome, the cultural pathology deemed "cured" by Bush Sr following the Gulf War of 1991. We may be given the illusion, in Vietnam, in the first Gulf War and the second, that we can witness it all firsthand, in its gritty realism, but the great frustration is that we cannot: that what can be shown is never equivalent to what *is*. And again, it is the unsettling persistence of this fact that is brought to bear in the emergent and continuing cinematic critiques of the war in Iraq.

REDACTED: THE BRIDGE TO GULF WAR II

The techniques of storytelling deployed by Conrad and Coppola, as well as the aesthetic developments they enable, played out at the level of both popular cultural production and news coverage and evolved even further as the anti–Iraq War film made its debut on the silver screen. In these films, the leading directors are all too aware of the constraints of representation and willing to use that awareness to full advantage. In some of the best Iraq War films, as in *Apocalypse Now*, the viewer involvement I described with respect to *Black Hawk Down*, which elicited an unthinking complicity with militarism in an age that questioned grand narrative (namely, the "legitimate defense of one's own life"[25]), is brought directly to the forefront, only to be turned against the hegemonic paradigm itself, creating a new "syndrome" hardly different from its predecessor.

The end of "grand narratives," as the postmodernists say, and as I've discussed throughout this book, is connected to Jameson's "weakening of history" and a "mutation in space" for which we lack the "perceptual equipment";[26] it removes the "mediating" element in the subject–object relationship, rendering all the more urgent Lyotard's question: "Where, after the metanarratives, can legitimacy reside?"[27] As Eagleton notes, the West has become "disabled at the very moment when it needs to affirm its universal authority," having "embarked on a more ambitiously aggressive foreign policy than ever before," and it "needs some spiritual legitimation for this project at just the time when it is threatening to come apart at the cultural seams."[28] Hence, as discussed, the War on Terror: as Philip Hammond notes, war since 1991 has been "driven by attempts on the part of Western leaders to recapture a sense of purpose and meaning, both for themselves and their societies."[29] It has furnished (to some extent) the metaphysical, narrative grounds of crime, resolution, and punishment that epitomized an earlier, more optimistic global outlook, one that not only put its wholehearted faith in the explanatory power of narrative – whether the detective narrative or the frontier western – but that also posited a teleology, a utopian goal that would herald the pinnacle of "progress." Less has changed between the late nineteenth century and the early twenty-first than we might assume. "Freedom" and "free trade," now commonly conflated in the term "the free market," are used interchangeably in the grand narrative of Western neo-imperialism, and the promise of the War on Terror was a world in which "our children and our children's children"[30] would know a degree of security and prosperity unimaginable on 11 September 2001.

I cannot overstate the centrality of the aesthetics attached to this narrative and to the structure of feeling that sustains it, even if now, in a globalized world – or in the cultural imaginary of a globalized world – one cannot go "beyond" the frontier, so "the rest" is as much inside us as "the West" and cannot be so easily mapped out. The aesthetics of posthistory has undergone a corresponding shift in its mediating forms and functions, indeed in many cases to the point at which, as I have argued, there would seem to be no mediation at all. Yet again, as this chapter points out, these forms and functions are a double-edged sword: while the ostensible absence of a mediating narrative can on the one hand, as seen, be deployed to perpetuate a politics of fear (*Black Hawk Down*), it can equally be used to reveal the hopeless inadequacy of our "grand narrative" frameworks, and this is what films like *Redacted*, *The Battle for Haditha*, and *The Hurt Locker*, among others, have achieved.

Brian de Palma's *Redacted* (2007), with its hyper-awareness of the camera as the storytelling medium and its deliberate, documentary-inspired placement of the viewer in the "first-person" position, retains something of the western in that its protagonists are sent to reinforce and guard the "frontier" of global capitalism, but "going native" has now lost its terrifying/exhilarating exoticism. With communism gone, and frontier capitalism pushing up against its limits, the "crisis in legitimation" already described has reached new heights, and in this context even the politics of fear is increasingly unconvincing. In the absence of a credible link between Iraq and Islamic terrorist networks, and given the failure to find Saddam's purported weapons of mass destruction, "self-defence" no longer seemed a reason to be at war. Further, as the situation in Iraq spiralled grimly out of control, the alleged "altruism" of the occupiers in itself had come into question.

Legitimation requires narrative, and narrative requires leadership (at least insofar as plot can be described as a function of character), and it is to a considerable extent the vacuum in leadership that brought into question America's willingness to invade Iraq on the suspect premises that it did. What *Redacted* and its generation of antiwar films present is not, as in *Apocalypse Now*, only a problem of leadership gone mad but of leadership gone altogether. *Redacted*, *In the Valley of Elah*, *The Battle for Haditha*, and similar films feature young, inexperienced troops with no clear direction and little security but equipped, importantly, with a grotesque excess of firepower. This same lack of leadership comes through in the films' cinematic techniques that emphasize the gritty, hyperrealistic, deceptively amateurish first-person perspective, as they did in *Black Hawk Down* but without reference to the "humanitarian" mission that supposedly contextualized the latter. The viewer has only Michaels's "subject position" to rely on, the ethos of "kill or be killed" that structures the experience of first-person video games. And instead of supporting the grand narrative, as it does in Scott's and Spielberg's films, the first-person aesthetic is exploited precisely to accentuate the confusion, the disorientation, the absence of the sort of spiritual legitimation America so badly needs.

Redacted as a text is fully aware of the impossibility of representation and thereby even more acutely of its own narrativity, and this comes through in its unrelenting self-reflexivity, its metafictional claims. Through the camera-vision of a young recruit aspiring to become a filmmaker, much of the action is depicted in amateur documentary style, resulting in a grainy, first-person aesthetic quite familiar to much of its target audience. De Palma also inserts other mediated forms: an intrusive cinematic narrative presented by French journalists attempting to document the war, footage from an Arabic news channel, online footage posted by insurgents, surveillance footage from the base camp as well as from military interrogation and psychological examination rooms, YouTube videos posted by Americans back home, and so forth. The ubiquity of cameras is far from lost on de Palma, who brings a keen, if sometimes too obvious, awareness of narrativity to the film as a whole. Nor is the ubiquity of *redaction* lost on him, and I do not mean "redaction" at the level of plot alone or as limited to administrative cover-ups and the "bad apples" narrative. Rather, de Palma recognizes that every narrative has its counter-narrative, one that must be discarded for the purposes of narrative integrity. The resulting cubist framework thus reveals the war as more than the sum of its component narratives, as more than what the administration – or anyone – would have us believe it is. Redaction for de Palma is, in other words, a *structural necessity* of narration, the absent evidence of what remains untold; the drive toward authenticity here really does break though the "aura" in the way that Benjamin saw as potentially emancipatory (even though this breakthrough is so far confined to the theatre). The removal of the mediating "context" so central to the distance between narrator and narratee makes the viewer complicit in a horror to which he or she would rather not be privy, in this case the vicious rape and murder of a fifteen-year-old girl and the killing of her family. In each instance of narration, de Palma implies that out of sheer structural necessity, a thing cannot be conveyed without simultaneously leaving another thing out – in other words, that redaction is inherent to narrative. And in a twist on the aesthetic that structured *Black Hawk Down*, the uncompromising realism that this generation of viewers demands, de Palma gives more than is bargained for – complicity not just in warfare but in crime straight out, as well as in the cover-up that follows. This is why de Palma's message, even though delivered with a sledgehammer, is so important: it seizes on that video-game realism to which viewers are increasingly accustomed and turns it 180 degrees to make the viewers not the victims (as in *Black Hawk Down*) but the victimizers. The detective paradigm is so reversed as to present the crime *instead* of its solution; the paradigm of the Wild West may remain but only to reveal how utterly degraded that paradigm has become.

Thus, in *Heart of Darkness* Marlow (or his narrator) "redacts" to the extent that the meaningless is given a meaning; the reader is complicit in the undercurrent of desire upon which the narrative is based; the sense of an ending is critical to the genre, and Marlow as a "storyteller" of the epic variety knows this. In *Apocalypse Now*, the viewer is told that he or she "cannot judge" – and having participated in the Valkyries scene, having succumbed to the sublimity and terror with a kind of *jouissance*, the viewer really cannot, even if he or she looks for meaning all the same. In *Redacted*, by virtue of the almost exclusive first-person presentation and the inevitable direction of the narrative, the viewer is now fully complicit in a horrendous crime; the detective story, in the frontier land of capitalist expansion, has been turned quite inside out. It seems that for these films, the greater their awareness of their own narrativity, the greater the viewer's involvement such that, in the case of a film like *Redacted*, the viewer responds in disgust instead of mindless, credulous fear. Whereas the very same aesthetic (first-person perspective, the "subject position)," as skilfully crafted in *Black Hawk Down*, can be used to evoke a militaristic response, in such films the absence of an *awareness* of narrativity precludes a properly critical viewpoint on the part of the viewer. By contrast, the narrative layers and self-awareness combined with that same aesthetic in a film like *Redacted* make a harrowing statement connecting power to madness and cruelty of the most unthinkable kind, embedding the viewer in a traumatized regiment without leadership or direction, trapped in a "wilderness" for reasons unclear, able to reassert "masculinity" through only the most cowardly and senseless of acts. There is certainly no more of a "grand narrative" in *Redacted* than there is in *Black Hawk Down*, but their respective political orientations are utterly opposed. That Iraq War films had only limited distribution does not undermine the effectiveness of the critique that they impose. On the contrary, it is at this aesthetic level – not at the level of plot, story, or official rhetoric or even of pictures beamed around the world from Abu Ghraib – that a glimmer of hope (however faint) can be detected. It is at the sensory level, the level at which the viewer is drawn in on a more than purely cerebral level, that a space is opened up for resistance, which may represent a "tapping in" to that more emancipatory dimension of the political unconscious. In a way, to change the "subject position" in what once seemed a desperate fight for one's life is to change, in effect, the subject itself, and this opens up a possibility, however minuscule it may seem, for real change. At the very least, it does raise the moral spectres of Vietnam and the cultural malaise that followed, and Vietnam Syndrome, while by no means a product of the cinema alone, certainly had a role in foreign policy decisions prior to 9/11. In other words, "Iraq

Syndrome" – of which, admittedly, antiwar cinema is only one facet – could potentially take on a similar role.

The same is true of Nick Broomfield's *Battle for Haditha*, which may be among the most well-rounded of the antiwar films. *Haditha*'s camera-narrator is a unified one, unlike DePalma's, but it switches between two principal narratives or narrative perspectives: that of a particular American Marines unit and that of a group of Iraqi citizens in Haditha, two of whom, a father and son, have become involved with al-Qaeda (which they themselves deem "crazy," suggesting that in post-invasion Iraq aiding the mujahedeen is often one of few ways to earn money) and planted an IED in a populated area. The event is based on a true story – the bomb was remotely detonated on 19 November 2005, killing one American and wounding two others, and in the subsequent few hours Americans shot and killed, indiscriminately, some twenty-four men, women, and children. The narrative of the American unit – including the reasons that some of the soldiers joined the Marines and the overall lack of understanding of why they are there – is interspersed with the narrative of a large Iraqi family celebration, and it is at, and following, the moment of explosion that the narrative switches most rapidly from one side to the other, giving perhaps more balanced coverage to both than any other film at the time. Neither side is completely innocent – the two who planted the roadside bomb are not associated with the group of civilians now under fire and had forced the evacuation of a house, American-style, in order to secure a vantage point from which to await the American convoy and detonate the bomb. The Americans, for their part, are a group of young, inexperienced, mostly frightened recruits (one joined simply to escape a dead-end existence in Philadelphia, another had been seriously wounded but resumed duty because he would have received just 10 per cent of his pay after his release), and their actions, horrific as they are, are driven largely by confusion and fear. It is an American drama insofar as the troops have clearly reached a breaking point, but equal or greater sympathy is shown to the Iraqi victims, mostly innocent, as they grieve their losses and take desperate measures to escape the gunfire. The usual trope of the badly injured American talking to a photo of his wife or girlfriend back home is undermined by the silencing of his words beneath the ambient noise and the sound of the Iraqis mourning their own dead. This is very different from *Black Hawk Down*, with the putative "enemy" an encroaching, uniformly hostile force whose own suffering is never depicted. The bomber, for his part, is seized by remorse as he watches the events unfold, even after a cleric assures him that the innocents are martyrs. One soldier displays visible guilt at what has just transpired, but this parallels rather than undermines the guilt of the father and son who planted the IED. Each point in favour of America has a counterpoint on the Iraqi side, and the viewer is given an equal dose of both.

The cold fact of American military superiority, including the ability to kill from a control room, is not concealed, while the knee-jerk terror of an IED attack on the ground is simultaneously invoked, not to exonerate the Marines but to suggest how desperately chaotic the situation had become on all sides. In this sense, *Haditha* is probably one of the better Western films about Iraq, and its presentation of much of the action from the side of what is usually depicted as foreign and inscrutable – the "Oriental" side – partially redeems an industry that for decades has produced and reproduced Engelhardt's victory narrative, the narrative of "justified" slaughter following an ambush on American troops. Whatever "victory" was achieved – and there was no clear victory insofar as the bombers evaded capture – is hollow to the core. When the Americans go mad, in other words, it is not only they who suffer – as is alleged by some critics of *Apocalypse Now* and by Chinua Achebe[31] with respect to *Heart of Darkness*.

Most important, the cinematic perspective gives us an aesthetic that is often "first-person," like Scott's in *Black Hawk Down*, only in this instance it is not exclusively the *American* "first person" who sees. Thus, the gritty realism of the film's aesthetic is far more conducive to critical response than that provided in films like *Black Hawk Down* in which only one perspective – the Western one – can be said to dominate and in which, despite mistakes on the part of the Americans, there remains an element of hierarchy and leadership. This too, then, is a 180 degree turn – evident in form as in content – that makes *Haditha* one of the more potentially radical films to emerge in the midst of a foundering war.

It is certainly true that, as many a Hollywood critic is apt to point out, films like *Redacted* and *Rendition* were not given the exposure of the typical blockbuster; even *The Hurt Locker*, which came up against James Cameron's *Avatar* in the 2010 Academy Awards, was far less widely distributed than the latter. Yet this does not undermine its critical potential. Indeed, *The Hurt Locker*, like a number of its contemporaries, invoked the anxieties associated with a Vietnam (or Iraq) Syndrome without providing the resolution that even *Redacted* managed to (*Redacted*, after all, featured a character who maintained an almost implausible moral integrity in the face of the crime and its subsequent cover-up). Its aesthetic is the fully involving one of films like *Redacted* and *Battle for Haditha*, repeatedly "embedding" the viewer in the immediate radius of any of a number of IED blasts. As in 24, the ticking-time-bomb intensity is brought into play, but the solution, importantly, is not torture, even though the head of the bomb disposal unit displays the rugged individualism and contempt for protocol of his televisual counterpart Jack Bauer. Indeed, unlike in the show 24, there is no visible subject *to* torture. And in no case is the tension put to rest with any finality; neither the occupiers nor the occupied partake in any illusion of collectivity of the sort that sustains the "psychic horse-trading"[32] Jameson sees as fundamental to the success of any blockbuster film. On the contrary, the main character is irresponsible, erratic, and unpredictable in what should be a leadership role, causing conflict and miscommunication within his unit to the point where they not quite jokingly contemplate the possibility of killing him "accidentally." Nor are the Iraqis, for their part, shown as a collective, good or evil; they are mainly spectators, idly lining the rooftops and balconies, either resigned to or mildly interested in the chaos inflicted by the placement and defusion of IEDs. Rarely are they depicted as the "enemy." Many are mere children. There is no simplistic narrative in which order is imposed on chaos, in which unity is achieved in the face of peril. The inability to define the enemy – a "they" group – undermines any success in defining a "we" group, an American self. Although it can be plausibly argued, as Achebe did with *Heart of Darkness*, that the "other" is no more than a backdrop for a Western drama, the non-linearity and chaos of the drama sets the film apart from the conventional imperialist trope and places it, plotless and with its implication of sameness without end, squarely in the antiwar camp. It is not, as some have suggested, an implicit endorsement of American intervention, or at least an implicit exoneration of America on the basis of its putative "good intentions," but rather, again, an exposure of lack of leadership, indicating ignorance at the highest levels and leading only to further chaos on the ground. The main character is sickened, much as Kurtz and Marlow are; for him, the chaos has become addictive, and it can only be assumed that any continuation of the "story," such as it is, would be a continuation of the same, in real life as onscreen.

The film's jarring perspectives and, perhaps more important, its occasional 180-degree portrayal of the enemy's point of view (as depicted, for instance, in the seemingly interminable desert shoot-out scene) invokes the appropriate level of anxiety but does not, as in mainstream films, defuse it, thus leaving no clear distinction between the "docile" Iraqis and the militant ones, no guarantee that on their next mission the protagonists will not be blown to pieces. The film, like its contemporaries, presents the conflicting subject positions that Michaels describes rather than a single subject position (that of the American point of view) and with no grand narrative to unite them, no overarching ideology to account for the disparate situations in which the bomb disposal unit finds itself throughout the film. It is a conflict of identities in which neither side appears more "justified" than the other. Neither side can be "known" or "deciphered" from a distinctly American viewpoint, as becomes evident with the unit leader's vigilante mission after a mistaken-identity situation convinces him that a young boy he knows has been senselessly and brutally killed. Further, there is no indication that the viewer must simply *accept* the reality of American military intervention in foreign countries as the right and honourable course of action, even when the intervention does not go as planned. The audience is given instead a world of conflicting identities, a world fraught with tension, and a tension ultimately unresolved. A collective is not re-established even at the level of the domicile, the family – a unit often invoked in war films to bring symbolic resolution to a fractured situation. Lack of leadership and lack of narrative intertwine once again to reveal the stark reality that in a "posthistorical" world, the spiritual legitimation required by the West to justify its endeavours is nowhere to be found.

AND THE BOX OFFICE HITS? *AVATAR* IN THE POSTHISTORICAL CONTEXT

For all that these antiwar films challenge the dominant ideology by means of its own principal aesthetic, they did not approach the box-office returns of the undisputed blockbuster of 2009, James Cameron's *Avatar*. For some, this high-tech mega-spectacle, with its references to "fighting terror with terror" and "shock and awe," as well as its critique of resource-driven imperialism, seemed evidence of a new sensibility following eight years of failure in American foreign policy. And to some extent it was. I will not dwell on the typical criticism of Cameron's films – that they are impressive in their visual effects while short on character development, trite in plot, and stilted in dialogue; that sort of criticism belongs elsewhere. Nor, however, will I attempt to argue that the film is unequivocally radical, as some have suggested, or indeed radical at all.

The 3D technology so effectively employed in *Avatar* eliminates the "mediating" distance even more than "embedded" reporting or the most grittily "realistic" of war films do, and this elimination of distance, as noted, can be used for progressive as well as reactionary purposes. And, indeed, it seemed overly "progressive" to the political right, which interpreted the film all too credulously as a direct allegory for the wars on Iraq and Afghanistan, condemning it as a "Big, Dull, America-Hating, PC Revenge Fantasy"[33] that asks "the audience to root for the defeat of American soldiers at the hands of an insurgency."[34] There is, of course, some truth to this judgment; like *Dances With Wolves* (if a little bit too much like *Dances With Wolves*), it presents imperialism from the perspective (largely) of the victims, a daring move in wartime – yet not radical, since the action unfolds on a fictional planet. On the surface, indeed, it can be sensibly argued that *Avatar* is a critique of America's actions abroad, linking space-age frontier capitalism with the brand we already know (Earth's own frontiers having presumably been transcended). And it certainly resonated in Palestine, where in February 2010 a number of protesters dressed as Na'vi to demonstrate against Israeli-imposed barriers separating them from the bulk of their farmland. Even leftist critics Arundhati Roy and Slavoj Žižek have discussed *Avatar* in relation to the struggles of the Dongria Kondh people in India, and China and Brazil have both seen appropriations of the film for the purposes of popular protest. As Henry Jenkins notes, "digital media has [*sic*] allowed many more consumers to take media into their own hands, hijacking culture for their own purposes. Shared narratives provide the foundation for strong social networks, generating spaces where ideas get discussed, knowledge gets produced, and culture gets created." For him, "the meaning of a popular film such as *Avatar* lies at the intersection between what the author wants to say and how the audience deploys his creation for their own communicative purposes."³⁵ In other words, despite my own – and others' – scepticism about a portrayal of the film as "radical," the ways in which it has since been politically appropriated speak to the potential it contains.

I would be quick to qualify this, of course, by pointing out the racist trope that links the Na'vi of the film with Native Americans (as "noble savages"), or that the film's "radicalism" is undermined by the fact that it takes place on another planet, with a fictional society standing in for the victims of imperialism here on Earth, or that it takes a conscientious American to ensure that the "evil corporation" and the American army are sent packing at the end of the film. The integration of the main character, Jake, into the body of his Na'vi avatar, as well as his marriage to the chief's daughter, brings a palpably symbolic resolution to the tension and unease evoked by the unwanted incursion of the military-industrial complex into the utopian society that is Pandora. Further, what is perhaps most profoundly regressive about the film is the pastoral mythology that structures it and that brings about its harmonious resolution. Combined with the technology that immerses the viewer in the fictional world the film generates, the play on the age-old trope of the American pastoral responds to a mythical organicist yearning that can indeed overwhelm the progressive "critique" of that country's endeavours abroad. The "psychic horse-trading" of which Jameson speaks is here at its most blindingly effective; anxieties are necessarily acknowledged and evoked but only to the point at which they can be safely re-contained in the myth of the communal, the pastoral, the integration of a Western (and inherently expansion-driven) value system with a nostalgic, organicist tradition that goes back, in America at least, to the Golden Age of Emerson and Thoreau. Moreover, like most collective nostalgias, it is a nostalgia for a time that never existed and that now exists only in the realm of the imaginary. The ostensible "critique," effete as it may be, is the proverbial piece of meat thrown, as McLuhan once put it, to "distract the watchdog of the mind"³⁶ as the real burglary takes place. The neo-liberal fantasy of a harmonious collective is what ultimately defuses the anxiety produced within the film, the tension invoked by the incursion of American weaponry into an idealized, organic society.

The above qualification is important; yet, as Jameson also argues, there may be within the organicist yearning a kernel of genuine desire for collectivity. Collectivity, of course, is by no means inherently a good thing: it can manifest itself, as indeed it has, in xenophobia, exclusivity, even violence toward the "other," the one who does not belong. On the other hand, in an age of social atomization and disintegration, such a yearning can be mobilized as a means of overcoming social barriers in a genuinely radical way. One might argue, that is, that the desire for community persists, in however "degraded" a form, and that the movie has to make this concession to a political unconscious – however feeble, in the end – is grounds for hope in spite of knee-jerk cynicism. Since I have never attended a protest dressed as a Na'vi, it is ultimately not up to me to condemn or to valorize the reception of the film from various cultural standpoints. Finally, whatever its drawbacks (and they are numerous), the ideological distance between *Avatar* at the end of the decade and *Black Hawk Down* at the beginning is, to say the least, quite substantial.

Why *The Hurt Locker* triumphed over *Avatar* at the Oscars is ultimately up to the critics; if the results were based on box-office revenues alone, then needless to say, Cameron's epic would have won by far. But *Avatar*'s overwhelming popularity does not mean that sensibilities concerning war, cultural identity, and peace are not undergoing a process of change. To what extent such change – located as it is for the most part in the cinema – will affect actual foreign policy is not, of course, measurable at this point. Yet alongside *The Hurt Locker* are all of its contemporaries, which also present both viewpoints and depict senseless slaughters and atrocities carried out by American troops. Atrocities are committed in every war, of course, and the lack of a cohesive "grand narrative" is not a precondition for terror, trauma, vigilantism, and breakdown (or for their portrayal). But in the cultural *representation* of war, and imperial war in particular, the lack of "grand narrative" in these recent films (notwithstanding *Avatar*) merges with both the dominant posthistorical aesthetic and the contradictions that undermine it. The comparative failure of antiwar films at the box office was not primarily due to lack of interest in the subject matter[37] but rather a result of the production and distribution system that governs the release of Hollywood films. And at any rate, the triumph of *The Hurt Locker* over *Avatar* may indicate that the critics, at least, are ready for material that engages more directly with the spirit and events of our time.

SPECULATIONS ON AESTHETIC POSSIBILITIES AT THE "END OF HISTORY"

It was not possible in this analysis to do a comprehensive assessment of every film to come out of Hollywood over the past decade. But the trend is striking. The ostensible absence of a mediating narrative that on the one hand was deployed to perpetuate the politics of fear – in *Black Hawk Down* and its ilk – has also been used to reveal the hopeless inadequacy of our "grand narrative" frameworks. In an already globalized world – some would argue a system without a centre, which is not a system at all[38] – the barriers between "us" and "them," the "West" and the "rest," are, *pace* Huntington, undermined to the point that a correspondingly dualistic narrative, pitting forces of good against forces of evil, may be quite nearly forced to adopt a fictional planet as its setting (although I retain my reservations about the "radicality" of such a move). With the erosion of legitimacy and leadership depicted in the present generation of antiwar films, the weakness of the "few bad apples" theory has become increasingly apparent; if the Abu Ghraib scandal of 2004 was to some extent incorporated into the grand narrative (and only to some extent) as an example of "bad apple" behaviour, it might be because it was only the first to so shake the American public's moral foundations. But the entire armed forces is not composed of "bad apples," and films like *Redacted* do not absolve the administration but rather condemn it in its drive to conceal the truth. The same is true of films such as *In the Valley of Elah* and *Stop-Loss*, which, taking place in America, explore the effects of trauma on soldiers while unavoidably condemning the system that sends them to war in the first place. It has indeed been suggested that one of the most stressful things a soldier can face in wartime is a lack of leadership,[39] and in each of these films a connection can be drawn between the chaotic nature of modern warfare and the notion that just maybe, in a broader geopolitical context, the soldiers should never have been sent there to begin with. The historical context of imperialism, while not always explicitly engaged, is still brought into question much as it was by *Apocalypse Now* and the book that inspired it. And this is in large part a function of the very same aesthetic that promoted a paranoid, militaristic reaction in *Black Hawk Down*; narrativity is now turned on its head, jarring viewers into a disturbingly altered consciousness of what narrative does and what it means and thereby inviting a critical perspective that undermines the dominant narrative.

The im/mediacy of instant mediation, then, can work against the hegemonic imperative quite as effectively as it can work for it, and it is indeed at this level of the image transmitted instantaneously, recorded, retained, and rebroadcast, as well as used for artistic purposes, that the latest imperial war has encountered one of its greatest challenges at the level of popular culture. The "authenticity" that inheres in the aesthetics of hegemony is equally conducive to an aesthetics that counters it, and while in a film like *Black Hawk Down* this aesthetics is indeed a one-way street, a film like *Redacted* – concluding, as it does, with censored (redacted) images from the actual conflict – presents us with the undeniable reality that the absence of mediation, of a consistent, monolithic narrative, combined with the capacity of the "enemy" to avail themselves of the same technologies as the "protagonists," can only undercut that illusion of dominance at the moment when the ruling powers most need it. The same technologies that enable surveillance of "insurgents," real or constructed as such, enable a corresponding counter-surveillance; the same technologies that keep troops in contact with their families at home are used by insurgents to promote their own agendas; the same technologies enlisted to reinforce our "grand narrative" by means of "embedded" reporting can be turned against it with the proliferation of Arabic networks equally global in their reach. This very reality is refracted by popular culture and brings about the unease of a new Vietnam Syndrome; the excess of imperialistic warfare is brought "home," by instant transmission, to the American consumer to counter the narratives of national security and altruism, and recent war films exploit this with undeniable clarity. *Redacted* is only one of the films that transposes the trope of imperialistic excess that informed films such as *Apocalypse Now* and *The Deer Hunter* and unravels the faith in linearity and narrative as they are articulated in conventional fiction. In particular, the capacity of narrative to articulate the horrors of imperialistic warfare is brought directly into question, as it was in both Conrad's text and Coppola's film.

Errol Morris's documentary *Standard Operating Procedure*, which presents the Abu Ghraib scandal of 2004 in a stark but understated way, demonstrates the power of the image – in its relation to the truth – to raise more questions than it answers. As Susan Sontag remarked in *The Guardian* on the initial release of the Abu

Ghraib photographs, it is ultimately not *what happens* in Iraq but what can be legitimately *told* about it that matters above all else: that is, for every image beamed around the world, there were countless others consigned to invisibility. The images, distasteful as they are, were ultimately incorporated into "our" narrative of the war; indeed, as she notes, the "focus of regret" on the release of those images "seemed the damage to America's claim to moral superiority, to its hegemonic goal of bringing 'freedom and democracy' to the benighted Middle East." Yet the increasing evidence of failure in Iraq and the recent efforts of contemporary filmmakers undermine this claim to moral superiority, a message to which viewers are becoming increasingly receptive, as the success of *The Hurt Locker* might suggest. A "culture of shamelessness" permeates the images from Iraq and gives increasing credibility to films like *Redacted* and *Battle for Haditha* that expose the rot at the core of the American endeavour. No leadership, no authorities – no ambassadors of the "law" – are present to retrace and retell the crimes, to bring culprits on either side to justice, to give the stories coherence and meaning; there is only "the horror," as Kurtz so cryptically informs Conrad's readers: the horror of checkpoints, the horror of rapes and murders, the horror of beheadings, the horror of indiscriminate slaughter. "Where once photographing war was the province of photojournalists," Sontag noted in her 2004 response, "now soldiers themselves are all photographers – recording their war, their fun ... their atrocities, and emailing them all over the globe."[40] The micromanagement of imagery by the Pentagon and the administration has given way to what for them must be a devastating loss of control: "embedded reporting" has gone one step too far, in a direction unanticipated by the architects of the new "journalism." The lack of authority thus comes to pervade all aspects of the war, including its coverage. The effects of this new dynamic are slow to unfold, but the dominant line, by the time of Obama's election in 2008, no longer had the hold on the popular imagination that it once did.

These films, both fiction and documentary, illustrate with astonishing clarity the absence of leadership, of co-ordination, of agreement among perpetrators and participants concerning the purpose of either the barbaric acts themselves or recording and disseminating them, highlighting the culture of mismanagement, permissiveness, and lack of accountability, not to mention the sickness, stress, and rage that accompany the living conditions of American troops and the lack of any clear rules of engagement, instructions, or restrictions. *Standard Operating Procedure*, notes W.J.T. Mitchell in *Harper's Magazine*, "provides almost no outside perspective ... [immersing] us in the testimony of the 'bad apples' who were present at the events ... [penetrating] into the interior of a famous historical event, and [leaving] the external narrative almost completely unstated and invisible."[41] This absolves neither the perpetrators nor the administration, and other films clearly incriminate the latter. Yet as the young filmmaker in *Redacted* eagerly proclaims, there is "no Hollywood action film, no narrative to make sense of it all," only a revelation of the failure of authority, an absence that parallels the absence of a mediating narrative in both films.

These films are by no means alone in their critique of the years following the Bush administration, and more can be expected as current and future administration efforts to solve the problems in Afghanistan and leave Iraq in a state of relative order, as well as carry on "overseas contingency operations,"[42] continue. As noted, this book is primarily a retrospective on the Bush years, particularly the post-9/11 years, not a prognosis for a "New American Century" that may well never materialize. And films – whatever the power of both the "aestheticization of politics" and its inverse – will never in and of themselves bring about the required change in the cultural and political climate; they must form part of a larger picture of far greater complexity and magnitude than what can be found on the screen. However, as more films emerge, ever more on the "blockbuster" scale – such as Ridley Scott's *Body of Lies* and Paul Greengrass's *Green Zone*, to name just two – it will become easier to gauge the popular cultural response, with greater hindsight, to the War on Terror and what it has meant to America. Thus far, such films have not depicted the heroism of combat against the "enemies of freedom," or even the brotherhood that forms among soldiers on the front, but rather a sprawling sort of despair, a horror, not unlike what we witnessed in Vietnam and its representations. The "heart of darkness" re-emerges in recent war narratives – a cyclical recurrence or "return of the repressed" whereby what seems at first to be a solid narrative promising a satisfactory conclusion becomes, through sheer excess, what Peter Brooks would call "unreadable": there is a disconnect between representation and reality that widens to the point that the consumption-satisfaction of the conventional narrative is fully disabled. In the end, there is no "solution," much less a moral certitude of the sort that the "conventional" narrative mode provides. From the Congo, then, into Vietnam and now Iraq: the "horror" undoes the narrative itself, reminding us that behind the safe world of representation and consumption-satisfaction is a chasm quite possibly too awful to contemplate. It may be too awful, and yet it is undeniably necessary and ultimately impossible to avoid, for in that very disconnect – one glossed over by the apodictic character of the aesthetics of hegemony – is a space that, by giving the lie to the "interpellation" of the subject and the illusion of collectivity, compels the politics of fear to yield to a politics proper, a politics that, like the outrage following the attacks of September 11, might eventually merge with an altered sensibility to bring about the social change so desperately needed.

Conclusion

On 17 September 2001, six days after the crime of the "official" master narrative – 9/11 – President George W. Bush declared to reporters at the Pentagon that "there [are] no rules."[1] He was referring to the actions of the 9/11 terrorists: "It's barbaric behavior. They slit throats of women on airplanes in order to achieve an objective that is beyond comprehension. And they like to hit and then they like to hide out ... And we're adjusting our thinking to the new type of enemy. These are terrorists that have no borders." No borders, no mediation, no distance: the enemy is already within. And as films like *Redacted* and images from Guantánamo and Abu Ghraib clearly demonstrate, the enemy *is* already within. It was Lyotard who insisted that "when there are no rules, there is no game,"[2] and when there is no game, there is no narrative. What *Heart of Darkness* seems to tell us is that there never *was* a game, that beneath the veneer of one – what Marlow calls the "idea" behind the "conquest of the earth, which is not a pretty thing when you look into it too much"[3] – lurks a darkness that, in Bush's own words, is fully "beyond comprehension" and verbalization. Whether we've had to "adjust our thinking to the new type of enemy" or whether we harboured it all along is what we ask ourselves as evidence of atrocity and destruction illuminates the gaps in the tightly controlled, micromanaged narrative of America's "just war." The footage on our screens has given way from the initial "shock and awe" of a bombing campaign reminiscent of Gulf War I to a seemingly endless barrage of conflict and chaos in a moral, ideological, and literal desert. Certain filmmakers, as noted above, have been quick to grasp this contradiction and expose it, if only to a limited number of viewers in contrast to films like *Avatar*, but this "war" cannot go on forever without greater numbers mobilizing against it, whether through battle fatigue more generally or in light of the paradigm shift imposed by the deployment of the hyper-realist aesthetic against its own initial aims. That is, if the subversion of the realist aesthetic in popular culture cannot by itself prevent further brutality on either side of the conflict or even dissuade America from undertaking further foreign endeavours, it can nonetheless destabilize the ostensible moral certitude invoked to justify such projects, bringing about a Vietnam Syndrome updated to reflect our age – a malaise allegedly "kicked" by Gulf War I, in the words of Bush Sr – and undermining America's official justificatory strategies in the process. Certainly, as Mitchell notes, the Abu Ghraib photographs were never enough to bring the war to an end, in part because of the "bad apples" hypothesis,[4] but, he points out, "[t]he images credited with bringing the war in Vietnam to an end ... did not have their effect immediately. It took time for their meaning to sink in with the American public, and it took even more time for the political process to catch up with their meaning."[5] Transformation of the sort that the war's opponents anticipate is bound to take time, particularly as the current administration redefines its mission as "overseas contingency operations" and withdraws from Iraq while fortifying the American presence in Afghanistan. Yet our metanarratives of liberation from tyranny and self-defence against terrorism seem ever more absurd in light of the emerging truths of the war.

As I have argued, the War on Terror represented not a new era but an intensification and acceleration of America's long-standing political and economic strategies and a final attempt at realizing what has been known, since the nineteenth century, as its "manifest destiny." Even its ideological co-ordinates, the terms of which imply a mission to "civilize" a barbarous world, are by no means a novelty, having long been used to characterize earlier forms of imperialism. What is unique to the present era is the deployment of such a strategy within a Western socio-economic and cultural context that seems to admit of no alternatives and the particular effect this seems to have on politics as such. I have therefore tried to present the post–Cold War era, from the first Gulf War onward, as constituted at the level of "lived reality" by a particular cultural "structure of feeling," one premised on some of the spatio-temporal characteristics of late capitalism and that consequently cannot be seen to have begun with the end of the Cold War but instead served as the ideal backdrop for it, as well as for George H.W. Bush's declaration of a "new world order." However, despite the promise of a new era of security and stability that this "new world order" and its supporting structure of feeling implied, the 1990s instead offered an intensification of cultural fear – a fear quite unlike that premised on the Cold War "balance of terror" but centred instead on a host of diverse and shifting objects, all of which seemed to portend death and destruction on both an individual and a mass scale.

What has since happened, I would conclude, is that the contradiction between the Enlightenment ideal of "progress" and the imperatives of the socio-economic system intended to sustain it has been pressed, in posthistory, to an undesirable extreme. This is the broadest way in which I can contextualize not the rise of terrorism itself or the emergence of the "war" against it but rather the impact of both on American popular culture, the precise ways in which they are received and perceived, and the reasons for their effectiveness as an instrument of ideological justification in relation to what is ultimately a new stage of US-led capitalist imperialism. There is nothing new about the "paranoid style" in American politics, the strategy of tapping into amorphous, diffuse anxieties and fears in order to justify a militaristic endeavour. There is nothing new about the "politics of fear." There is nothing new about American militarism, even though it has accelerated and intensified following the terrorist attacks of 11 September. The underlying dynamic – namely, the inherently expansive imperative of capitalism – has long been with us. The enemy has changed, but there is a clear ideological continuity between the "evil empire" and the "axis of evil." In many ways, then, even the terms have not changed. It is, rather, the context that has changed. The posthistorical structure of feeling, in other words, permeates the popular experience of both terrorism and the "war" against it down to its very marrow.

To summarize, this structure of feeling initially facilitated the presentation of a "new world order" to which there could be no alternatives – and indeed to which no alternatives were required. With the Cold War over, liberal-democratic capitalism could easily be presented as the only viable system, both for the West and for the "rest." Although the "rest" had yet to catch up, a new era of peace and security seemed to glimmer on the horizon. No threats to American dominance seemed to exist – none, at least, that could challenge it economically or militarily. And when any threat to stability emerged, such as Iraq's invasion of Kuwait in August 1990, it could be swiftly defused by means of America's unparalleled military might, backed with the blessing of the harmonious "family of nations." Gulf War I, accordingly, was presented as evidence of the viability of Bush Sr's "new world order," both in the official rhetoric and on the network news. The media not only explicitly supported the administration and the Pentagon in its presentation of the war but also processed it as a spectacular, real-time commodity, thereby abstracted from its historical context. Further, the commodity-form of the coverage predetermined the construction of an illusion of solidarity premised on a spatial rather than a temporal axis, an illusion produced and consumed aesthetically and according to which progress in anything other than a quantitative sense would be no longer necessary. The real-time coverage, moreover, coincided with a "writing" of history that took place simultaneously with its unfolding, a "writing" whereby the future was discounted into a perpetual present, the present of "instant history," and thereby discounted altogether.

This illusion of harmony between events, ideology, and structure of feeling, however, soon gave way to pervasive cultural fear. And it was, I argued, the same spatial and temporal co-ordinates in lived experience, or in other words the same structure of feeling, that now came to inform a host of amorphous and constantly shifting anxieties that only a narrative of decay and decline seemed able to impose any coherence or intelligible form upon. A quasi-conspiracist mindset took hold according to which social life, in the absence of any narrative of "progress" toward a desirable goal, was headed straight for the proverbial dogs; the only question that remained was whether the world would end with a bang (as per the disaster film) or a whimper. Indeed, the increasing popularity of these films over the 1990s seemed to portend the former, whether as the endpoint of the narrative of decline or, alternatively, as a sudden, unforeseeable, and cataclysmic "event." In both cases, one of the effects of the proliferation of media scares and disaster films was to reconstitute the subject, individual and collective, against a non-subjective, viral threat that could be conceived as inhering within or without but that was always in any case immediate and inevitable. Thus, the same structure of feeling of *im/mediacy* that allowed for the celebration of posthistory during Gulf War I could also be held to account for the proliferation of panic terrors over the rest of the decade.

It was this generalized cultural fear that was appropriated as an instrument of social control following the terrorist attacks of 11

September, a "traumatic" and apparently apocalyptic event in itself, at least at the level of the image. The fear of another imminent, real-time attack, combined with the fear of an enemy quite as diffuse and amorphous as the manifold objects of fear over the 1990s, lent itself easily to such an appropriation, and the War on Terror quickly became the new raison d'être of the American global project. The Bush administration, it seemed, had found the perfect solution to the crisis in legitimation that had plagued the first posthistorical decade. Now, the always somewhat questionable trio of free markets, free elections, and human rights that had served the Clinton administration over the preceding years was expanded to include a fourth co-ordinate – "homeland security." Once the terrorism had been located in poverty and oppression and the solution to these scourges located in the boundless benevolence of the free market, America could now license itself – legally or not – to pursue its interests far and wide. Further, with the added element of the terrorist threat, it could now pursue these interests independently of the wishes of the international community and with utter disregard for the "outdated" question of national sovereignty. And all this could be done with the consent of much of the American public. As for the rest, their silence – certainly at the beginning – was enough to imply consent, and silence was more or less enforced (even if only through a lack of media coverage) wherever America's mission was not wholeheartedly embraced.

What confronts us throughout is a structure of feeling that validates the ideological proposition that there can be no alternative but the present configuration. And the ideological sleight of hand that presents the current system as the only viable one is effected, by and large, through the concealing of real and properly historical economic forces under the blanket term of "modernity." The defeat of communism brings with it the suppression of the *idea* of capitalism, because there is no longer anything, ideologically, for capitalism to define itself against, and without "capitalism" we are left with the vacuous term "modernity," substituted with increasing frequency for the economic forces that make disruption, dispossession, and the erosion of social bonds the order of the day. In the absence of a qualitatively different future, "modernity," as Jameson accurately notes, is "used precisely to cover up the absence of any great collective social hope, or *telos*, after the discrediting of socialism. For capitalism itself has no social goals. To brandish the word "modernity" in place of "capitalism" allows politicians, governments, and political scientists to pretend that it does, and so to paper over that terrifying absence."[6]

Further, it is "modernity" that confirms the illusion of *no alternative* insofar as the past is not an option; it is "modernity" that replicates on the broadest ideological level the logic of the "forced choice." As Jameson says elsewhere, "[i]f free-market positions can be systematically identified with modernity and habitually grasped as representing what is modern, then the free-market people have won a fundamental victory which goes well beyond the other ideological victories ... The holders of the opposite position have nowhere to go terminologically."[7]

The pre-emption of an "opposite position" effected by the emphasis on "modernity" is simply another manifestation of the "choice" that is offered, by the "politics" of fear, between life and death, between what is and its negation. In its very disavowal of capitalism as a driving force, modernity is central to the posthistorical structure of feeling, manifesting itself in numerous ways across the spectrum of mainstream popular representations of history.

It is only through the disavowal of what Walter Benjamin has called the "necessities that rule our lives"[8] that the contemporary situation and its corresponding structure of feeling can come to present the current system – "modernity" – as the only viable one. Indeed, there is nothing wrong with "modernity" as such: genuine progress has been made in a number of critical areas – medicine, suffrage, and civil rights, to name a few. However, when the *term* "modernity" is invoked to reaffirm the global social order as it stands against a barbaric, primitive past as its only alternative, "ideology" would seem to disavow itself most effectively indeed. That the "holders of the opposite position have nowhere to go terminologically" is evident in John Kerry's assertion, noted previously, that the "difference" between the Vietnam War and the War on Terror is that the former conflict was "ideological" whereas the present one is not.

The disavowal of capitalism works on several other levels as well. Among them is an inability to attribute real, material social anxieties to any correspondingly real, material force; they have instead been re-projected onto external threats, such as viruses, enemies, or indeed viral enemies. Further, even when certain fears are indeed legitimate – such as the fear of terrorism, however amplified it might have been in the wake of 9/11 – they are manipulated in such a way as to serve the same function that the "other" does in Hollywood films: that is, they are no longer so much a real, historical entity in themselves as a spectacular projection of the same real, material anxieties onto an external and all-pervasive threat. Indeed, almost immediately following the death of bin Laden in May 2011, threats were released from "beyond the grave," indications that the "treasure trove" discovered in his compound included plans for a terrorist attack to commemorate 9/11.

Further and more ominously still, such projections can all too easily prefigure a regression into the politics of exclusion – into "identity politics," one might say, in some of its less emancipatory manifestations. Huntington's focus on cultural identity as the "fault line" of global conflict in the coming century depends on his own disavowal of capitalism as implying an ideology in itself. Much as Fukuyama airbrushes class conflict out of the picture in order to proclaim the end of history, so too does Huntington "aestheticize" capitalism out of existence, and he is consequently unable to account for global conflict save against a carefully constructed "map" of incommensurable global identities. His model, consequently, is reducible to one of the "self" (the "West") against the "other" (the "rest"), and it is only the reconstitution and reaffirmation of the former against a now "multi-civilizational" set of "others" that can guarantee its, or rather "our," survival. Although Huntington's thesis is arguably more nuanced than this, the paradigm he presents, finally, can all too easily be mobilized toward a "politics" of hatred and intolerance – a "politics," in other words, that does not merit the name.

What we are faced with, finally, is a contemporary situation that demands, with increasing urgency, the resurrection of politics proper, as is finally taking place (albeit still at the level of the cultural imaginary) in films like *Redacted*, *Battle for Haditha*, and *In the Valley of Elah*. After all, it is the death of politics – felled by the same "invisible hand" that brought about the death of history and ideology alike – that reduces the situation to one of what "is" versus its senseless negation and in such a way as to effectively silence dissent.

What is thereby concealed, moreover, is quite a "primitive" mechanism in itself – namely, capitalism's strategies of "accumulation by dispossession"[9] and the imperial violence they often entail. Capitalism, as Harvey notes, "must perpetually have something 'outside of itself' in order to stabilize itself" and "necessarily and always creates its own 'other.'"[10] For Harvey, the "predatory practices of 'primitive' or 'original' accumulation" continue to prevail, backed by "[t]he state, with its monopoly of violence and definitions of legality,"[11] and America's foreign policy strategies following the Second World War and particularly the Cold War have consistently supported these "predatory practices" in the pursuit of American interests more broadly. To date, the "primary vehicle for accumulation by dispossession," according to Harvey, has been "the forcing open of markets throughout the world by institutional pressures exercised through the IMF and the WTO, backed by the power of the United States (and to a lesser extent Europe) to deny access to its own vast market to those countries that refuse to dismantle their protections."[12]

Note, here, that "those countries that refuse to dismantle their protections" are also quite often those countries that refuse to *modernize* – that is, those countries that appear to reject the only viable option, a rejection, by the logic of the "forced choice," that is already invalid. And it is increasingly such states that now become the targets of the new, American-led imperialism, as the attempt to impose a free-market utopia on the "clean slate" of an Iraq wiped clear of both its governing regime and its historical treasures aptly demonstrates.

The War on Terror seems to offer an opportunity to submerge the *idea* of capitalism once and for all, fusing a vacuous "freedom" with the "free market" as a solution to poverty worldwide. And by fusing this in turn with an imminent and immediate threat to the survival of the self (as the next potential victim of terror) and of the nation (as the "beacon of hope and opportunity" that by its sheer brightness attracts the unwanted attentions of freedom's "enemies"), the Bush administration seemed to have resolved, if only temporarily, the crisis in legitimation that posthistory presented. That this legitimation is once again in crisis seems apparent, but the crisis is left to his successor to defuse, and only time will tell whether the Democratic administration's response, framed though it may be in different rhetoric, will be substantially different.

Ultimately, the only hope lies in insisting that politics has not yet died, that its ostensible demise is little more than a function of triumphant capitalist ideology itself. Only then can the possibility of a real alternative be reasserted; only by insisting on the fundamental role of capitalism in the world's perennial ills can any viable solution to these ills ever be devised. Thus, finally, the ultimately apolitical difference between "what is and its negation" could yield once more to politics proper as the difference between *what is and what could be*. If the current and growing backlash is only a beginning, it is nonetheless a critical one, and if what this takes in a culture saturated through and through by images is in part a resistance on the level of the aesthetic, then the increasingly visible dissent and opposition are precisely what is needed for just this beginning. Combined with an American fatality count of more than 5,000 in Iraq and Afghanistan – concealed at the level of the image by administrative decree but nonetheless beginning to make its appearance in (presumably "illicit") photographs of flag-draped coffins returning to the "homeland" – the early signs of cultural climate change may be emerging at last. One can only hope that these early shifts in the prevailing winds can be harnessed toward genuinely progressive ends.

Afterword

It was as I was preparing the final draft of this manuscript that the news of Osama bin Laden's death hit the airwaves. At this time we cannot know what the longer-term implications may be for US–Pakistani relations. As could be expected, there were celebrations on the streets in America at the outset, but they were quickly curtailed on the premise that what differentiates the liberal West from the terrorist "rest" is that the former does not glorify or celebrate violence – an interesting premise, following a decade of war. But there may be other, better justifications for the president's injunction against "gloating" in the wake of the al-Qaeda leader's death: the fact, perhaps, that it had taken the US ten years to find him; the fact that "enhanced interrogation," surely one of the more tasteless euphemisms to enter the lexicon over the past decade, had had nothing to do with the operation; the fact that bin Laden's assassination was not, narratively speaking, the culmination of a decade of conflict, with innumerable casualties on both sides; and perhaps the fact that, in the end and despite CNN's computer-generated reconstruction of the Navy SEALs' raid, interspersed with still shots of blood stains in the compound, there was no single image to counter that of the Twin Towers in flames on 11 September 2001. Even had images of the dead bin Laden been released, they could not have compared in scale or scope to the media spectacle of that day. Terrorism, if we are to (wrongly) interpret bin Laden's death as the end of the story, effectively won the War on Terror, and the Western media proved to be among its greatest weapons.

Notes

INTRODUCTION

1 Johnson, *Blowback*.
2 According to David Gross ("Survey"), "Only television news still outpaces the Internet, with 78 percent of respondents saying they watch local news and 73 percent saying they view a national network or cable news channel like CNN, Fox News or MSNBC."
3 A revealing look at these statistics is offered in Lobe, "TV News Bad for Truth about Iraq."
4 Ignatieff, "America's Empire Is an Empire Lite" and *Empire Lite*.
5 Holloway, *Cultures of the War on Terror*.
6 Benjamin, *Illuminations*, 242.
7 Engelhardt, *The End of Victory Culture*.

CHAPTER ONE

1 Fukuyama, "The End of History?"
2 Fukuyama, *The End of History*.
3 Ibid., 45.
4 Ibid., 55.
5 Anderson, *A Zone of Engagement*, 283.
6 Niethammer, *Posthistoire*.
7 Anderson, *A Zone of Engagement*, 281.
8 Philip Hammond, in *Media, War & Postmodernity*, offers an in-depth analysis of the US's self-redefinition throughout the 1990s that is highly relevant to and substantiates the present investigation.
9 George H.W. Bush, 11 September 1990.

10   Again, see Hammond for a more substantive discussion of these
      "redefinitions."

11   Fukuyama, *The End of History*, 276.

12   Huntington, "The Clash of Civilizations?" and *The Clash of Civilizations*.

13   Anderson, *A Zone of Engagement*, 335.

14   Fukuyama, "The Primacy of Culture," 9 (emphasis mine).

15   Fukuyama, *The End of History*, 45 (emphasis mine).

16   Ibid., 36.

17   Fukuyama, "The Primacy of Culture," 10.

18   Fukuyama, *The End of History*, 283.

19   Eagleton, *The Idea of Culture*, 53.

20   Fukuyama, "After Neoconservatism."

21   Fukuyama, "Has History Restarted?"

22   Huntington, *The Clash of Civilizations*, 254.

23   Again, see Hammond.

24   Fukuyama, *The End of History*, 39–54.

25   Ibid.

26   Huntington, *The Clash of Civilizations*, 20–1.

27   Fukuyama, *The End of History*, xi (emphasis mine).

28   Bell, *The End of Ideology*.

29   Dyer-Witheford, *Cyber-Marx*, 30–1.

30   Williams, *Marxism and Literature*, 130–1 (emphasis mine).

31   Ibid.

32   See also Pierre Bourdieu's concept of "habitus" as articulated in his *Out-
      line of a Theory of Practice*. Although less flexible than Williams's para-
      digm, it retains a certain relevance insofar as socio-ideological co-ordin-
      ates are concerned.

33   Williams, *Marxism and Literature*, 132 (emphasis mine).

34   Ibid., 122.

35   Although Engelhardt (*The End of Victory Culture*) sees the breakdown
      in the victory narrative as coinciding with the dropping of the A-bombs
      on Japan, I would argue that the paradigm shift thus effected (which pre-
      vailed during the Cold War) nonetheless differs from the post–Cold War
      "end of grand narratives," which does away with an ideological as well as
      a visibly identifiable enemy.

36   Again, see Hammond, who also sees the War on Terror as superseding
      the more fragile narratives of humanitarian intervention at the turn of the
      twenty-first century.

37   Jameson, *Postmodernism*, xiv.

38   Harvey, *The Condition of Postmodernity*, 204.

39   Ibid.
40   McLuhan, *The Gutenberg Galaxy.*
41   Harvey, *The Condition of Postmodernity,* 124–6. See this source for more detailed information on the economic crisis of 1973 and the transition from Fordism to "flexible accumulation."
42   Ibid., 147.
43   Ibid., 145.
44   Ibid., 175.
45   Jameson, *Postmodernism,* xxi.
46   Smith, *Millennial Dreams,* 10 (emphasis mine).
47   Mann, *Incoherent Empire,* 49.
48   Harvey, *The Condition of Postmodernity,* 232.
49   Ibid., 240 (first emphasis mine).
50   Ibid., 300.
51   Jameson, *Postmodernism,* 44.
52   Ibid., 38–9.
53   Harvey, *The Condition of Postmodernity,* 245–6.
54   Ibid., 249–50.
55   Ibid., 273.
56   Jameson, *Postmodernism,* 44. Incidentally, this merges with McLuhan's earlier assessment of the "electronic age" as well as much of the Vorticist aesthetic as elucidated in Wyndham Lewis's 1927 *Time and Western Man.*
57   Baudrillard, *Simulacra and Simulation.*
58   Harvey, *The Condition of Postmodernity,* 171.
59   Ibid., 285.
60   Ibid., 285–8.
61   McLuhan, *Understanding Media.*
62   McLuhan, *The Gutenberg Galaxy,* 11.
63   McLuhan, *Understanding Media,* 86–8.
64   Ibid., 145.
65   McLuhan, *The Gutenberg Galaxy,* 111.
66   Ibid., 125–6.
67   McLuhan, *Understanding Media,* 130.
68   Ibid., 137.
69   Ong, *Orality and Literacy,* 72.
70   Williams, *Television,* 86–7.
71   Jameson, *Postmodernism,* 38.
72   Williams, *Television,* 86–7.
73   Ong, 73.
74   McLuhan, *The Gutenberg Galaxy,* 22.

75 Eagleton, "Local and Global."

76 Harvey, *The Condition of Postmodernity*, 300.

77 Ong, 45.

78 Benjamin, *Illuminations*, 212.

79 Weber, *Mediauras*, 215–17.

80 Benjamin, 215–17.

81 Adorno and Horkheimer, *Dialectic of Enlightenment*, 120–67.

82 Pater, *The Renaissance*.

83 Harvey, *The Condition of Postmodernity*, 207.

84 While the Internet is increasingly a source of information that both reinforces and challenges this legitimation, much of web-based news production is backed by the corporate networks at any rate, and television still remains the primary source of news for the American public. It is for this reason that television, rather than the Internet, will remain the focus of the present inquiry. See this book's introduction and "The National Entertainment State."

85 Debord, *The Society of the Spectacle*, 1:24 (henceforth I will refer to the chapter and paragraph as organized in the online text).

86 Ibid., 1:34 (emphasis original).

87 Retort, *Afflicted Powers*, 19–20.

88 Ibid., 21.

89 Harvey, *The Condition of Postmodernity*, 288.

90 Debord, 6:147–54.

91 Jameson, *Postmodernism*, ix.

92 Ibid., 6.

93 Ibid., 44.

94 Ibid., 26–7.

95 Harvey, *The Condition of Postmodernity*, 149–50.

96 Comaroff and Comaroff, "Millennial Capitalism," 295.

97 Tronti, "The Strategy of Refusal," cited in Comaroff and Comaroff, 294.

98 Harvey, *The Condition of Postmodernity*, 153.

99 Ibid., 171.

100 Benjamin, 253–64.

101 Lyotard, *The Postmodern Condition*, xxiv.

102 Ibid., xxiv–v.

103 Eagleton, *The Idea of Culture*, 66–7.

104 Engelhardt, *The End of Victory Culture*, 4ff. Engelhardt sees the "end" of the victory narrative as manifesting itself following World War II; in my own work it appears at the end of the Cold War, when even an ideologically distinguishable enemy vanished from the scene.

105 In *The Pentagon's New Map*, Thomas Barnett sees this threat as having effectively come to an end in 1973 (37).

106 Engelhardt, *The End of Victory Culture*, 55ff.

107 Barnett argues that the realization that parts of the world could come under Soviet regimes without an ensuing "domino effect" signalled the effective end of the Cold War (91).

108 Not an unrealistic threat, nor one that has come to pass.

109 Jameson, *Postmodernism*, 46.

110 Jameson, "Reification and Utopia in Mass Culture," 133–8.

111 Harvey, *The Condition of Postmodernity*, 302–3.

112 Weber, 126.

113 Of course, there were dissenting voices during the first Gulf War, and scenes such as the infamous "turkey shoot" as Iraqi forces retreated to Basra undermined the illusion of "good intentions" on the part of the first Bush administration. However, because the aim of this book is to examine the mainstream response to the events, I will focus on network coverage and spontaneous displays of collective solidarity as "Vietnam Syndrome" came to an "end" with the "liberation" of Kuwait.

CHAPTER TWO

1 *War in the Gulf*.

2 Baudrillard, *The Gulf War Did Not Take Place*.

3 George H.W. Bush, 11 September 1990.

4 Ibid. (emphasis mine).

5 Anderson, "Force and Consent," 7.

6 George H.W. Bush, 11 September 1990.

7 Ibid. Note he is at pains to emphasize that there is no conflict between the West and "Moslems" or between the West and "Arabs."

8 Ibid.

9 Perry Anderson points to the use of economic inducements to secure Security Council approval in the case of the first Gulf War and beyond, noting that "[b]y the late nineties, the UN had become virtually as much an arm of the State Department as the IMF is of the Treasury." See "Force and Consent," 8.

10 George H.W. Bush, 11 September 1990.

11 Ibid.

12 Anderson, "Force and Consent," 7.

13 Official rhetoric, bolstered by televised news coverage, repeatedly emphasized this comparison; see CBS's *Desert Triumph*, CNN's *War in the Gulf*, and MacArthur's *Second Front* for a more in-depth analysis.

14 Debord, *The Society of the Spectacle*, 1:6.

15 George H.W. Bush, 11 September 1990. Barnett (*The Pentagon's New Map*) points out that the Pentagon and the military-industrial complex more broadly would not be allowed to suffer the blow of reduced defence spending in the wake of the Soviet collapse.

16 George H.W. Bush, 16 January 1991.

17 Ibid.

18 George H.W. Bush, 11 September 1990.

19 MacArthur, *Second Front*, 70.

20 George H.W. Bush, 16 January 1991.

21 MacArthur, 59.

22 George H.W. Bush, 29 January 1991.

23 Douglas Kellner presents substantial evidence that the Bush administration refused to consider such a solution from the outset, even though it feigned reluctance to engage in combat. For a complete account of the lost diplomatic opportunity, see Kellner, *The Persian Gulf TV War*, ch.1, 19–20. (Hereafter, excerpts from this book will be cited as per their online chapter designations.)

24 George H.W. Bush, 16 January 1991.

25 Kellner, *The Persian Gulf TV War*.

26 George H.W. Bush, 16 January 1991.

27 Ibid.

28 Ibid.

29 Ibid.

30 George H.W. Bush, 29 January 1991.

31 Ibid.

32 Ibid.

33 Ibid.

34 Kellner, *The Persian Gulf TV War*, ch.7.

35 Ibid., ch.8.

36 George H.W. Bush, cited in Kellner, *The Persian Gulf TV War*, ch. 8.

37 It took a while before the live burial of "hundreds, possibly thousands" of trapped, retreating forces would become public knowledge. MacArthur, 200–1.

38 George H.W. Bush, 6 March 1991.

39 Ibid.

40 George H.W. Bush, 15 December 1992.

41 Ibid.

42 Ibid.

43 Ibid.

44   MacArthur, 37–43.

45   Ibid., 41.

46   Anderson, "Force and Consent," 7.

47   Ibid., 9.

48   Many critics have highlighted the centrality of the spectre of the Viet-
     nam War to representations of the Persian Gulf War, citing both Bush and
     Schwarzkopf as promising that there would not be a repeat of the ear-
     lier conflict. See, for instance, Kendrick, "The Never Again Narratives,"
     129–30.

49   MacArthur, 113ff. See also Sobel, *The Impact of Public Opinion*, and
     Ryan and Dumbrell, *Vietnam in Iraq*.

50   See Link, "Maintaining Normality," 59.

51   George H.W. Bush, 11 September 1990.

52   J. Comaroff and J.L. Comaroff, "Millennial Capitalism," 333.

53   Said, *Orientalism*.

54   Barnett, *The Pentagon's New Map*.

55   See CNN's *War in the Gulf* and/or CBS's *Desert Triumph* for visual and
     textual examples.

56   George H.W. Bush, 8 August 1990.

57   Zunes, "The Gulf War: 8 Myths."

58   George H.W. Bush, 16 January 1991.

59   According to Zunes (see note 57), Iraq in the American media progressed
     in mid-1990 from having the ability to develop a nuclear weapon in "five
     to seven years" to gaining nuclear capability "within months" by Novem-
     ber, "when public opinion polls first indicated that this was the one rea-
     son that most Americans felt could justify a military attack against Iraq."
     Further, Hussein had "for some time been calling for a nuclear-free zone
     in all of the Middle East" and, unlike Israel and Pakistan, had signed the
     Nuclear Non-Proliferation Treaty and opened its nuclear sites to inter-
     national inspection teams.

60   Morin, "Decision to Go to War."

61   Kellner, *The Persian Gulf TV War*, ch. 2.

62   Anderson, "Force and Consent," 5–6.

63   Ibid., 7.

64   Kubursi, "Oil and the Gulf War," and Barnett, *The Pentagon's New
     Map*.

65   Mann, *Incoherent Empire*, 82.

66   MacArthur, 141.

67   Ibid., 142.

68   Ibid., 143.

69 The print media in particular were not exactly pleased with the pool system; *Harper's* and others had launched a lawsuit prior to the beginning of the war.

70 Chesterman, "Ordering the New World."

71 Kellner, "The Crisis in the Gulf," 42.

72 Kellner, *The Persian Gulf TV War*, ch. 2.

73 MacArthur, 151.

74 Hiebert, "Public Relations as a Weapon of Modern Warfare," 30–1.

75 O'Heffernan, "Sobering Thoughts on Sound Bites," 22.

76 Kellner, *Media Culture*, 213.

77 MacArthur, 220.

78 Kellner, *The Persian Gulf TV War*, ch. 2.

79 In most cases, though, the protests came too late. See MacArthur, 231.

80 Kellner, *The Persian Gulf TV War*, ch.2.

81 MacArthur, 200.

82 Ibid.

83 Ibid., 217.

84 However, as MacArthur notes, the Big Three networks lost revenue during the war (220). According to Wells and Hakanen, the "cable revolution" – which by 1990 provided 65 per cent of the public with CNN's uninterrupted coverage – was in large part to blame for this, as well as the fact that during "extensive news coverage" the networks "can not often cut away to commercials and, consequently, lose a fortune in potential advertising revenue" (*Mass Media and Society*, 248.)

85 There were, of course, exceptions: Pentagon guides sometimes became lost on their pool "tours," and reporters were often delayed to the point where they missed any "action" entirely. See MacArthur, 221.

86 Engelhardt, "The Gulf War as Total Television," 84.

87 Ibid., 87.

88 Ibid., 84–5.

89 Ibid., 85.

90 Ibid., 93.

91 Chesterman.

92 Link, "Maintaining Normality," 55–7.

93 Kendrick, "The Never Again Narratives," 135.

94 O'Heffernan, 26.

95 MacArthur, 184.

96 Kellner, *The Persian Gulf TV War*, ch.2.

97 Cheney, "We're Talking War," 69.

98 Lyotard, *The Postmodern Condition*, xxv.

99   George H.W. Bush, 11 September 1990.
100   MacArthur, 161.
101   Jameson, "Globalization and Political Strategy," 53.
102   Jameson, "Reification and Utopia in Mass Culture," 131.
103   Wark, "Engulfed by the Vector," 66.
104   Benjamin, *Illuminations*, 235.
105   Ibid., 234.
106   Ibid., 240.
107   Ibid., 224.
108   Ibid., 234.
109   Retort, *Afflicted Powers*, 21.
110   R. Berman, *Modern Culture and Critical Theory*, 41.
111   Benjamin, 226.
112   Ibid., 233.
113   Ibid., 229.
114   Jameson, "Reification and Utopia in Mass Culture," 141.
115   Ibid.
116   Ibid.
117   Ibid., 142.
118   Ibid., 144.
119   Retort, 21.
120   Benjamin, 243.
121   Weber, *Mass Mediaurus*, 102.
122   J. Schulte-Sasse and L. Schulte-Sasse, "War, Otherness, and Illusionary Identification with the State," 82–3.
123   Ibid., 72.
124   Benjamin, 234.
125   Eagleton, *The Ideology of the Aesthetic*, 347.
126   Žižek, *The Sublime Object of Ideology*, 126.
127   Ibid., 125.
128   Link, "Maintaining Normality," 59.
129   Ibid., 62.
130   Said, *Orientalism*, 6.
131   Ibid., 7.
132   Ibid, 207.
133   Link, "Fanatics, Fundamentalists, Lunatics, and Drug Traffickers," 34.
134   Ibid.
135   J. Schulte-Sasse and L. Schulte-Sasse, 85 (emphasis original).
136   *War in the Gulf*.
137   Said, *Orientalism*, 319.

138 J. Schulte-Sasse and L. Schulte-Sasse, 90.
139 Link, "Fanatics, Fundamentalists, Lunatics, and Drug Traffickers," 39.
140 Chesterman.
141 George H.W. Bush, 5 January 1993.
142 *Desert Triumph*.
143 Hüppauf, "Experiences of Modern Warfare," 73–4.
144 Ibid., 75.
145 Wark, 70.
146 Scarry, "Watching and Authorizing the Gulf War," 63.
147 Kellner, *The Persian Gulf TV War*, ch.3.
148 Gerbner, "Persian Gulf War, the Movie," 244.
149 Ibid., 245.
150 McLuhan, *The Gutenberg Galaxy*, 6.
151 Harvey, *The Condition of Postmodernity*, 291.
152 Benjamin, 217.
153 Ibid., 229.
154 Baudrillard, *Selected Writings*, 166.
155 Debord, ch.1.
156 Gerbner, 244.
157 Weber, 126.
158 Žižek, *The Sublime Object of Ideology*, 128.

CHAPTER THREE

1 Baudrillard, *The Gulf War Did Not Take Place*.
2 Barnett, *The Pentagon's New Map*.
3 Clinton, 25 January 1994.
4 Clinton, 4 February 1997.
5 Anderson, "Force and Consent," 9.
6 Ibid., 9–11.
7 Clinton, 24 January 1995.
8 Ibid.
9 Clinton, 23 January 1996.
10 MacArthur, *Second Front*, 55–7.
11 I borrow this term from O'Donnell, *Latent Destinies*, 20.
12 For more on this topic, see Orford, *Reading Humanitarian Intervention*; Price, *Forging Peace*; Bouvier, *Globalization of U.S.–Latin American Relations*.
13 Clinton, 23 January 1996.
14 Huyssen, *Present Pasts*, 23.

15 Finkelstein, *The Holocaust Industry*. See also J. Berman, *Holocaust Agendas*.
16 Fukuyama, "Reflections," 29.
17 Barnett.
18 The abstraction from history, it should be noted, also makes of the Holocaust an inexplicable aberration, disconnected from the logic of modernization and rationalization that to a considerable extent informed it.
19 Clinton, 23 January 1996.
20 Clinton, 4 February 1997.
21 Ibid.
22 Ibid.
23 Ibid.
24 Clinton, 23 January 1996.
25 Fukuyama, *The End of History*, 283.
26 Huntington, *The Clash of Civilizations*, 21.
27 Ibid., 20.
28 Ibid., 125.
29 Ibid., 20–1.
30 Huntington's book was on the *New York Times* bestseller list for 31 weeks initially and appeared again on the list after 9/11; Fukuyama's book was also on the bestseller list for several months after its publication.
31 Klein, *In Search of Narrative Mastery*, 275.
32 Eagleton, "Local and Global."
33 Barnett (*The Pentagon's New Map)* claims to have foreseen the danger caused by "disconnected" peoples at the beginning of the 1990s, if not before.
34 Michaels, "Posthistoricism," 4.
35 Michaels, "Political Science Fictions," 651–2.
36 Huntington, *The Clash of Civilizations*, 43.
37 Michaels, "Political Science Fictions," 649.
38 Althusser, *Lenin and Philosophy and Other Essays*, 17.
39 Eagleton, *The Idea of Culture*, 54–5.
40 Ibid., 54.
41 Eagleton, "Local and Global."
42 Ibid.
43 Lyotard, *The Postmodern Condition*.
44 Michaels, "Political Science Fictions," 652 (emphasis original).
45 Ibid., 654.
46 See Fish, "Postmodern Warfare."
47 Huntington, *The Clash of Civilizations*, 142.

48 Lyotard, xxiii–xxiv.
49 Ibid., 10.
50 Rorty, *Objectivity, Relativism, and Truth*, 31.
51 Ibid., 29.
52 Huntington, *The Clash of Civilizations*, 304–5.
53 Klein, 283.
54 Huntington, *The Clash of Civilizations*.
55 Michaels, "Empires of the Senseless," 106 (emphasis original).
56 Huntington, *The Clash of Civilizations*, 22–7.
57 This too is where Barnett (*The Pentagon's New Map*) gets his idea of "disconnectivity" among "the rest" as posing the military threat for the twenty-first century.
58 Buckley, *Remaking the World Order*.
59 Glassner, *The Culture of Fear*, xxi.
60 Ibid., 4.
61 Ibid, 27.
62 Ibid., 70.
63 Jameson, "Reification and Utopia in Mass Culture," 144. Jameson is referring to the shark in Steven Spielberg's film *Jaws*, although the same applies to other "natural" threats for which illness in particular serves as an ideal metaphor.
64 Massumi, *The Politics of Everyday Fear*, 4.
65 Glassner, 4.
66 Massumi, 10.
67 Ibid.
68 Ibid., 9–11.
69 Engelhardt, *The End of Victory Culture*, 98.
70 Massumi, 12.
71 Eagleton, "Local and Global."
72 Jameson, "Cognitive Mapping," 357.
73 O'Donnell, 12.
74 Ibid., 13–14.
75 Jameson, *Postmodernism*, 44.
76 O'Donnell, 19.
77 Melley, "Agency Panic and the Culture of Conspiracy," 60.
78 Sontag, *Illness as Metaphor*, 150–1.
79 Link, "Fanatics, Fundamentalists, Lunatics, and Drug Traffickers," 39–40.
80 Eagleton, *After Theory*, 217.
81 Rogin, *Kiss Me Deadly*, 3.
82 Ibid., 3.

83 Knight, *Conspiracy Culture*, 174–5.
84 Engelhardt, *The End of Victory Culture*.
85 Knight, 175–7.
86 Link, "Maintaining Normality," 60.
87 Link, "Fanatics, Fundamentalists, Lunatics, and Drug Traffickers," 36.
88 Engelhardt, *The End of Victory Culture*.
89 See also George Monbiot, "Both Saviour and Victim."
90 Link, "Fanatics, Fundamentalists, Lunatics, and Drug Traffickers," 41–2.
91 Ibid., 42–3.
92 Michaels, "Political Science Fictions," 655–6.
93 Monbiot.
94 Wetta and Novelli, "Now a Major Motion Picture," 864–5.
95 Ibid., 861.
96 Ibid., 865.
97 *Black Hawk Down*.
98 Weber, *Mass Mediaurus*, 102.
99 Keane, *Disaster Movies*, 73.
100 A good account of the connection between disaster films and the nuclear threat appears in Sontag, "The Imagination of Disaster."
101 An increase in religious apocalypticism has no doubt taken place, with Tim LaHaye's and Jerry B. Jenkins's *Left Behind* series becoming a veritable industry for the Christian Right. However, because I consider this demographic still on the fringe, I focus on the secular version as manifested in mainstream Hollywood films.
102 Daniel Wojcik, *The End of the World as We Know It*, 97.
103 See Boyer, *When Time Shall Be No More*.
104 Nye, *American Technological Sublime*, 225–6.
105 Engelhardt, *The End of Victory Culture*.
106 Lifton and Mitchell, *Hiroshima in America*, 305.
107 Ibid., 314 (emphasis original).
108 Sontag, "The Imagination of Disaster," 212.
109 Lyotard, 81.
110 Burke, *A Philosophical Inquiry*, 58.
111 Kant, *Critique of Judgment*, 99.
112 Eagleton, *Holy Terror*, 44.
113 Kant, 86 (emphasis original).
114 Burke, 133.
115 This is central to the experience of the sublime; it would also be central, Jameson might say, to the subjective experience of contemporary capitalism.

116 Lyotard, 78.

117 Sontag, "The Image-World," 359.

118 Eagleton, *Ideology of the Aesthetic*, 54.

119 Eagleton, *Holy Terror*, 44–5.

120 Jameson, *Postmodernism*, 36.

121 Jameson, "Cognitive Mapping," 356.

122 Virilio, *City of Panic*, 63 (emphasis original).

123 Jameson, *The Cultural Turn*, 50.

124 Ibid., 59.

125 Ibid., 60.

126 Ibid., 60–1.

127 Sontag, "The Imagination of Disaster," 227.

128 Virilio, 28 (emphasis original).

129 Michaels, "Empires of the Senseless," 109.

130 Jameson, "Reification and Utopia in Mass Culture," 46.

131 Ibid., 41.

132 Jameson, *Postmodernism*, 27.

133 J. Schulte-Sasse and L. Schulte-Sasse, *War, Otherness, and Illusionary Identification with the State*, 89.

134 Link, "Maintaining Normality," 61.

135 Michaels, "Empires of the Senseless," 109.

136 Link, "Maintaining Normality," 59.

CHAPTER FOUR

1 Virilio, *City of Panic*, 27.

2 Venn, "World Dis/Order," 121.

3 Lacan, *Écrits*, 324.

4 *America Remembers*.

5 Ibid.

6 *Merriam-Webster*, online. See also Kaplan, *Homeland Insecurities*, 83.

7 Breithaupt, "Rituals of Trauma," 67.

8 Ibid., 69.

9 Engelhardt, *The End of Victory Culture*.

10 Baudrillard, *The Spirit of Terrorism*, 31.

11 Leys, *Trauma*, 68.

12 *What We Saw*.

13 *America Remembers*.

14 *What We Saw*.

15 Freud, *The Uncanny*, 125.

16   Ibid., 132 (emphasis mine).

17   Ibid.

18   Žižek, *Welcome to the Desert of the Real*, 22.

19   Baudrillard, *The Spirit of Terrorism*, 5–7 (emphasis original).

20   Ibid., 6.

21   Žižek, *Welcome to the Desert of the Real*, 17.

22   Ibid., 18–19 (emphasis original).

23   Ibid., 16–17 (emphasis original).

24   Ibid., 12.

25   Freud's *Beyond the Pleasure Principle* articulates the satisfaction, or symbolic mastery, afforded by compulsive repetition as explained earlier.

26   Spiegelman, *In the Shadow of Two Towers*.

27   George W. Bush, 15 September 2001, cited in McCaleb, "Bush Tours Ground Zero."

28   George W. Bush, 20 September 2001.

29   Croft, *Culture, Crisis and America's War on Terror*.

30   George W. Bush, 11 September 2001.

31   George W. Bush, "There's No Rules," 17 September 2001.

32   Badiou, *Infinite Thought*, 143.

33   *National Security Strategy*.

34   George W. Bush, "There's No Rules," 17 September 2001.

35   George W. Bush, 20 September 2001.

36   Croft describes the "decisive intervention" that assured the alternative narratives would not gain centre stage.

37   Croft, 40.

38   Ibid., 44.

39   Ibid., 66.

40   Ibid., 69.

41   Engelhardt, *The End of Victory Culture*.

42   Croft, 76.

43   Engelhardt sees this as a key element in America's narratives of "victory culture," beginning with the "western" narrative and extending through to Pearl Harbor.

44   Baudrillard, *The Spirit of Terrorism*, 34.

45   Croft, 83.

46   Ibid., 93.

47   Ibid., 101.

48   See Faludi's *The Terror Dream* for an elucidation of these "traditional values."

49   George W. Bush, "President Holds Prime Time News conference," 11 October 2001.

50   George W. Bush, 8 November 2001.

51   Ibid.

52   George W. Bush, 29 January 2002.

53   Ibid.

54   George W. Bush, "President Holds Prime Time News Conference," 11 October 2001.

55   Kakutani, "An Identity Crisis for Norman Rockwell America."

56   Žižek, *Welcome to the Desert of the Real*, 33.

57   George W. Bush, 8 November 2001.

58   Croft, 104.

59   George W. Bush, "Islam Is Peace," 17 September 2001.

60   Dick Cheney, in "The Vice President Receives."

61   George W. Bush, "President Holds Prime Time News Conference," 11 October 2001.

62   George W. Bush, 8 November 2001.

63   George W. Bush, 7 October 2001.

64   *National Security Strategy.*

65   Michaels, "Empires of the Senseless," 106.

66   George W. Bush, "There's No Rules," 17 September 2001.

67   George W. Bush, 20 October 2001.

68   George W. Bush, 20 September 2001.

69   George W. Bush, 11 September 2001.

70   George W. Bush, 10 November 2001.

71   Croft, 280.

72   Cited in Croft, 279.

73   George W. Bush, "There's No Rules," 17 September 2001.

74   George W. Bush, 7 November 2001.

75   George W. Bush, "President Bush at Pentagon Memorial," 11 October 2001.

76   George W. Bush, 15 September 2001.

77   Link, "Fanatics, Fundamentalists, Lunatics, and Drug Traffickers," 39.

78   Eagleton, *After Theory*, 217.

79   George W. Bush, 20 September 2001.

80   Žižek, *Welcome to the Desert of the Real*, 3.

81   Fink, *The Lacanian Subject*, 50.

82   George W. Bush, "President Holds Prime Time News Conference," 11 October 2001.

83   George W. Bush, "There's No Rules," 17 September 2001.

84   Engelhardt, *The End of Victory Culture.*

85   Cited in Garamone, "Rumsfeld Says No Evidence Bin Laden Is Dead."

86   Link, "Fanatics, Fundamentalists, Lunatics, and Drug Traffickers," 36.

87   George W. Bush, "There's No Rules," 17 September 2001.

88   George W. Bush, 8 November 2001.

89   Eagleton, "Holy Terror."

90   Baudrillard, *The Spirit of Terrorism*, 30.

91   George W. Bush, 29 January 2002.

92   George W. Bush, 8 November 2001.

93   *24*, seasons 1–3. Although the first season, which dealt with terrorism in the more limited context of a political assassination, was produced prior to the terrorist attacks of 11 September, the second and third series – produced following the attacks – came to address terrorism on a mass scale and according to the ticking-time-bomb logic of the Bush administration.

94   Spiegelman, 1.

95   CNN *Presents: Nuclear Terror.*

96   Ibid.

97   Lattman, "Justice Scalia Hearts Jack Bauer."

98   It is less that there are no alternatives than that "the more liberal elements" find a ticking-time-bomb scenario highly unlikely and (rightly) question the validity of information obtained under duress, but when asked whether the torture of one man is justified if it would without a doubt save a million innocent lives, they are hard-pressed to come up with a solution. *Unthinkable* addresses this question in an interesting way.

99   *Rendition* addresses this question and will be discussed in the following chapter.

100 George W. Bush, "President Holds Prime Time News Conference," 11 October 2001.

101 *National Security Strategy*, 3.

102 O'Donnell, *Latent Destinies*, 12.

103 George W. Bush, 29 January 2002.

104 Associated Press, "Poll: 70% believe Saddam, 9-11 Link."

105 "CBS News Poll."

106 O'Donnell, 20.

107 See also Jackson, *Writing the War on Terrorism*, 44.

108 George W. Bush, 20 September 2001.

109 O'Donnell, 20.

110 Engelhardt, *The End of Victory Culture.*

111 O'Donnell, 20.

112 Gerbner, "Persian Gulf War, the Movie," 244.

113   Hofstadter, *The Paranoid Style in American Politics*.

114   Melley, "Agency Panic and the Culture of Conspiracy," 60.

115   Ibid., 62.

116   O'Donnell, 13.

117   "Office of Homeland Security Fact Sheet."

118   Kaplan, 85–7.

119   Ibid., 90.

120   Freud, *The Uncanny*, 132.

121   George W. Bush, "President Holds Prime Time News Conference," 11 October 2001.

122   George W. Bush, 28 January 2003.

123   Ibid.

124   George W. Bush, 7 October 2002.

125   Ibid.

126   Ibid.

127   Ibid. (emphasis mine).

128   George W. Bush, 6 March 2003.

129   Baier et al., "Saddam Captured 'Like a Rat.'"

130   "About PEJ."

131   "Embedded Reporters."

132   "Inside the Numbers."

133   "Embedded Reporters," para. 7.

134   *War in Iraq*.

135   Jameson, "Reification and Utopia in Mass Culture," 145.

136   *War in Iraq*.

137   Retort, *Afflicted Powers*, 27.

138   Ibid.

139   George W. Bush, 18 May 2004.

140   Retort, 16 (emphasis original).

141   George W. Bush, 24 May 2004.

142   "A Background of Abu Ghraib."

143   "US President George Bush Planned to Bomb Aljazeera."

144   George W. Bush, 28 August 2005.

145   Ibid.

146   "United States Military Casualties of War."

147   Retort, 35–7 (emphasis original).

148   "Kerry: Closing Loopholes."

149   Eagleton, "Holy Terror."

150   Fukuyama, *The End of History*, 276.

151   George W. Bush, 7 September 2003.

152 Burkeman, "Obama Administration Says Goodbye to 'War on Terror.'"
153 Badiou, *L'être et l'événement*, 195.
154 See, again, Hammond, *Media, War and Postmodernity*.
155 Kaplan, 89.
156 Anderson, *A Zone of Engagement*, 335.
157 Anderson, "Internationalism," 8.
158 Ibid., 23.
159 George W. Bush, 1 May 2001.
160 Rather, "Introduction."

CHAPTER FIVE

1 The failure to find WMDS (2004) and the catastrophic failure of the administration during and after Hurricane Katrina (2005) no doubt contributed to this growing disillusionment.
2 *The Iraq Study Group Report*, xiii.
3 George W. Bush, 28 January 2003.
4 See Žižek, *The Borrowed Kettle*.
5 George W. Bush, 10 January 2007.
6 Cited in Novak, "Hagel's Grim Iraq Assessment."
7 "Bush Says US 'Does Not Torture People.'"
8 I.e., not in the Foucauldian sense.
9 Jameson, *The Political Unconscious*.
10 Alford, *Reel Power*, 17.
11 Alford examines several examples, including *Black Hawk Down*, in what is by and large a convincing critique but one that underestimates the potential for genuine progress in the industry.
12 Brooks, *Reading for the Plot*.
13 Todorov, *The Typology of Detective Fiction*, 122–3.
14 Brooks, 25.
15 Doyle, "The Adventures of the Musgrave Ritual."
16 Brooks, xi–xii.
17 Ibid., 249.
18 Conrad, 70.
19 Ibid., 49–50.
20 Brooks, 238.
21 Engelhardt, *The End of Victory Culture*.
22 Kays, "A Critique of the U.S. Department of Defense's Documentary."
23 Cook, *Lost Illusions*, 62.
24 *Apocalypse Now*.

25 Link, "Fanatics, Fundamentalists, Lunatics, and Drug Traffickers" 42–3.
26 Jameson, *Postmodernism*, ix.
27 Lyotard, *The Postmodern Condition*, xxiv–xxv.
28 Eagleton, *The Idea of Culture*, 66–7.
29 Hammond, *Media, War, and Postmodernity*, 11.
30 George W. Bush, 4 February 2002.
31 Achebe, "An Image of Africa."
32 Jameson, "Reification and Utopia in Mass Culture," 141.
33 Nolte, "Review."
34 Podhoretz, "Avatarocious."
35 Jenkins, "Avatar Activism."
36 McLuhan, *Understanding Media*, 32.
37 After all, video games featuring first-person "modern" warfare constitute a multi-million-dollar industry. See Suellentrop, "War Games."
38 Eagleton, "Local and Global."
39 Gabriel, *No More Heroes*, 55.
40 Sontag, "What Have We Done?"
41 Mitchell, "The Fog of Abu Ghraib," 82.
42 Obama's new name for the War on Terror.

CONCLUSION

1   George W. Bush, 17 September 2001.
2   Lyotard, *The Postmodern Condition*, 10.
3   Conrad, *Heart of Darkness*, 10.
4   Mitchell, "The Fog of Abu Ghraib," 86.
5   Ibid.
6   Jameson, "Globalization and Political Strategy," 62.
7   Jameson, *A Singular Modernity*, 9–10.
8   Benjamin, *Illuminations*, 229.
9   Harvey, *The New Imperialism*, 137–82.
10 Ibid., 140–1.
11 Ibid., 144–5.
12 Ibid., 181.

Bibliography

24, Season One (2001), DVD, directed by Jon Cassar et al. (Fox Video 2002)

24, Season Two (2002), DVD, directed by Jon Cassar et al. (Fox Video 2003)

24, Season Three (2003), DVD, directed by Jon Cassar et al. (Fox Video 2004)

"About PEJ." Journalism.org, http://www.journalism.org/who

Achebe, Chinua. "An Image of Africa: Racism in Conrad's 'Heart of Darkness.'" *Massachusetts Review* 18 (1977), reprinted online, http://kirbyk.net/hod/image.of.africa.html

Adorno, Theodor, and Max Horkheimer. *Dialectic of Enlightenment.* Trans. John Cumming. London and New York: Verso 1997

Alford, Matthew. *Reel Power: Hollywood Cinema and American Supremacy.* London: Pluto 2010

Althusser, Louis. *Lenin and Philosophy and Other Essays.* Trans. Ben Brewster. New York: Monthly Review Press 1971

America Remembers: The Events of September 11 and America's Response, DVD (TimeInc Home Entertainment 2003)

Anderson, Perry. "Force and Consent." *New Left Review* 17 (2002): 5–30

– "Internationalism: A Breviary." *New Left Review* 14 (2002): 525

– *A Zone of Engagement.* London: Verso 1992

Apocalypse Now (1979), DVD, directed by Francis Ford Coppola (Zoetrope Corporation 2000)

Associated Press. "Poll: 70% Believe Saddam, 9-11 Link." *USA Today* (6 September 2003) http://www.usatoday.com/news/washington/2003-09-06-poll-iraq_x.htm

Avatar (2009), DVD, directed by James Cameron (Twentieth Century Fox Home Entertainment 2010)

"A Background of Abu Ghraib." Canadian Broadcasting Corporation, *the fifth estate* (16 November 2005) http://www.cbc.ca/fifth/badapples/history.html

Badiou, Alain. *L'être et l'événement*. Paris: Éditions du Seuil 1988

– *Infinite Thought: Truth and the Return to Philosophy*. Trans. Oliver Feltham and Justin Clemens. London: Continuum 2003

Baier, Bret, et al. "Saddam Captured 'Like a Rat' in Raid." *FOXNews.com* (14 December 2003) http://www.foxnews.com/story/0,2933,105706,00.html

Barnett, Thomas. *The Pentagon's New Map: War and Peace in the Twenty-First Century*. New York: Penguin 2004

Battle for Haditha (2007), DVD, directed by Nick Broomfield (Paradox 2007).

Baudrillard, Jean. *The Gulf War Did Not Take Place*. Trans. Paul Patton. Bloomington: Indiana University Press 1995

– *Selected Writings*. Ed. Mark Poster. Stanford, CA: Stanford University Press 1998

– *Simulacra and Simulation*. Trans. Sheila Faria Glaser. Ann Arbor, MI: University of Michigan Press 1994

– *The Spirit of Terrorism*. Trans. Chris Turner. London: Verso 2002

Bell, Daniel. *The Cultural Contradictions of Capitalism*. Twentieth Anniversary edn. New York: Basic Books 1996

– *The End of Ideology: On the Exhaustion of Political Ideas in the Fifties*. New York: The Free Press of Glencoe, 1960

Benjamin, Walter. *Illuminations: Essays and Reflections*. Trans. Harry Zohn and Hannah Arendt. New York: Schocken 2007

Berman, Judith E. *Holocaust Agendas, Conspiracies and Industries? Issues and Debates in Holocaust Memorialization*. London: Valentine Mitchell 2006

Berman, Russell. *Modern Culture and Critical Theory: Art, Politics, and the Legacy of the Frankfurt School*. Madison: University of Wisconsin Press 1989

Black Hawk Down (2001), DVD, directed by Ridley Scott (Revolution Studios Distribution Co. 2003)

Body of Lies (2008), DVD, directed by Ridley Scott (Warner Home Video 2009)

Bourdieu, Pierre. *Outline of a Theory of Practice*. Trans. Richard Nice. Cambridge: Cambridge University Press 1977

Bouvier, Virginia M. *The Globalization of U.S.–Latin American Relations: Democracy, Intervention, and Human Rights*. Westport, CT: Praeger 2002.

Boyer, Paul. *When Time Shall Be No More: Prophecy Belief in Modern American Culture*. Cambridge, MA: Harvard University Press 2002

Breithaupt, Fritz. "Rituals of Trauma: How the Media Fabricated September 11." In *Media Representations of September 11*, edited by Steven Chernak, Frankie Y. Baily, and Michelle Brown, 67–81. Westport, CT, and London: Praeger 2003

Brooks, Peter. *Reading for the Plot: Design and Intention in Narrative*. Cambridge, MA: Harvard University Press 1984

Buckley, Sandra. "Remaking the World Order: Reflections on Huntington's *Clash of Civilizations*." *Theory and Event* 2, no. 4 (1998) http://muse.jhu.edu/journals/theory_and_event/v002/2.4buckley.html

Burke, Edmund. *A Philosophical Inquiry into the Origin of Our Ideas of the Sublime and the Beautiful*. Ed. J.T. Boulton. Oxford: Blackwell 1987

Burkeman, Oliver. "Obama Administration Says Goodbye to 'War on Terror.'" *The Guardian* (25 March 2009) http://www.guardian.co.uk/world/2009/mar/25/obama-war-terror-overseas-contingency-operations

Bush, George H.W. "Address on Iraq's Invasion of Kuwait (August 8, 1990)." The Miller Center for Public Affairs, Scripps Library and Multimedia Archive, http://millercenter.org/scripps/archive/speeches/detail/5529

– "Address before a Joint Session of Congress." (11 September 1990) The Miller Center for Public Affairs, Scripps Library and Multimedia Archive, http://millercenter.org/scripps/archive/speeches/detail/3425

– "Address to the Nation on the Invasion of Iraq (January 16, 1991)." The Miller Center for Public Affairs, Scripps Library and Multimedia Archive, http://millercenter.virginia.edu/scripps/diglibrary/prezspeeches/ghbush/ghb_1991_0116.html

– "State of the Union Address (January 29, 1991)." The Miller Center for Public Affairs, Scripps Library and Multimedia Archive, http://millercenter.virginia.edu/scripps/diglibrary/prezspeeches/ghbush/ghb_1991_0129.html

– "Address before a Joint Session of Congress on the End of the Gulf War (March 6, 1992)." The Miller Center for Public Affairs, Scripps Library and Multimedia Archive, http://millercenter.virginia.edu/scripps/diglibrary/prezspeeches/ghbush/ghb_1991_0306.html

– "Remarks at Texas A&M University (December 15, 1992)." The Miller Center for Public Affairs, Scripps Library and Multimedia Archive, http://millercenter.virginia.edu/scripps/diglibrary/prezspeeches/ghbush/ghb_1992_1215.html

– "Address at West Point (January 5, 1993)." The Miller Center for Public Affairs, Scripps Library and Multimedia Archive, http://millercenter. virginia.edu/scripps/diglibrary/prezspeeches/ghbush/ghb_1993_0105. html

Bush, George W. "Remarks by the President to Students and Faculty at National Defense University." The White House (1 May 2001) http:// www.whitehouse.gov/news/releases/2001/05/20010501-10.html

– "Text of Bush's Address." *CNN.com* (11 September 2001) http:// archives.cnn.com/2001/US/09/11/bush.speech.text

– "President Urges Readiness and Patience." The White House (15 September 2001) http://www.whitehouse.gov/news/releases/2001/09/ 20010915-4.html

– "Islam Is Peace, Says President." Remarks by the President at the Islamic Center, Washington, DC (17 September 2001) http://www.whitehouse. gov/news/releases/2001/09/20010917-11.html

– "There's No Rules." *CNN.com* (17 September 2001) http://articles.cnn. com/2001-09-17/us/gen.bush.transcript_1_ strong-symbol-safe-havens-military-police?_s=PM:US

– "Transcript of President Bush's Address." *CNN.com* (20 September 2001) http://archives.cnn.com/2001/US/09/20/gen.bush.transcript/index.html

– "Presidential Address to the Nation." The White House (7 October 2001) http://www.whitehouse.gov/news/releases/2001/10/20011007-8. html

– "President Bush at Pentagon Memorial." *OnlineNewsHour, PBS.org* (11 October 2001) http://www.pbs.org.newshour/bb/terrorism/bush_ pentagon_memorial.html

– "President Holds Prime Time News Conference." The White House (11 October 2001) http://www.whitehouse.gov/news/releases/2001/ 10/20011011-7.html

– "Bush: No Isolation from Evil." *CNN.com* (20 October 2001) http:// archives.cnn.com/2001/US/10/20/gen.bush.speech/index.html, para. 19

– "President Announces Crackdown on Terrorist Financial Network." The White House (7 November 2001) http://www.whitehouse.gov./news/ releases/2001/11/20011107-4.html

– "President Discusses War on Terrorism." The White House (8 November 2001) http://www.whitehouse.gov/news/releases/2001/11/20011108-13. html

– "U.S. President Bush's Speech to United Nations." *CNN.com* (10 November 2001) http://archives.cnn.com/2001/US/11/10/ret.bush. un.transcript

- "Bush State of the Union Address." *CNN.com* (29 January 2002) http://
  transcripts.cnn.com/2002/ALLPOLITICS/01/29/bush.speech.txt
- "Remarks on Arrival in Daytona Beach, Florida." Bnet (4 February
  2002) http://findarticles.com/p/articles.mi_m2889/is_5_38/ai_83762163
- "Bush: Don't Wait for Mushroom Cloud." *CNN.com* (7 October 2002)
  http://archives.cnn.com/2002/ALLPOLITICS/10/07/bush.transcript.index.
  html
- "Bush's State of the Union Speech." *CNN.com* (28 January 2003) http://
  edition.cnn.com/2003/ALLPOLITICS/01/29/sotu.transcript.index.html
- "Transcript of Bush News Conference on Iraq." *CNN.com* (6 March
  2003) http://edition.cnn.com/2003/US/03/06/bush.speech.transcript/
  index.html
- 7 September 2003. The White House, http://www.whitehouse.gov/news/
  releases/2003/09/20030907-1.html
- "President Speaks to the American Israel Public Affairs Committee."
  The White House (18 May 2004) http://www.whitehouse.gov/news/
  releases/2004/05/20040518-1.html
- "President Outlines Steps to Help Iraq Achieve Democracy and Freedom." The White House (24 May 2004) http://www.whitehouse.gov/
  news/releases/2004/05/20040524-10.html
- "President Discusses Hurricane Katrina, Congratulates Iraqis on Draft
  Constitution." The White House (28 August 2005) http://www.
  whitehouse.gov/news/releases/2005/08/20050828-1.html
- "President's Address to the Nation." The White House (10 January
  2007) http://www.whitehouse.gov/news/releases/2007/01/20070110-7.
  html
"Bush Says U.S. 'Does Not Torture People.'" *MSNBC.com* (5 October
  2007) http://www.msnbc.msn.com/id/21148801/#slice-2
Butler, Judith. *Frames of War: When Is Life Grievable?* London: Verso 2010
- *Precarious Life: The Powers of Mourning and Violence.* London: Verso
  2004
"CBS News Poll, March 15–18, 2008." *Polling.com* (14 July 2008) http://
  www.pollingreport.com/iraq.htm
Cheney, George. "We're Talking War: Symbols, Strategies, and Images." In
  Desert Storm and the Mass Media, edited by Bradley S. Greenberg and
  Walter Gantz, 61–73. Cresskill, NJ: Hampton Press 1993
Chesterman, Simon. "Ordering the New World: Violence and its Re/
  presentation in the Gulf War and Beyond." *Postmodern Culture* 8,
  no. 3 (1998) http://muse.jhu.edu/journals/postmodern_culture/v008/
  8.3chesterman.html

Clinton, William J. "State of the Union Address (January 25, 1994)."
    The Miller Center of Public Affairs, Scripps Library and Multimedia
    Archive, http://millercenter.virginia.edu/scripps/diglibrary/prezspeeches/
    clinton/wjc_1994_0125.html, para 61
– "1995 State of the Union Address." *Washington Post* (24 January 1995)
    http://www.washingtonpost.com/wp-srv/politics/special/states/docs/
    sou95.htm
– "1996 State of the Union Address." *Washington Post* (23 January 1996)
    http://www.washingtonpost.com/wp-srv/politics/special/states/docs/
    sou96.htm
– "1997 State of the Union Address." *Washington Post* (4 February 1997)
    http://www.washingtonpost.com/wp-srv/politics/special/states/docs/
    sou97.htm
CNN *Presents: Nuclear Terror* (CNN 2004)
Comaroff, Jean, and John L. Comaroff. "Millennial Capitalism: First
    Thoughts on a Second Coming." *Public Culture* 12, no. 2 (2000):
    291–323
Conrad, Joseph. *Heart of Darkness*. New York: Norton 2006
Cook, David A. *Lost Illusions: American Cinema in the Shadow of Water-
    gate and Vietnam 1970–1979*. Berkeley: University of California Press
    2002
Croft, Stuart. *Culture, Crisis, and America's War on Terror*. Cambridge:
    Cambridge University Press 2006
Debord, Guy-Ernest. *The Society of the Spectacle*. Trans. and ed.
    Red & Black (1994) http://library.nothingness.org/articles/SI/en/
    display
Desert Triumph: The Complete Study of the Persian Gulf War, VHS (CBS
    Video Presentation 1991)
Doyle, A.C. "The Adventures of the Musgrave Ritual." *Classic Literature
    Library*, http://sherlock-holmes.classic-literature.co.uk/the-musgrave-
    ritua./ebook-page-06.asp
Dyer-Witheford, Nick. *Cyber-Marx: Cycles and Circuits of Struggle in
    High-Technology Capitalism*. (1999) http://www.fims.uwo.ca/people/
    faculty/dyerwitheford/Chatper2.pdf
Eagleton, Terry. *After Theory*. London: Allen Lane 2003
– "The Art of Terror." *The Guardian* (30 November 2002) http://www.
    guardian.co.uk/comment/story/0,3604,851051,00.html
– *Holy Terror*. Oxford: Oxford University Press 2005
– *The Idea of Culture*. Oxford: Blackwell 2000
– *The Ideology of the Aesthetic*. Oxford: Blackwell 1990

- "Local and Global." http://www.usm.maine.edu/~bcj/issues/three/eagleton.html
"Embedded Reporters: What Are Americans Getting?" Journalism.org (3 April 2003) http://www.journalism.org/resources/research/reports/war/embed/default.asp
Engelhardt, Tom. *The End of Victory Culture: Cold War America and the Disillusioning of a Generation*. Amherst: University of Massachusetts Press 1995
- "The Gulf War as Total Television." In *Seeing through the Media*, edited by Susan Jeffords and Lauren Rabinovitz, 81–95. New Brunswick, NJ: Rutgers University Press 1994
Faludi, Susan. *The Terror Dream: Fear and Fantasy in Post 9/11 America*. New York: Metropolitan Books 2007
Fink, Bruce. *The Lacanian Subject: Between Language and Jouissance*. Princeton, NJ: Princeton University Press 1995
Finkelstein, Norman. *The Holocaust Industry*. 2nd edn. New York: Verso 2003
Fish, Stanley. "Postmodern Warfare: The Ignorance of Our Warrior Intellectuals." *Harper's Magazine* (July 2002): 33–40
Freud, Sigmund. *Beyond the Pleasure Principle*. Trans. and ed. James Strachey. New York and London: Norton 1990
- *The Uncanny*. Trans. David McLintock. New York: Penguin 2003
Fukuyama, Francis. "After Neoconservatism." *New York Times* (19 February 2006) http://www.nytimes.com/2006/02/19/magazine/neo.html?ex=1298005200&en=4126fa38fefd8ode&ei=5090&partner=rssuserland&emc=rss
- "The End of History?" *The National Interest* (Summer 1989): 3–18
- *The End of History and the Last Man*. New York: Free Press 2006
- "Has History Restarted since September 11?" *The Nineteenth Annual John Bonython Lecture* (Melbourne, 8 August 2002) http://www.cis.org.au/Events
- "The Primacy of Culture." *Journal of Democracy* 6, no. 1 (1995): 7–14
- "Reflections on 'The End of History,' Five Years Later." In *After History: Francis Fukuyama and His Critics*, edited by Timothy Burns. Lanham, MD: Rowman and Littlefield, 1994
Gabriel, Richard A. *No More Heroes: Madness and Psychiatry in War*. New York: Hill and Wang 1987
Garamone, Jim. "Rumsfeld Says No Evidence Bin Laden Is Dead." American Forces Information Service, United States Department of

Defense (20 January 2002) http://www.defenselink.mil/news/Jan2002/ n01202002_200201202.html

Gerbner, George. "Persian Gulf War, the Movie." In *Triumph of the Image*, edited by George Gerbner, Hamid Mowlana, and Herbert Schiller, 243–65. Boulder, CO: Westview Press 1992

Glassner, Barry. *The Culture of Fear: Why Americans Are Afraid of the Wrong Things*. New York: Basic Books 1999

Green Zone (2010), DVD, directed by Paul Greengrass (Universal Pictures 2010)

Gross, David. "Survey: More Americans Get News from Internet Than Newspapers or Radio." *CNN.com* (1 March 2010) http://edition.cnn. com/2010/TECH/03/01/social.network.news/index.html

Hammond, Philip. *Media, War, and Postmodernity*. London: Routledge 2007

Harvey, David. *The Condition of Postmodernity: An Enquiry into the Origins of Cultural Change*. Cambridge, MA, and Oxford: Blackwell 1990

– *The New Imperialism*. Oxford: Oxford University Press 2003

Hiebert, Ray Eldon. "Public Relations as a Weapon of Modern Warfare." In *Desert Storm and the Mass Media*, edited by Bradley S. Greenberg and Walter Gantz, 29–36. Cresskill, NJ: Hampton Press 1993

Hofstadter, Richard. *The Paranoid Style in American Politics and Other Essays*. Cambridge, MA: Harvard University Press 1996

Holloway, David. *Cultures of the War on Terror: Empire, Ideology, and the Remaking of 9/11*. Montreal: McGill-Queen's University Press 2008

The Hunt for Red October (1990), DVD, directed by John McTiernan (Paramount 2005)

Huntington, Samuel P. "The Clash of Civilizations?" *Foreign Affairs* 72, no. 3 (1993): 22–50

– *The Clash of Civilizations and the Remaking of World Order*. New York: Touchstone 1996

Hüppauf, Bernd. "Experiences of Modern Warfare and the Crisis of Representation." *New German Critique* 59 (1993): 41–76

The Hurt Locker (2008), DVD, directed by Kathryn Bigelow (Summit Entertainment 2010)

Huyssen, Andreas. "Present Pasts: Media, Politics, Amnesia." *Public Culture* 12, no. 1 (2000): 21–38

Ignatieff, Michael. "America's Empire Is an Empire Lite." *New York Times Magazine* 10 (Jan. 2003)

– *Empire Lite: Nation-Building in Bosnia, Kosovo and Afghanistan*. Toronto: Penguin Canada 2003

In the Valley of Elah (2007), DVD, directed by Paul Haggis (Warner 2009)

Independence Day (1996), DVD, directed by Roland Emmerich (Fox 2001)

"Inside the Numbers." Journalism.org (3 April 2003) http://www.
journalism.org

Invasion of the Body Snatchers (1956), DVD, directed by Don Siegel
(Republic Pictures 1998)

The Iraq Study Group Report. United States Institute of Peace (6 December 2006) http://www.usip.org/isg/iraq_study_group_report/report/
1206/index.html

Jackson, Richard. *Writing the War on Terrorism: Language, Politics, and
Counter-Terrorism*. Manchester: Manchester University Press 2005

Jameson, Fredric. "Cognitive Mapping." In *Marxism and the Interpretation of Culture*, edited by Cary Nelson and Lawrence Grossberg,
347–57. Champaign: University of Illinois Press 1988

– *The Cultural Turn: Selected Writings on the Postmodern*. London: Verso
1998

– "Globalization and Political Strategy." *New Left Review* 4 (2000):
49–68

– *The Political Unconscious: Narrative as a Socially Symbolic Act*. London: Routledge 1983

– *Postmodernism, or The Cultural Logic of Late Capitalism*. Durham, NC:
Duke University Press 1991

– "Reification and Utopia in Mass Culture." *Social Text* 1 (1979): 130–48

– *A Singular Modernity: Essay on the Ontology of the Present*. London:
Verso 2002

Jenkins, Henry. "Avatar Activism: Pick Your Protest." *Globe and Mail*
(18 September 2010) http://www.theglobeandmail.com/news/opinions/
avatar-activism-pick-your-protest/article1712766/singlepage

Johnson, Chalmers. *Blowback: The Costs and Consequences of American
Empire*. 2nd edn. New York: Holt Paperbacks 2004

Kakutani, Michiko. "An Identity Crisis for Norman Rockwell America."
New York Times (28 May 2004) http://www.nytimes.com/2004/05/28/
books/28BOOK.html

Kant, Immanuel. *Critique of Judgment*. Trans. and ed. J.H. Bernard. New
York: Hafner Press 1951

Kaplan, Amy. "Homeland Insecurities: Reflections on Language and
Space." *Radical History Review* 85 (2003): 82–93

Kays, John, "A Critique of the U.S. Department of Defense's Documentary: Why Viet-Nam?" *News Blaze* http://newsblaze.com/story/
20090412110017kays.nb/topstory.html

Keane, Stephen. *Disaster Movies: The Cinema of Catastrophe*. London: Wallflower 2001

Kellner, Douglas. "The Crisis in the Gulf and the Lack of Critical Media Discourse." In *Desert Storm and the Mass Media*, edited by Bradley S. Greenberg and Walter Gantz, 37–47. Cresskill, NJ: Hampton Press 1993

– *Media Culture: Cultural Studies, Identity and Politics between the Modern and the Postmodern*. London: Routledge 1995

– *The Persian Gulf TV War*. Boulder, CO: Westview Press 1992, reprinted online, http://www.gseis.ucla.edu/faculty/kellner/kellnerhtml.html. The chapters of *The Persian Gulf TV War* are available as individual PDF documents on this site, and references pertain to the chapter and page numbers provided there.

Kendrick, Michelle. "The Never Again Narratives: Political Promise and the Videos of Operation Desert Storm." *Cultural Critique* 28 (1994): 129–47

"Kerry: Closing Loopholes Will Help Fuel Promises." *CNN.com* (16 October 2004) http://edition.cnn.com/2004/ALLPOLITICS/10/15/kerry.interview/index.html

Klein, Kerwin Lee. "In Search of Narrative Mastery: Postmodernism and the People without History." *History and Theory* 34, no. 4 (1995): 275–98

Knight, Peter. *Conspiracy Culture: From Kennedy to the X Files*. London: Routledge 2000

Kubursi, Atif A. "Oil and the Gulf War: An 'America Century' or a 'New World Order.'" *Arab Studies Quarterly* 15 (1993) HighBeam Encyclopedia, http://www.encyclopedia.com/doc/1G1-16075106.html

Lacan, Jacques. *Écrits*. Trans. Bruce Fink. New York and London: Norton 1996

Lattman, Peter. "Justice Scalia Hearts Jack Bauer." *Wall Street Journal Law Blog* (20 June 2007) http://blogs.wsj.com/law/2007/06/20/justice-scalia-hearts-jack-bauer

Lewis, Wyndham. *Time and Western Man*. Berkeley, CA: Gingko 1993

Leys, Ruth. *Trauma: A Genealogy*. Chicago: University of Chicago Press 2000

Lifton, Robert Jay, and Greg Mitchell. *Hiroshima in America: A Half-Century of Denial*. New York: Avon Books 1996

Link, Jürgen. "Fanatics, Fundamentalists, Lunatics, and Drug Traffickers – The New Southern Enemy Image." *Cultural Critique* 19 (1991): 33–53

– "Maintaining Normality: On the Strategic Function of the Media in Wars of Extermination." *Cultural Critique* 19 (1991): 55–65

Lobe, Jim. "TV News Bad for Truth about Iraq." *IPSNews*.net (2 October 2003) http://ipsnews.net/interna.asp?idnews=20438

Lyotard, Jean-François. *The Postmodern Condition: A Report on Knowledge*. Trans. Geoff Bennington and Brian Massumi. Manchester: Manchester University Press 1999

MacArthur, John. *Second Front: Censorship and Propaganda in the 1991 Gulf War*. Berkeley and Los Angeles: University of California Press 1992, 2004

McCaleb, Ian Christopher. "Bush Tours Ground Zero in Lower Manhattan." *CNN.com* (14 September 2001) http://archives.cnn.com/2001/US/09/14/bush.terrorism

McLuhan, Marshall. *The Gutenberg Galaxy*. Toronto: University of Toronto Press 1962

– *Understanding Media: The Extensions of Man*. New York: Signet 1964

Mann, Michael. *Incoherent Empire*. London: Verso 2003

Massumi, Brian, ed. "Everywhere You Want to Be: Introduction to Fear." In *The Politics of Everyday Fear*, edited by Brian Massumi, 3–37. Minneapolis: University of Minnesota Press 1999

Melley, Timothy. "Agency Panic and the Culture of Conspiracy." In *Conspiracy Nation*, edited by Peter Knight, 57–84. New York: New York University Press 2002

Michaels, Walter Benn. "Empires of the Senseless: (The Response to) Terror and (the End of) History." *Radical History Review* 85 (2003): 105–113

– "Political Science Fictions." *New Literary History* 31 (2000): 649–64

– "Posthistoricism: The End of the End of History." *Transitions* 70 (1996): 4–19

Mitchell, W.J.T. "The Fog of Abu Ghraib: Errol Morris and the 'Bad Apples.'" *Harper's Magazine* (May 2008): 81–6

Monbiot, George. "Both Saviour and Victim." Monbiot.com. First published in *The Guardian* (29 January 2002) http://www.monbiot.com/archives/2002/01/29/both-saviour-and-victim

Morin, Richard. "Decision to Go to War Given Initial Support; Post–ABC Poll Finds 76% Approval." *Washington Post* (17 January 1991) http://www.washingtonpost.com

"The National Entertainment State." *The Nation* (3 July 2006) http://www.thenation.com/doc/20060703/mediachart

National Security Strategy. The White House (2002) http://www.whitehouse.gov/nsc.nss.html

Niethammer, Lutz. *Posthistoire: Has History Come to an End?* Trans.
 Patrick Camiller. London: Verso 1992

Nolte, John. "Review: Cameron's 'Avatar,' Big Hollywood." http://
 bighollywood.breitbart.com/jjmnolte/2009/12/11/review-camerons-
 avatar-is-a-big-dull-america-hating-pc-revenge-fantasy

Novak, Robert. "Hagel's Grim Iraq Assessment." *Pittsburgh Tribune
 Review*, http://pittsburghlive.com/x/pittsburghtrib/opinion/columninsts/
 guest/s_505015.html

Nye, David E. *American Technological Sublime*. Cambridge, MA: MIT
 Press 1994

O'Donnell, Patrick. *Latent Destinies: Cultural Paranoia and Contemporary U.S. Narratives*. Durham, NC: Duke University Press 2000

"Office of Homeland Security Fact Sheet." http://www.thirdworldtraveler.
 com/Homeland_Security/Homeland_Security_EPIC.html

O'Heffernan, Patrick. "Sobering Thoughts on Sound Bites Seen Round the
 World." In *Desert Storm and the Mass Media*, edited by Bradley
 S. Greenberg and Walter Gantz, 19–28. Cresskill, NJ: Hampton Press
 1993

Ong, Walter J. *Orality and Literacy: The Technologizing of the Word*.
 London: Routledge 1982

Orford, Anne. *Reading Humanitarian Intervention: Human Rights and
 the Use of Force in International Law*. Cambridge: Cambridge University Press 2007

Pater, Walter. *The Renaissance: Studies in Art and Poetry*. Ed. Alfred J.
 Drake. The Victorian Web, http://www.victorianweb.org/authors/pater/
 renaissance/html

Podhoretz, John. "Avatarocious." *Weekly Standard* (28 December 2009)
 http://www.weeklystandard.com/Content/Public/Articles/000/000/017/
 350fozta.asp?page=2&pg=1

Price, Monroe E., and Mark Thompson. *Forging Peace: Intervention,
 Human Rights, and the Management of Media Space*. Bloomington:
 Indiana University Press 2002

Rather, Dan. "Introduction." In *What We Saw – The Events of September
 11, 2001 – In Words, Pictures, and Video*. CBS Worldwide. New York:
 Simon and Schuster 2002

Redacted, DVD, directed by Brian De Palma (Magnolia 2008)

Rendition (2007), DVD, directed by Gavin Hood (New Line Home Video
 2008)

Retort. *Afflicted Powers: Capital and Spectacle in a New Age of War*.
 London: Verso 2005

Rogin, Michael. "Kiss Me Deadly: Communism, Motherhood, and Cold War Movies." *Representations* 6 (1984): 1–36

Rorty, Richard. *Objectivity, Relativism, and Truth: Philosophical Papers, Volume I*. Cambridge: Cambridge University Press 1991

Ryan, David, and John Dumbrell, eds. *Vietnam in Iraq: Tactics, Lessons, Legacies and Ghosts*. New York: Routledge 2007

Said, Edward. *Culture and Imperialism*. New York: Vintage 1994

– *Orientalism*. Twenty-Fifth Anniversary edn. New York: Vintage 2004

Saving Private Ryan (1998), DVD, directed by Steven Spielberg (Dreamworks 2006)

Scarry, Elaine. "Watching and Authorizing the Gulf War." In *Media Spectacles*, edited by Marjorie Garber, Jann Matlock, and Rebecca L. Walkovitz, 57–76. New York: Routledge 1993

Schindler's List (1993), DVD, directed by Steven Spielberg (Universal 2005)

Schulte-Sasse, Jochen, and Linda Schulte-Sasse. "War, Otherness, and Illusionary Identifications with the State." *Cultural Critique* 19 (1991): 67–95

Smith, Paul. *Millennial Dreams: Contemporary Culture and Capital in the North*. London: Verso 1997

Sobel, Richard. *The Impact of Public Opinion on U.S. Foreign Policy since Vietnam*. New York: Oxford University Press 2001

Sontag, Susan. *Illness as Metaphor/AIDS and Its Metaphors*. New York: Picador 2001

– "The Image-World." In *A Susan Sontag Reader*, 350–67. New York: Vintage 1983

– "The Imagination of Disaster." In *Against Interpretation and Other Essays*, 209–25. New York: Picador 2001

– "What Have We Done?" *The Guardian* (24 May 2004) http://www.commondreams.org/views04/0524-09.htm

Spiegelman, Art. *In the Shadow of No Towers*. New York: Viking 2004

Standard Operating Procedure, DVD, directed by Errol Morris (Columbia/Tristar 2008)

Stop-Loss (2008), DVD, directed by Kimberly Peirce (Paramount 2008)

Suellentrop, Chris. "War Games." *New York Times* (8 September 2010) http://www.nytimes.com/2010/09/12/magazine/12military-t.html

The Sum of All Fears (2002), DVD, directed by Phil Alden Robinson (Paramount 2002)

Todorov, Tzvetan. "The Typology of Detective Fiction." In *The Narrative Reader*, edited by Martin McQuillan. New York: Routledge 2000

Tronti, Mario. "The Strategy of Refusal." Semiotext(e) 3, no. 3: 28–35, cited in Jean Comaroff and John L. Comaroff, "Millennial Capitalism: First Thoughts on a Second Coming," *Public Culture* 12, no. 2 (2000): 291–323

True Lies (1994), DVD, directed by James Cameron (Fox Home Video 1994)

United 93 (2006), DVD, directed by Paul Greengrass (Universal 2006)

"United States Military Casualties of War." *Wikipedia*, http://en.wikipedia. org/wiki/United_States_military_casualties_of_war

Unthinkable (2010), DVD, directed by Gregor Jordan (Sony Pictures 2010)

"US President George Bush Planned to Bomb Aljazeera, British Newspaper the *Daily Mirror* Has Reported." GlobalResearch.ca (24 November 2005) http://www.globalresearch.ca/index.php?context=viewArticle& code-20051124&articleId=1318

The Usual Suspects (1995), DVD, directed by Bryan Singer (Fox Video 2009)

Venn, Couze. "World Dis/Order: On Some Fundamental Questions." *Theory, Culture and Society* 19 (2002): 121–36

"The Vice President Receives the International Republican Institute's 2001 Freedom Award." The White House (23 October 2001) http://www. whitehouse.gov/vicepresident/news-speeches/speeches/vp20011023.html

Virilio, Paul. *City of Panic*. Oxford and New York: Berg 2005

War in Iraq: The Road to Baghdad, DVD (TimeInc Home Entertainment 2003)

War in the Gulf, VHS (Cable News Network 1991)

Wark, McKenzie. "Engulfed by the Vector." *New Formations* 21 (1994): 64–79

Weber, Samuel. *Mass Mediauras: Form, Technics, Media*. Stanford, CA: Stanford University Press 1996

Wells, Alan, and Ernest A. Hakanen. *Mass Media and Society*. Santa Barbara, CA: Greenwood 1997

Wetta, Frank J., and Martin A. Novelli, "Now a Major Motion Picture: War Films and Hollywood's New Patriotism." *Journal of Military History* 67 (2003): 861–82

What We Saw – The Events of September 11, 2001 – In Words, Pictures, and Video, DVD (CBS 2002)

Williams, Raymond. *Marxism and Literature*. Oxford: Oxford University Press 1977

– *Television: Technology and Cultural Form*. New York: Schocken Books 1975

Wojcik, Daniel. *The End of the World as We Know It: Faith, Fatalism, and Apocalypse in America*. New York: New York University Press 1997

World Trade Center, DVD, directed by Oliver Stone (Paramount 2006)

Žižek, Slavoj. *The Borrowed Kettle*. New York: Verso 2005

– *The Sublime Object of Ideology*. London: Verso 1989

– *Welcome to the Desert of the Real*. London: Verso 2002

Zunes, Stephen. "The Gulf War: 8 Myths." *Foreign Policy in Focus* (1 January 2001) http://www.fpif.org/articles/the_gulf_war_8_myths

Index